The Book of
JOY

The Book of
JOY

Lasting Happiness in a
Changing World

HIS HOLINESS THE DALAI LAMA
AND ARCHBISHOP DESMOND TUTU
with Douglas Abrams

RANDOM HOUSE
LARGE PRINT

Front cover photograph and photographs on
pp. iv, 248, 454, and 526 copyright © Miranda
Penn Turin. Back cover photograph and photographs
on pp. x, xiv, 14, 38, 94, 114, 278, 408, and 430
copyright © Tenzin Choejor.

The Library of Congress has established a
Cataloging-in-Publication record for this title.

ISBN: 978-1-5247-0863-4

www.randomhouse.com/largeprint

FIRST LARGE PRINT EDITION

Printed in the United States of America

10 9 8 7 6 5 4 3

This Large Print edition published in accord with
the standards of the N.A.V.H.

CONTENTS

DAYS 2 & 3
The Obstacles to Joy 115

DAYS 4 & 5
The Eight Pillars of Joy 279

The Invitation
to Joy

To celebrate one of our special birthdays, we met for a week in Dharamsala to enjoy our friendship and to create something that we hope will be a birthday gift for others. There is perhaps nothing more joyous than birth, and yet so much of life is spent in sadness, stress, and suffering. We hope this small book will be an invitation to more joy and more happiness.

No dark fate determines the future. We do. Each day and each moment, we are able to create and re-create our lives and the very quality of human life on our planet. This is the power we wield.

Lasting happiness cannot be found in pursuit of any goal or achievement. It does not reside in fortune or fame. It resides only in the human mind and heart, and it is here that we hope you will find it.

Our cowriter, Douglas Abrams, has kindly agreed to assist us in this project and interviewed us over the course of a week in Dharamsala. We have asked him to weave our voices together and offer his own as our narrator so that we can share not only our views and our experience but also what scientists and others have found to be the wellsprings of joy.

You don't need to believe us. Indeed, nothing we say should be taken as an article of faith. We are sharing what two friends, from very different worlds, have witnessed and learned in our long lives. We hope you will discover whether what is included here is true by applying it in your own life.

Every day is a new opportunity to begin again. Every day is your birthday.

May this book be a blessing for all sentient beings, and for all of God's children—including you.

TENZIN GYATSO,
HIS HOLINESS THE DALAI LAMA

DESMOND TUTU,
ARCHBISHOP EMERITUS OF
SOUTHERN AFRICA

INTRODUCTION

By Douglas Abrams

As we stepped off the plane at the small airport, the howl of the jet engines deafening and the snowcapped foothills of the Himalayas looming behind us, two old friends embraced. The Archbishop touched the Dalai Lama's cheeks tenderly, and the Dalai Lama pursed his lips as if blowing the Archbishop a kiss. It was a moment of enormous affection and friendship. In the yearlong preparations for this visit, we were quite aware of what the meeting might mean for the world, but we never realized what a week together might mean for the two of them.

It has been a profound privilege and a daunting responsibility to convey the remarkable week of dialogues that took place in Dharamsala, India, at the Dalai Lama's residence in exile. In this book I have tried to share with you their intimate conversations, which were filled with seemingly endless laughter and punctuated by many poignant moments of recalling love and loss.

Although they had met only half a dozen times, the men shared a bond that transcended these brief visits, and each considered the other his "mischievous spiritual brother." Never before, or likely after, would they have a chance to spend so much time in each other's company, reveling in the joy of their friendship.

The heavy footsteps of mortality were never far from our conversations. Our trip itinerary had to be reworked twice so that the Archbishop could attend funerals for his peers. As health and global politics have conspired to keep them apart, we recognized that this might be their last time together.

For a week we sat in a pool of soft light, arranged carefully to avoid hurting the Dalai Lama's sensitive eyes, as five video cameras filmed around us. During our quest to understand joy, we explored many of the most profound subjects in life. We were in search of true joy that was not dependent on the vicissitudes of circumstance. We knew that we would need to tackle the obstacles that can so often make joy elusive. During the dialogues they outlined eight pillars of joy—four pillars of the mind and four pillars of the heart. These two great leaders agreed on the most important principles, and offered illuminating differences, as we attempted to gather insights that might help readers to find lasting happiness in an ever-changing, and often aching, world.

We had an opportunity each day to sip warm Darjeeling tea and to break bread—Tibetan flat bread. All who were working on filming the interviews were invited to join these daily teas and lunches. One exceptional morning, the Dalai Lama even introduced the Archbishop to his meditation practice in his private residence, and the Archbishop gave the Dalai Lama communion, a rite generally reserved for those who are within the Christian faith.

Finally, at the end of the week, we celebrated the Dalai Lama's birthday at the Tibetan Children's Village, one of the boarding schools for children who have fled Tibet, where the Chinese authorities have prevented them from receiving an education based on Tibetan culture and language. The children are sent by their parents over the mountain passes with guides who promise to deliver them to one of the Dalai Lama's schools. It is hard to imagine the heartbreak of parents sending their children away, knowing that they will not see them again for more than a decade, if ever.

In the midst of this traumatized school, more than two thousand students and their teachers cheered as the Dalai Lama, who is prohibited by his monastic vows from dancing, took his first tentative shimmy encouraged by the Archbishop's irrepressible boogie.

The Dalai Lama and the Archbishop are two of the great spiritual masters of our time, but they are also moral leaders who transcend their own traditions and speak always from a concern for humanity as a whole. Their courage and resilience and dogged hope in humanity inspire millions as they refuse to give in to the fashionable cynicism that risks engulfing us. Their joy is clearly not easy or superficial but one burnished by the fire of adversity, oppression, and struggle. The Dalai Lama and the Archbishop remind us that joy is in fact our birthright and even more fundamental than happiness.

"Joy," as the Archbishop said during the week, "is much bigger than happiness. While happiness is often seen as being dependent on external circumstances, joy is not." This state of mind—and heart—is much closer to both the Dalai Lama's and the Archbishop's understanding of what animates our lives and what ultimately leads to a life of satisfaction and meaning.

The dialogues were about what the Dalai Lama has called the very "purpose of life"—the goal of avoiding suffering and discovering happiness. They shared their hard-won wisdom of how to live with joy in the face of life's inevitable sorrows. Together they explored how we can transform joy from an ephemeral **state** into an enduring **trait**, from a fleeting feeling into a lasting way of being.

From the beginning this book was envisioned as a three-layer birthday cake.

The first layer is the Dalai Lama's and Archbishop Tutu's **teachings** on joy: Is it really possible to be joyful even in the face of our daily
troubles—from frustration with morning traffic to fears of not being able to provide for our
families, from anger at those who have wronged
us to grief at the loss of those we love, from the
ravages of illness to the abyss of death? How
do we embrace the reality of our lives, deny
nothing, but transcend the pain and suffering
that is inescapable? And even when our lives
are good, how do we live in joy when so many
others are suffering: when crushing poverty
robs people of their future, when violence and
terror fill our streets, and when ecological devastation endangers the very possibility of life on
our planet? This book is an attempt to answer
these questions and many more.

The second layer is made up of the latest **science** on joy and also on all the other qualities
that they believe are essential for enduring happiness. With new discoveries in brain science
and experimental psychology, there are now
many profound insights into human flourish-
ing. Two months before the trip I had lunch
with neuroscientist Richard Davidson, a pio-

neer researching happiness. He has studied meditators in his lab and found that meditation confers measurable benefits for the brain. We sat at an outdoor table at a Vietnamese restaurant in San Francisco, the ever-present wind blowing the gray-black locks of his boyish haircut. As we ate spring rolls, Davidson said that the Dalai Lama had once confessed to him that he found the science on meditation inspiring, especially when getting out of bed to sit in the early morning. If the science helps the Dalai Lama, it can help the rest of us even more.

Too often we see spirituality and science as antagonistic forces, each with its hand at the other's throat. Yet Archbishop Tutu has expressed his belief in the importance of what he calls "self-corroborating truth"—when many different fields of knowledge point to the same conclusion. Similarly, the Dalai Lama was adamant about the importance of making sure that this was not a Buddhist or Christian book, but a universal book supported not only by opinion or tradition but also by science. (Full disclosure: I am Jewish, although I also identify as secular—it sounds a little like a

joke: A Buddhist, a Christian, and a Jew walk
into a bar . . .)

The third layer of the birthday cake is the
stories of being in Dharamsala with the Dalai
Lama and the Archbishop throughout the
week. These up-close and personal chapters are
meant to allow the reader to join the journey
from the first embrace to the final goodbye.

We have also included a selection of joy practices at the end of the book. Both teachers
shared with us their daily practices, the anchors
of their own emotional and spiritual lives. The
goal here is not to create a recipe for a joyful
life but to offer some of the techniques and traditions that have served the Dalai Lama and
the Archbishop and countless others over the
millennia in their respective traditions. These
practical exercises will hopefully help you take
the teachings, the science, and the stories and
incorporate them into your daily life.

I have had the privilege of working with many
of the great spiritual teachers and scientific
pioneers of our time, helping them convey their
insights about health and happiness for others.

(Many of these scientists have generously contributed their research to this book.) I am sure that my fascination—okay, obsession—with joy began while growing up in a loving home that was shadowed by the black dog of depression. Having witnessed and experienced such pain from a very young age, I know that so much of human suffering occurs within our own head and heart. The week in Dharamsala felt like an extraordinary and challenging peak in this lifelong journey to understand both joy and suffering.

As the people's ambassador, I sat there for five days of interviews, staring into the eyes of two of the most compassionate people on the planet. I am very skeptical about the magical sensations that some attribute to being in the presence of spiritual teachers, but from the very first day I found my head starting to tingle. It was startling, but perhaps it was simply an example of how my mirror neurons, those special empathic brain cells, were internalizing what I was witnessing in the eyes of these two extremely loving men.

Fortunately, I was not alone in the daunting task of distilling their wisdom. Thupten

Jinpa, the Dalai Lama's principal translator for more than thirty years and a Buddhist scholar, accompanied me from start to finish. For many years he was a Buddhist monk, but he gave up his robes for a life of marriage and family in Canada, making him the perfect partner for translating between worlds as well as languages. We sat together during the dialogues, but Jinpa also helped me to prepare the questions and interpret the answers. He has become a trusted collaborator and a dear friend.

The questions were not ours alone. We invited the world to ask their questions about joy, and although it turned out we had only three days to collect them, we received more than a thousand. It was fascinating that the most asked question was not about how we could discover our own joy but how we could possibly live with joy in a world filled with so much suffering.

During the week their fingers were often wagging at each other teasingly, moments before their hands were clasped together affectionately. During our first lunch the Archbishop told the story of a talk they were giving together. As they were getting ready to walk on stage, the Dalai Lama—the world's icon of compassion and peace—pretended to choke his spiritual older brother. The Archbishop turned to the Dalai Lama and said, "Hey, the cameras are on us, act like a **holy** man."

These two men remind us that how we choose to act each day is what matters. Even holy men have to act like holy men. But how we think holy men act, serious and severe, pious and reserved, is hardly how these two greet the world, or each other.

The Archbishop has never claimed sainthood and the Dalai Lama considers himself a simple monk. They offer us the reflection of real lives filled with pain and turmoil in the midst of which they have been able to discover a level of peace, of courage, of joy that we can aspire to in our own lives. Their desire for this book is not just to convey their wisdom but their humanity as well. Suffering is inevitable, they said, but how we respond to that suffering is our choice. Not even oppression or occupation can take away this freedom to choose our response.

Right until the very last minute we did not know if the Archbishop's doctors would allow him to travel. The prostate cancer had returned and was slow, this time, to respond to treatment. The Archbishop is now on an experimental protocol to see if it will hold the cancer at bay. As we were landing in Dharamsala, what surprised me most was the excitement, anticipation, and perhaps a touch of concern, on the Archbishop's face that could be seen in his wide grin and twinkling blue-gray eyes.

Arrival:
We Are Fragile Creatures

We are fragile creatures, and it is from this weakness, not despite it, that we discover the possibility of true joy," the Archbishop said as I handed him his sleek black cane with the silver handle shaped like a greyhound. "Life is filled with challenges and adversity," the Archbishop continued. "Fear is inevitable, as is pain and eventually death. Take the return of the prostate cancer—well, it does focus the mind."

One of the side effects of the medicine the Archbishop was taking is fatigue, and he had slept for most of the flight to India, a beige blanket pulled up over his head. We had planned to talk on the flight, but sleep was most important, and now he was trying to share his thoughts quickly as we approached Dharamsala.

We had stopped off in Amritsar for the night so he could rest and because the airport in Dharamsala was open for only a couple of hours a day. This morning we had visited the famed Harmandir Sahib, the Sikh religion's holiest site. The upper stories are clad in gold, resulting in its popular name, the Golden Temple. There are four doors to get into the **gurdwara,** which symbolizes the tradition's openness toward all people and all religions. This seemed like an appropriate place to pay our respects, as we were embarking on an interfaith meeting that would bring two of the world's great religions, Christianity and Buddhism, into deep dialogue.

As we were swallowed into a throng of the temple's one hundred thousand daily visitors, we got the call. The Dalai Lama had decided to meet the Archbishop at the airport, a rare honor that he bestows on very few of the endless stream of visiting dignitaries. We were told that he was already on his way. We raced to get out of the temple and back to the airport as we pushed the Archbishop in his wheelchair, his bald head covered by an orange handkerchief, a required sign of respect at the temple, which made him look like a Day-Glo pirate.

The van tried to inch its way through the traffic-choked streets of Amritsar as a symphony of car horns played, the mass of cars, pedestrians, bicycles, scooters, and animals all jostling for position. Concrete buildings lined the roads, their rebar sticking out in an always unfinished state of expansion. We finally made it to the airport and onto the plane. We wished that the twenty-minute flight would go even faster, concerned now that the Dalai Lama would be waiting on the tarmac.

"Discovering more joy does not, I'm sorry to say," the Archbishop added, as we began our descent, "save us from the inevitability of hardship and heartbreak. In fact, we may cry more easily, but we will laugh more easily, too. Perhaps we are just more alive. Yet as we discover more joy, we can face suffering in a way that ennobles rather than embitters. We have hardship without becoming hard. We have heartbreak without being broken."

I had witnessed both the Archbishop's tears and his laughter so many times. Well, more his laughter than his tears, in truth, but he does

cry easily and often, for that which is not yet
redeemed, for that which is not yet whole. It
all matters to him, it all affects him deeply.
His prayers, in which I have been enveloped,
reach around the world to all who are in need
and suffering. One of his book editors had a
grandson who was ill and on the Archbishop's
very long daily prayer list. Several years later,
the editor asked if he would once again pray
for his grandson, because the child's illness had
returned. The Archbishop replied that he had
never stopped praying for the boy.

From the plane, we could see the snow-
covered mountains that are the postcard back-
drop to the Dalai Lama's home in exile. After
the Chinese invasion of Tibet, the Dalai Lama
and a hundred thousand other Tibetans fled
to India. These refugees were temporarily settled in the lowlands of India, where the heat
and mosquitos led a great many to become
ill. Eventually the government of India established the Dalai Lama's residence in Dharamsala,
and the Dalai Lama was very grateful for the
higher altitude and the cooler weather. Over
time many Tibetans came to settle here as
well, as if the community was heartsick for

the mountainous landscape and high altitude of their home. And of course most of all, they wanted to be close to their spiritual and political leader.

Dharamsala is in the north Indian state of Himachal Pradesh, and the British, when they ruled India, also used to come here to escape the relentless heat of the Indian summer. As we approached this former British hill station, we could see the green carpet of pine trees and agricultural fields below. Dense storm clouds and fog often close the small airport, as it did on my last visit. But today the sky was blue, the wisps of clouds held at bay by the mountains. We descended for the steep landing.

One great question underlies our existence," the Dalai Lama had said before the trip. "What is the purpose of life? After much consideration, I believe that the purpose of life is to find happiness.

"It does not matter whether one is a Buddhist like me, or a Christian like the Archbishop, or any other religion, or no religion at all. From the moment of birth, every human being wants to discover happiness and avoid suffering. No differences in our culture or our education or our religion affect this. From the very core of our being, we simply desire joy and contentment. But so often these feelings are fleeting and hard to find, like a butterfly that lands on us and then flutters away.

"The ultimate source of happiness is within us. Not money, not power, not status. Some of my friends are billionaires, but they are very unhappy people. Power and money fail to bring inner peace. Outward attainment will not bring real inner joyfulness. We must look inside.

"Sadly, many of the things that undermine our joy and happiness we create ourselves. Often it comes from the negative tendencies of the mind, emotional reactivity, or from our inability to appreciate and utilize the resources that exist within us. The suffering from a natural disaster we cannot control, but the suffering from our daily disasters we can. We create most of our suffering, so it should be logical that we also have the ability to create more joy. It simply depends on the attitudes, the perspectives, and the reactions we bring to situations and to our relationships with other people. When it comes to personal happiness there is a lot that we as individuals can do."

We lurched forward as the brakes seized the tires, and then the plane rumbled and shook, stopping quickly on the short runway. Out the window of the airplane we could see the Dalai Lama standing on the tarmac, a large yellow umbrella held over his head to protect him from the bright Indian sun. He was wearing his maroon robe and red shawl, although we could see a small patch of saffron yellow on his sleeveless vest. An entourage of office staff and airport officials in suits flanked him. Indian soldiers in khaki uniforms were providing security.

The media had been kept outside of the airport. This was going to be an intimate reunion with only the Dalai Lama's personal photographer taking pictures. As the Archbishop hobbled down the steep stairs in his blue blazer and signature fisherman's cap, the Dalai Lama approached.

The Dalai Lama was smiling, his eyes sparkling behind his large square-framed glasses.

He bowed low and then the Archbishop spread his arms out, and they embraced. They separated and held each other's shoulders, gazing into each other's eyes, as if trying to convince themselves that they were really together again.

"I haven't seen you in a long while," Archbishop Tutu said as he touched the Dalai Lama's cheek tenderly with the tips of his fingers and inspected him closely. "You look very good."

The Dalai Lama, still holding the Archbishop's small shoulders, puckered as if to blow him a kiss. The Archbishop raised his left hand, gold wedding ring shining, and clasped the Dalai Lama's chin as one might do to one's precious grandchild. Then the Archbishop went in for a kiss on the cheek. The Dalai Lama, not used to kisses from anyone, flinched but also laughed with delight, which was quickly accompanied by the Archbishop's high-pitched cackle.

"You don't like a kiss," the Archbishop said, and gave him another on the other cheek. I wondered how many kisses the Dalai Lama had received in his whole life, taken from his parents at age two and raised in a rarefied realm far away from kisses.

They stopped for the formal presentation of **khata** (a white scarf), a Tibetan custom of greeting and respect. The Dalai Lama bowed with hands pressed together at his heart, the gesture of welcome that recognizes our oneness. The Archbishop took off his fisherman's cap and bowed in return. The Dalai Lama then draped the long white silk scarf around the Archbishop's neck. They whispered into each other's ears, trying to talk over the noise of the jet still droning in the background. The Dalai Lama took the Archbishop's hand, and then they were more eight than eighty, laughing and making jokes together as they strolled toward the terminal, yellow umbrella sheltering above them.

Even though the Archbishop's white scarf was bunched around his neck, it still hung all the way down his small body. The size of the **khata** one gives is a sign of the esteem that one holds for the recipient, high lamas receiving the longest ones. This **khata** was the longest one I had ever seen. The Archbishop joked throughout the week, as **khata** after **khata** was draped around his neck, that he felt like a human coat rack.

We were ushered into a small room with a couple of brown couches set aside for the Dalai Lama to await his often delayed or canceled flights out of Dharamsala. We could see the media gathered outside the airport, lining the glass wall waiting for a chance to snap a photograph or ask a question. It was only then that I recalled how newsworthy and even historic this trip was. It had been so easy to get lost in the logistics and to forget that their time together was an important event for the world.

In the lounge, the Archbishop relaxed into a couch while the Dalai Lama was perched in a large chair beside him. Next to the Archbishop sat his daughter Mpho, who was dressed in a brilliant green and red African print dress, her head wrapped with a matching fabric. The youngest of four children, she followed her father into the ministry and was now the executive director of the Desmond and Leah Tutu Legacy Foundation. During our trip Mpho would get down on bended knee and propose to her girlfriend, Marceline van Furth. The trip was only a couple months before the U.S. Supreme Court made its landmark ruling legalizing gay marriage, but the Archbishop had supported gay rights for decades. He famously had said that he would refuse to go to a "homophobic" heaven. What many forget—especially those who find themselves on the receiving end of his moral censure—is that the Archbishop decries any form of oppression or discrimination, wherever he might find it. Shortly after the marriage, Mpho was stripped of her ministry because the South African Anglican Church does not recognize gay marriage.

"I was really looking forward to coming to your birthday," the Dalai Lama said, "but your government had some difficulties. At that time you expressed some very strong words," the Dalai Lama said as he put his hand on the Archbishop's forearm. "And I appreciated it." **Strong words** was an understatement.

The week in Dharamsala to celebrate the Dalai Lama's birthday had its origins four years earlier, when Archbishop Tutu celebrated his own eightieth birthday in Cape Town, South Africa. The Dalai Lama had been invited to be the guest of honor, but the South African government bowed to pressure from the Chinese government and was unwilling to issue the Dalai Lama a visa. China is one of the major buyers of South African minerals and raw materials.

The Archbishop was daily on the front page of the South African newspapers leading up to the celebration, railing against the government for their perfidy and duplicity. He even compared the ruling African National Congress—the party whose members he fought for decades to help bring out of exile and imprisonment—to the long-hated apartheid government. He said they were actually worse, because at least in the case of the apartheid government the villainy was overt.

"I always try to avoid any inconvenience," the Dalai Lama said with a grin, and then pointed to the Archbishop, "but I was happy someone else was willing to be an inconvenience. I was very happy."

"I know," the Archbishop said. "You use me. That's the trouble. You use me, and I don't learn."

The Archbishop then put out his hand and took the Dalai Lama's tenderly.

"When the South Africans refused to let you come for my eightieth birthday, it made the whole event all the more spectacular, because we had Google hosting our conversation, and there was a lot more press interest than there might have otherwise been. But never mind—wherever you are, there is a lot of interest. I'm not jealous.

"You know, I remember when we were in Seattle, they were looking for a venue that would be large enough for the people who wanted to come to see you, and it ended up that they found a football stadium. There were seventy thousand people who wanted to come hear this man, and he can't even speak English properly."

The Dalai Lama let out a big belly laugh.

"It's really not nice," the Archbishop continued. "You really need to pray that I become a little more popular like you."

To tease someone is a sign of intimacy and friendship, to know that there is a reservoir of affection from which we all drink as funny and flawed humans. And yet their jokes were as much about themselves as about each other, never really putting the other down, but constantly reinforcing their bond and their friendship.

The Archbishop wanted to thank and introduce each of the people who had helped make the trip possible. He introduced his daughter Mpho, philanthropist and peace builder Pam Omidyar, and me, but the Dalai Lama said he already knew all of us. Then he introduced my wife, Rachel, as his American doctor; Pat Christian, a colleague of Pam's from the Omidyar Group; and his daughter's soon-to-be fiancée, Marceline, a pediatrician and professor of epidemiology in Holland. He did not need to introduce the final member of our party, the Venerable Lama Tenzin Dhonden, who was a member of the Dalai Lama's own Namgyal Monastery.

Now the Dalai Lama was rubbing the Archbishop's hand warmly, as he would throughout the week. They were talking about the flight itinerary and our stopover in Amritsar. "This is very good. Necessary to rest," the Dalai Lama said. "I always sleep eight to nine hours a night."

"But you get up very early, don't you?" the Archbishop asked.

"That's right. Three o'clock."

"Three o'clock?"

"Always."

"And you pray five hours?" The Archbishop was holding up five fingers for emphasis.

"Yes."

The Archbishop looked upward and shook his head. "No, that's too much."

"Sometimes I do meditation on the nature of self using what is known as the 'sevenfold analysis,'" the Dalai Lama said. Jinpa later explained that this is a Buddhist contemplative practice in which one searches for the true nature of the self by analyzing the relationship between oneself and the physical and mental aspects of our body and mind. "For example," the Dalai Lama continued, "now when I look at you, and I analyze, I see that this is my dear, respected friend Bishop Tutu. No, this is his body, not himself. This is his mind, but not himself." The Dalai Lama leaned in to emphasize his point, presenting a paradoxical riddle as old as Buddhism. "Where is Bishop Tutu's self? We can't find it." He slapped the Archbishop's forearm playfully.

The Archbishop looked a little mystified and a little bemused. **"Really?"**

"So now," the Dalai Lama concluded, "in quantum physics, they also have a similar view. Any objective thing does not really exist. There is nothing ultimately we can find. This is similar to analytical meditation."

The Archbishop put his hands over his face in bewilderment. "I couldn't do that." The Dalai Lama may have been arguing against there being an essential Bishop Tutu, but at the same time there **was** a person, a friend that was special to him in a way that, despite his friendliness to all, was unique and clearly important to him. Jinpa and I discussed what it was about this relationship that probably meant so much. For both of them, it was rare to have a true friend. There are, after all, not many members of the moral leaders club. Their lives are filled with people who relate to them as icons. It must be a relief to find someone who is not looking for a photo op. Certainly, they also share values at a place where the core of all religions meet, and of course they share a fantastic sense of humor. I was beginning to see how central friendship, and relationship more generally, was in our experience of joy. This was a theme that would arise many times in our week together.

"I tell people," said the Archbishop, "that one of the greatest things about you is your serenity, and I say, 'Well, you know every day he spends those five hours in the morning meditating,' and it shows in how you respond to things that are agonizing—the pain of your country, and the pain of the world. As I say, I try, but five hours is too much." The Archbishop, characteristically humble and self-effacing, was dismissing his own three or four hours of prayer a day. It is true, he sleeps in . . . until four.

What is it, I wondered, about spiritual leaders that they are always getting up early to pray and meditate? It clearly makes a great difference in how they approach their day. When I first heard that the Dalai Lama got up at 3:00 a.m., I thought I was going to hear another story of superhuman devotion and learn that he slept only two or three hours a night. I was relieved to hear that he simply went to bed very early, typically by 7:00 p.m. (Not exactly practical for a householder who has children to feed and get to bed, I thought, but perhaps getting to bed an hour earlier and up an hour earlier was possible. Would it lead to more spiritual growth? Would it lead to more joy?)

The Dalai Lama held the Archbishop's hand up to his cheek. "So now we go to my home."

. . .

As we walked out of the airport, the media crowded around the two leaders and shouted questions about the Archbishop's trip. The Archbishop stopped to answer, and to use the attention of the media to shine a spotlight on injustice. He spoke as the clicks of cameras peppered his comments. "I am so glad to be with my dear friend. Often things and people try to keep us apart, but the love that we have for each other and the goodness of God's universe ensures that we shall meet. The first time that the South African government refused him a visa—when he was going to come to my eightieth birthday—I asked him, 'How many divisions do you have in your army? Why is China scared of you?' And that is what surprises me—maybe they are right— a spiritual leader is something that should be taken very seriously. We hope that God's world will become a better place, more hospitable to goodness, more hospitable to compassion, more hospitable to generosity, more hospitable to living together so we don't have what is happening now between Russia and the Ukraine, or what is happening with ISIS, or what is happening in Kenya or Syria. They make God weep."

The Archbishop turned to leave but then paused again as another journalist asked about the purpose of his trip. "We are together just to enjoy our friendship and to talk about joy."

The Archbishop and the Dalai Lama were whisked away by a waiting motorcade. The drive to the Dalai Lama's residence was about three-quarters of an hour. The streets had been closed to allow the Dalai Lama to go to the airport, and Tibetans, Indians, and a few tourists were lining the streets, hoping to get a glimpse of him and his special guest. I realized now why the Dalai Lama so rarely makes the pilgrimage to the airport. It is a major logistical operation that shuts down one of the main roads and impacts the whole city.

We were here to discuss joy in the face of life's challenges, and everywhere in Dharamsala were reminders that this was a community that had been traumatized by oppression and exile. The town clings to winding hillside roads, and craft stalls hang over the edges of sheer cliffs. Like construction throughout India and so much of the developing world, building codes and security precautions were waved aside to make room for the exploding population. I wondered

how these structures would fare in an earthquake, and feared that the whole city might be
shaken off the back of these mountains like a
leaf from a waking animal.

The motorcade snaked up as the lines of the
devout thickened, some burning incense and
many others with **mala** beads draped around
their prayerfully cupped hands. It is hard for
non-Tibetans to understand how much the
Dalai Lama means to the Tibetan people, and
this exile community in particular. He is both
the symbol of their national and political identity and also the embodiment of their spiritual aspirations. To be the embodiment of the
Bodhisattva of Compassion means in many
ways to be a Christlike figure. I can only imagine how challenging it must be for the Dalai
Lama to carry this responsibility while also trying to emphasize his being "nothing special,"
just one of the seven billion people.

The streets narrowed, and I wondered how
our speeding cars could possibly pass through
the throng of people, but we seemed to slow
only for the occasional sacred cow that mean-
dered into the street, perhaps also to get a better glimpse of the two holy men.

I wondered if the careening pace was due to security concerns or a desire to reopen the roads, but I guessed more likely the former. This city, like all of India's cities, is formed through the constant friction of tectonic layers of culture, shifting and jostling with each other in a vibrant and sometimes uneasy display of devotion and identity.

The Tibetan Buddhist hilltop town of McLeod Ganj, known also as Upper Dharamsala, is one more sedimentary level on top of the Indian Hindu city. Dharamsala, or Dharamshala, as it is pronounced in Hindi, means "spiritual dwelling," combining the word **dharma**, or spiritual teaching, with **shala**, which is a dwelling, and the whole name means "pilgrim's lodge or rest house." It is a fitting name for a city that is the site of so much pilgrimage today.

We hurried through the simple metal gates of the Dalai Lama's complex, where his offices and private residence are located. We arrived at a semicircular driveway surrounding a bed bursting with spring flowers. I had visited Dharamsala in January to meet with the Dalai Lama's office to plan this trip. At the time, the whole town was shrouded in clouds and freezing cold, but now the sun was shining brightly, the flowers all the more eager to bloom, as they always seem to be in the brief growing season at higher altitudes, their lives cut short, every day seemingly more urgent and appreciated.

As the beginning of the dialogues grew closer, I realized I was becoming increasingly nervous, but I also knew that I was not the only one. On one of our planning calls for the trip, I had been touched by the Archbishop's honest expression of concern about crossing wits with the Dalai Lama. "He is much more cerebral," he had said, referring to the Dalai Lama's great love of debate, intellectual inquiry, and scientific exploration. "I am more instinctual," he had said, and I remembered him saying that deep visceral knowing and prayerful surrender had guided all of the major turning points in his life and his mission in the struggle to end apartheid. I guess even great spiritual leaders get nervous when they are journeying into the unknown.

After a day of rest for the Archbishop, we would begin the dialogues on the nature of true joy.

Day 1:

The Nature of
True Joy

Why Are You Not Morose?

To begin, I invited the Archbishop to offer a prayer, since, in his tradition, that is the way to open any important conversation.

"Yes, thank you," the Archbishop began. "I always need all the help I can get.

"Let's be still for a moment. Come, Holy Spirit. Fill the hearts of thy faithful people and kindle in them the fire of thy love. Send forth thy spirit and they shall be made new and thou shalt renew the face of the earth. Amen."

"Amen," the Dalai Lama added. I then asked the Dalai Lama to share his hopes for our time together. He sat back and rubbed his hands. "Now we are in the twenty-first century. We are improving on the innovations of the twentieth century and continuing to improve our material world. While of course there are still a lot of poor people who do not have adequate food, generally the world is now highly developed. The problem is that our world and our education remain focused exclusively on external, materialistic values. We are not concerned enough with our inner values. Those who grow up with this kind of education live a materialistic life and eventually the whole society becomes materialistic. But this culture is not sufficient to tackle our human problems. The real problem is **here**," the Dalai Lama said, pointing to his head.

The Archbishop tapped his chest with his fingers to emphasize the heart as well.

"And **here**," the Dalai Lama echoed. "Mind and heart. Materialistic values cannot give us peace of mind. So we really need to focus on our inner values, our true humanity. Only this way can we have peace of mind—and more peace in our world. A lot of the problems we are facing are our own creation, like war and violence. Unlike a natural disaster, these problems are created by humans ourselves.

"I feel there is a big contradiction," the Dalai Lama continued. "There are seven billion human beings and nobody wants to have problems or suffering, but there are many problems and much suffering, most of our own creation. Why?" He was speaking now directly to the Archbishop, who was nodding in agreement. "Something is lacking. As one of the seven billion human beings, I believe everyone has the responsibility to develop a happier world. We need, ultimately, to have a greater concern for others' well-being. In other words, kindness or compassion, which is lacking now. We must pay more attention to our inner values. We must look inside."

He turned to the Archbishop and raised his hands, palms pressed together in a gesture of respect. "So now you, Archbishop Tutu, my longtime friend." He extended his hand to the Archbishop, who took it tenderly between both of his. "I think you have great potential—"

"Potential?!" the Archbishop responded with feigned outrage, retracting his hand.

"Great potential, yes. I mean great potential, you see, to create a happier humanity."

The Archbishop threw his head back, laughing. "Ah, yes."

"When people just look at your face," the Dalai Lama continued, "you are always laughing, always joyful. This is a very positive message." Now the Dalai Lama reached over and took the Archbishop's hand again and stroked it.

"Sometimes when you see political leaders or spiritual leaders, they have a very serious face—" He sat up in his chair frowning and looking very stern. "It makes one hesitant, but when they see your face—"

"It's the big nose," the Archbishop suggested, and they both giggled.

"So I really appreciate your coming to have this conversation," the Dalai Lama said. "In order to develop our mind, we must look at a deeper level. Everyone seeks happiness, joyfulness, but from outside—from money, from power, from big car, from big house. Most people never pay much attention to the ultimate source of a happy life, which is inside, not outside. Even the source of physical health is inside, not outside.

"So there may be a few differences between

us. You usually emphasize faith. Personally I am Buddhist, and I consider faith very important, but at the same time the reality is that out of seven billion people, over one billion people on the planet are nonbelievers. So we cannot exclude them. One billion is quite a large number. They are also our human brothers and sisters. They also have the right to become happier human beings and to be good members of the human family. So one need not depend on religious faith to educate our inner values."

"It's very difficult to follow your very profound pronouncements," the Archbishop began. "I thought you were going to say that, in fact, when you are pursuing happiness, you are not going to find it. It's very, very elusive. You don't find it by saying, I'm going to forget about everything and just pursue happiness. There's a title of a book by C. S. Lewis called **Surprised by Joy,** which I think expresses how it works.

"Many people look at you," the Archbishop continued, "and they think of all the awful things that have happened to you. Nothing can be more devastating than being exiled from your home, from the things that are really precious to you. And yet when people come to you, they experience someone who has a wonderful serenity . . . a wonderful compassion . . . a mischievousness—"

"That's the right word," the Dalai Lama added. "I don't like too much formality."

"Don't interrupt me," the Archbishop elbowed back.

"Oh!" The Dalai Lama laughed at his reprimand.

"It's wonderful to discover that what we want is not actually happiness. It is not actually what I would speak of. I would speak of joy. Joy subsumes happiness. Joy is the far greater thing. Think of a mother who is going to give birth. Almost all of us want to escape pain. And mothers know that they are going to have pain, the great pain of giving birth. But they accept it. And even after the most painful labor, once the baby is out, you can't measure the mother's joy. It is one of those incredible things that joy can come so quickly from suffering.

"A mother can be dead tired from work," the Archbishop continued, "and all of the things that have worried her. And then her child is ill. That mother will not remember her exhaustion. She can sit at the bedside of her sick child the night through, and when the child gets better you see that joy."

What is this thing called joy, and how is it possible that it can evoke such a wide range of feelings? How can the experience of joy span from those tears of joy at a birth to an irrepressible belly laugh at a joke to a serenely contented smile during meditation? Joy seems to blanket this entire emotional expanse. Paul Ekman, famed emotions researcher and long-time friend of the Dalai Lama, has written that joy is associated with feelings as varied as:

pleasure (of the five senses)
amusement (from a chuckle to a belly laugh)
contentment (a calmer kind of satisfaction)
excitement (in response to novelty or challenge)
relief (following upon another emotion, such as fear, anxiety, and even pleasure)

wonder (before something astonishing
  and admirable)
ecstasy or bliss (transporting us outside
  ourselves)
exultation (at having accomplished a
  difficult or daring task)
radiant pride (when our children earn a
  special honor)
unhealthy jubilation or <u>schadenfreude</u>
  (relishing in someone else's suffering)
elevation (from having witnessed an act
  of kindness, generosity, or compassion)
gratitude (the appreciation of a selfless act
  of which one is the beneficiary)

In his book on happiness, Buddhist scholar and
former scientist Matthieu Ricard has added
three other more exalted states of joy:

rejoicing (in someone else's happiness,
  what Buddhists call **mudita**)
delight or enchantment (a shining kind
  of contentment)
spiritual radiance (a serene joy born from
  deep well-being and benevolence)

This helpful mapping of the kingdom of joy conveys its complexity and its subtlety. Joy can span from the pleasure of others' good fortune, what Buddhists call **mudita,** to the pleasure in others' misfortune, what the Germans call **schadenfreude.** Clearly what the Archbishop was describing was more than mere pleasure and closer to the relief, wonder, and ecstasy of birth. Joy certainly does embrace all of these human experiences, but lasting joy—joy as a way of being—that one witnesses in the Archbishop and the Dalai Lama is probably closest to the "shining contentment" or the "spiritual radiance" born from deep well-being and benevolence.

I knew this complex topography of joy was what we were here to discover. Research conducted at the Institute of Neuroscience and Psychology at the University of Glasgow suggests that there are really only four fundamental emotions, three of which are so-called negative emotions: fear, anger, and sadness. The only positive one is joy or happiness. Exploring joy is nothing less than exploring what makes human experience satisfying.

. . .

s joy a feeling that comes and surprises us, or is it a more dependable way of being?" I asked. "For the two of you, joy seems to be something much more enduring. Your spiritual practice hasn't made you somber and serious. It's made you more joyful. So how can people cultivate that sense of joy as a way of being, and not just a temporary feeling?"

The Archbishop and the Dalai Lama looked at each other and the Archbishop gestured to the Dalai Lama. The Dalai Lama squeezed the Archbishop's hand and began. "Yes, it is true. Joy is something different from happiness. When I use the word **happiness,** in a sense I mean **satisfaction.** Sometimes we have a painful experience, but that experience, as you've said with birth, can bring great satisfaction and joyfulness."

"Let me ask you," the Archbishop jumped in. "You've been in exile fifty-what years?"

"Fifty-six."

"Fifty-six years from a country that you love more than anything else. Why are you not morose?"

"Morose?" the Dalai Lama asked, not understanding the word.

As Jinpa hurried to translate **morose** into Tibetan, the Archbishop clarified, "Sad."

The Dalai Lama took the Archbishop's hand in his, as if comforting him while reviewing these painful events. The Dalai Lama's storied discovery as the reincarnation of the Dalai Lama meant that at the age of two, he was swept away from his rural home in the Amdo province of eastern Tibet to the one-thousand-room Potala Palace in the capital city of Lhasa. There he was raised in opulent isolation as the future spiritual and political leader of Tibet and as a godlike incarnation of the Bodhisattva of Compassion. After the Chinese invasion of Tibet in 1950, the Dalai Lama was thrust into politics. At the age of fifteen he found himself the ruler of six million people and facing an all-out and desperately unequal war. For nine years he tried to negotiate with Communist China for his people's welfare, and sought political solutions as the country came to be annexed. In 1959, during an uprising that risked resulting in a massacre, the Dalai Lama decided, with a heavy heart, to go into exile.

The odds of successfully escaping to India were frighteningly small, but to avoid a confrontation and a bloodbath, he left in the night dressed as a palace guard. He had to take off his recognizable glasses, and his blurred vision must have heightened his sense of fear and uncertainty as the escape party snuck by garrisons of the People's Liberation Army. They endured sandstorms and snowstorms as they summited nineteen-thousand-foot mountain peaks during their three-week escape.

"One of my practices comes from an ancient Indian teacher," the Dalai Lama began answering the Archbishop's question. "He taught that when you experience some tragic situation, think about it. If there's no way to overcome the tragedy, then there is no use worrying too much. So I practice that." The Dalai Lama was referring to the eighth-century Buddhist master Shantideva, who wrote, "If something can be done about the situation, what need is there for dejection? And if nothing can be done about it, what use is there for being dejected?"

The Archbishop cackled, perhaps because it seemed almost too incredible that someone could stop worrying just because it was pointless.

"Yes, but I think people know it with their head." He touched both index fingers to his scalp. "You know, that it doesn't help worrying. But they still worry."

"Many of us have become refugees," the Dalai Lama tried to explain, "and there are a lot of difficulties in my own country. When I look only at that," he said, cupping his hands into a small circle, "then I worry." He widened his hands, breaking the circle open. "But when I look at the world, there are a lot of problems, even within the People's Republic of China. For example, the Hui Muslim community in China has a lot of problems and suffering. And then outside China, there are many more problems and more suffering. When we see these things, we realize that not only do we suffer, but so do many of our human brothers and sisters. So when we look at the same event from a wider perspective, we will reduce the worrying and our own suffering."

I was struck by the simplicity and profundity of what the Dalai Lama was saying. This was far from "don't worry, be happy," as the popular Bobby McFerrin song says. This was not a denial of pain and suffering, but a shift in perspective—from oneself and toward others, from anguish to compassion—seeing that others are suffering as well. The remarkable thing about what the Dalai Lama was describing is that as we recognize others' suffering and realize that we are not alone, our pain is lessened.

Often we hear about another's tragedy, and it makes us feel better about our own situation. This is quite different from what the Dalai Lama was doing. He was not contrasting his situation with others, but uniting his situation with others, enlarging his identity and seeing that he and the Tibetan people were not alone in their suffering. This recognition that we are all connected—whether Tibetan Buddhists or Hui Muslims—is the birth of empathy and compassion.

I wondered how the Dalai Lama's ability to shift his perspective might relate to the adage "Pain is inevitable; suffering is optional." Was it truly possible to experience pain, whether the pain of an injury or an exile, without suffering? There is a Sutta, or teaching of the Buddha, called the Sallatha Sutta, that makes a similar distinction between our "feelings of pain" and "the suffering that comes as a result of our response" to the pain: "When touched with a feeling of pain, the uninstructed, ordinary person sorrows, grieves, and laments, beats his breast, becomes distraught. So he feels two pains, physical and mental. Just as if they were to shoot a man with an arrow and, right afterward, were to shoot him with another one, so that he feels the pain of two arrows." It seems that the Dalai Lama was suggesting that by shifting our perspective to a broader, more compassionate one, we can avoid the worry and suffering that is the second arrow.

"Then another thing," the Dalai Lama continued. "There are different aspects to any event. For example, we lost our own country and became refugees, but that same experience gave us new opportunities to see more things. For me personally, I had more opportunities to meet with different people, different spiritual practitioners, like you, and also scientists. This new opportunity arrived because I became a refugee. If I remained in the Potala in Lhasa, I would have stayed in what has often been described as a golden cage: the Lama, holy Dalai Lama." He was now sitting up stiffly as he once had to when he was the cloistered spiritual head of the Forbidden Kingdom.

"So, personally, I prefer the last five decades of refugee life. It's more useful, more opportunity to learn, to experience life. Therefore, if you look from one angle, you feel, oh how bad, how sad. But if you look from another angle at that same tragedy, that same event, you see that it gives me new opportunities. So, it's wonderful. That's the main reason that I'm not sad and morose. There's a Tibetan saying: 'Wherever you have friends that's your country, and wherever you receive love, that's your home.'"

There was an audible gasp in the room at this poignant saying, and at its ability to ease, if not erase, the pain of a half century spent in exile.

"That's very beautiful," the Archbishop said.

"Also," the Dalai Lama continued, "whoever gives you love, that's your parent. So I consider you—although you are only four years older than me—as my father. I think you never could have had your children at the age of four, so you are not my real father. But I do consider you as a father."

"What you said is quite wonderful," the Archbishop began, still clearly moved by the Dalai

Lama's response to exile. "I think I would just add to it by saying to our sisters and brothers out there: Anguish and sadness in many ways are things that you cannot control. They happen. Supposing somebody hits you. The pain causes an anguish in you and an anger, and you might want to retaliate. But as you grow in the spiritual life, whether as a Buddhist or a Christian or any other tradition, you are able to accept anything that happens to you. You accept it not as the result of your being sinful, that you are blameworthy because of what has happened— it's part of the warp and woof of life. It's going to happen whether you like it or not. There are going to be frustrations in life. The question is not: How do I escape? It is: How can I use this as something positive? Just as you, Your Holiness, have just described. Nothing, I think, can be more devastating in many ways than being turfed out of your own country. And a country is not just a country, I mean it is part of you. You are part of it in a way that is very difficult to describe to other people. By rights, the Dalai Lama should be a sourpuss."

The Dalai Lama asked Jinpa for a translation of **sourpuss**.

The Archbishop decided to explain it himself: "It's when you do that face." He was pointing at the Dalai Lama's quizzical expression
and pursed lips, which did look a little like he
had bitten into a lemon. "Just that face, just
like that, you look like a real sourpuss."

The Dalai Lama was still trying to understand how one's puss could look sour, and Jinpa
was still trying to translate.

"And then when you smile your face lights up.
And it is because in a very large measure you
have transmuted what would have been totally
negative. You've transmuted it into goodness.
Because, again, you have not said, 'Well how
can I be happy?' You've not said that. You've
said, 'How can I help to spread compassion
and love?' And people everywhere in the world,
even when they don't understand your English,
they come and they fill stadiums. I'm not really
jealous. I speak far better English than you,
and I don't get so many people coming to hear
me as they come to you. And you know what?
I don't think they come to listen. They may
be doing that a bit. What they've come for is
that you embody something, which they feel,
because some of the things that you say, in a

sense, are obvious. Yet it's not the words. It's
the spirit behind those words. It is when you sit
and you tell people that suffering, frustration,
are not the determinants of who we are. It is
that we can use these things that are seemingly
negative for a positive effect.

"And I hope we can convey to God's children out there how deeply they are loved. How
deeply, deeply precious they are to this God.
Even the despised refugee whose name no one
seems to know. I look frequently at pictures
of people fleeing from violence, and there's so
much of it. Look at the children. I say that God
is crying, because that is not how God wanted
us to live. But you see again even in those circumstances, you have these people who come
from other parts of the world to try to help,
to make things better. And through the tears,
God begins to smile. And when God sees you
and hears how you try to help God's children,
God **smiles**." The Archbishop was now beam-
ing, and he whispered the word **smile** as if it
were the holy name of God.

"He wants to ask another question," the
Archbishop said, seeing that I was leaning forward. It was extraordinary to hear how deeply

they were engaging with joy and suffering, but at the rate we were going, we wouldn't get through one-tenth of the questions we needed to ask.

The Dalai Lama slapped the Archbishop's hand and said, "We have several days, so it's not a problem. If our interview is only thirty minutes or one hour, then we have to shorten our answers."

"**You** must shorten your answers," the Archbishop said. "**I am brief.**"

"First let's have tea, and then I will be brief."

Nothing Beautiful Comes
Without Some Suffering

Archbishop, you were talking about how the Dalai Lama has experienced great suffering in his exile. During apartheid, you and your country experienced great suffering, too. And even in your personal life, you've dealt with prostate cancer—you're dealing with it now. Many people, when they get ill, don't feel very joyful. You've been able to maintain that joy in the face of suffering. How have you been able to do it?"

"Well, I have certainly been helped by many other people. One of the good things is realizing that you are not a solitary cell. You are part of a wonderful community. That's helped very greatly. As we were saying, if you are setting out to be joyful you are not going to end up being joyful. You're going to find yourself turned in on yourself. It's like a flower. You open, you blossom, really because of other people. And I think some suffering, maybe even intense suffering, is a necessary ingredient for life, certainly for developing compassion.

"You know, when Nelson Mandela went to jail he was young and, you could almost say, bloodthirsty. He was head of the armed wing of the African National Congress, his party. He spent twenty-seven years in jail, and many would say, Twenty-seven years, oh, what a waste. And I think people are surprised when I say no, the twenty-seven years were necessary. They were necessary to remove the dross. The suffering in prison helped him to become more magnanimous, willing to listen to the other side. To discover that the people he regarded as his enemy, they too were human beings who had fears and expectations. And they had been molded by their society. And so without the twenty-seven years I don't think we would have seen the Nelson Mandela with the compassion, the magnanimity, the capacity to put himself in the shoes of the other."

While the racist apartheid government in South Africa imprisoned Nelson Mandela and so many other political leaders, the Archbishop became the de facto ambassador of the anti-apartheid struggle. Protected by his Anglican robes and the Nobel Prize that he received in 1984, he was able to campaign for an end to the oppression of blacks and other people of color in South Africa. During that bloody struggle, he buried countless men, women, and children, and tirelessly preached peace and forgiveness at their funerals.

After the release of Nelson Mandela and his election as the first president of a free South Africa, the Archbishop was asked to create the famed Truth and Reconciliation Commission to try to find a peaceful way to confront the atrocities of apartheid and pioneer a new future without revenge and retribution.

"And, in a kind of paradoxical way," the Archbishop continued, "it is how we face all of the things that seem to be negative in our lives that determines the kind of person we become. If we regard all of this as frustrating, we're going to come out squeezed and tight and just angry and wishing to smash everything.

"When I spoke about mothers and childbirth, it seems to be a wonderful metaphor, actually, that nothing beautiful in the end comes without a measure of some pain, some frustration, some suffering. This is the nature of things. This is how our universe has been made up."

Later I was amazed to hear from prenatal researcher Pathik Wadhwa that there is indeed a kind of biological law at work in these situations. Stress and opposition turn out to be exactly what initiate our development in utero. Our stem cells do not differentiate and become us if there is not enough biological stress to encourage them to do so. Without stress and opposition, complex life like ours would never have developed. We would never have come into being.

"If you want to be a good writer," the Archbishop concluded, "you are not going to become one by always going to the movies and eating bonbons. You have to sit down and write, which can be very frustrating, and yet without that you would not get that good result."

There was deep truth in what the Archbishop was saying, and yet I wanted to repeat back to him what he had said to the Dalai Lama. It's one thing to understand the value of suffering, and quite another to remember it when you are angry or frustrated or in pain. "Archbishop, take us with you to the hospital or to a doctor's appointment, and they're probing you and prodding you, and it's painful, and it's uncomfortable. And you're waiting, and it takes a long time. What do you do inside yourself not to feel angry or to complain or to wallow in your self-pity? It sounds like you're saying you can choose to be joyful even in the face of that difficulty. How do you do that?"

"I think we ought not to make people feel guilty when it is painful. It **is** painful, and you have to acknowledge that it is painful. But actually, even in the midst of that pain, you can recognize the gentleness of the nurse who is looking after you. You can see the skill of the surgeon who is going to be performing the operation on you. Yet sometimes the pain can be so intense that you do not have even the capacity to do that.

"The thing is, don't feel guilty. We have no control over our feelings. Emotions are spontaneous things that arise." This was a point that

the Archbishop and the Dalai Lama would
disagree on during the week: How much control do we have over our emotions? The Archbishop would say we have very little. The
Dalai Lama would say we have more than we
think.

"At some point, you will be in anguish,"
the Archbishop continued. "We are told in the
Christian tradition to offer up our suffering
and unite it with the anguish and pain of our
Savior and thus use it to improve the world.
It does help you not to be too self-centered. It
helps you to some extent to look away from
yourself. And it can help make that anguish
bearable. You don't have to be a believer in
any faith to be able to say, Oh, aren't I blessed
that I have doctors, that I have nurses qualified to look after me, and that I can be in a
hospital? That might just be the beginning of
moving away from being so self-centered and
concentrating too much on me, me, me, me.
You begin to realize, Hey, I'm not alone in this.
Look at all the many others, and there may be
some who are in greater pain. It's like being put
into a fiery furnace to be refined."

The Dalai Lama jumped in to affirm the

truth of what the Archbishop was saying. "Too much self-centered thinking is the source of suffering. A compassionate concern for others' well-being is the source of happiness. I do not have as much experience with physical pain as you have. Yet one day I was in Bodh Gaya, the place where the Buddha achieved enlightenment, to begin a series of important Buddhist teachings. Bodh Gaya is the holiest pilgrimage place for Buddhists.

"There were around one hundred thousand people who had come to attend the teachings, but suddenly I had intense pain in my abdomen. They did not know then that it was my gallbladder, but I was told I needed to go to the hospital urgently. When bouts of pain struck, it was so intense that I was sweating. We had to drive to the hospital in Patna, the capital city of the state of Bihar, which was two hours away. As we were driving, along the road we passed a lot of poverty. Bihar is one of the poorest states in India. I could see out the window that the children had no shoes, and I knew that they were not getting a proper education. Then as we approached Patna, under a hut I saw an old man lying on the ground. His hair was disheveled, his clothes were dirty, and he looked sick. He had no one to take care of him. Really, he looked as if he were dying. All the way to the hospital, I was thinking of this man and felt his suffering, and I completely forgot about my own pain. By simply shifting my focus to another person, which is what compassion does, my own pain was much less intense. This is how compassion works even at the physical level.

"So as you rightly mentioned, a self-centered attitude is the source of the problem. We have to take care of ourselves without selfishly taking care of ourselves. If we don't take care of ourselves, we cannot survive. We need to do that. We should have wise selfishness rather than foolish selfishness. Foolish selfishness means you just think only of yourself, don't care about others, bully others, exploit others. In fact, taking care of others, helping others, ultimately is the way to discover your own joy and to have a happy life. So that is what I call wise selfishness."

"You are wise," the Archbishop said. "I wouldn't just say wise selfish. You are wise."

. . .

The Buddhist practice of mind training, called **lojong** in Tibetan, is an important part of the Dalai Lama's tradition. One of the fundamental messages in the original twelfth-century **lojong** text echoes what the Dalai Lama and the Archbishop were saying about looking away from oneself: "All dharma teachings agree on one point—lessening one's self-absorption."

The text clarifies that when we focus on our ourselves we are destined to be unhappy: "Contemplate that, as long as you are too focused on your self-importance and too caught up in thinking about how you are good or bad, you will experience suffering. Obsessing about getting what you want and avoiding what you don't want does not result in happiness." The text includes the admonition: "Always maintain only a joyful mind."

So what, then, is this joyful mind? Jinpa, who wrote a translation and commentary on this revered text, explained as we were preparing for the trip that joy is our essential nature, something everyone can realize. We could say that our desire for happiness is, in a way, an attempt to rediscover our original state of mind.

It seems that Buddhists believe that joy is the natural state but that the ability to experience joy can also be cultivated as a skill. As we were hearing, so much depends on where we put our attention: on our own suffering or that of others, on our own perceived separation or on our indivisible connection.

Our ability to cultivate joy has not been scientifically studied as thoroughly as our ability to cultivate happiness. In 1978, psychologists Philip Brickman, Dan Coates, and Ronnie Janoff-Bulman published a landmark study that found that lottery winners were not significantly happier than those who had been paralyzed in an accident. From this and subsequent work came the idea that people have a "set point" that determines their happiness over the course of their life. In other words, we get accustomed to any new situation and inevitably return to our general state of happiness.

However, more recent research by psychologist Sonja Lyubomirsky suggests that perhaps only 50 percent of our happiness is determined by immutable factors like our genes or temperament, our "set point." The other half is determined by a combination of our circumstances, over which we may have limited control, and our attitudes and actions, over which we have a great deal of control. According to Lyubomirsky, the three factors that seem to have the greatest influence on increasing our happiness are our ability to reframe our situation more positively, our ability to experience gratitude, and our choice to be kind and generous. These were exactly the attitudes and actions that the Dalai Lama and the Archbishop had already mentioned and to which they would return as central pillars of joy.

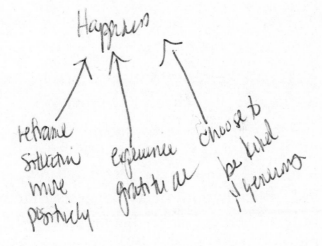

Have You Renounced Pleasure?

Most religions have a strong conviction that we cannot discover lasting happiness through our senses. So while temporary enjoyment can come through our senses, it is inevitably fleeting and not the source of enduring satisfaction. There is a Buddhist saying that trying to seek happiness through sensory gratification is like trying to quench your thirst by drinking saltwater. But what exactly is the relationship between joy and pleasure and between what the Dalai Lama has called happiness at the physical level and happiness at the mental level?

"Your Holiness, many believe that as a monk you have renounced pleasure or enjoyment."

"And sex," the Dalai Lama added, although that was not exactly where I was going.

"**What?**" the Archbishop said.

"**Sex, sex,**" the Dalai Lama repeated.

"**Did you just say that?**" the Archbishop said incredulously.

"Oh, oh," the Dalai Lama said with a laugh, noticing the Archbishop's surprise, and then reached over to reassure him, which caused the Archbishop to erupt in a gleeful cackle.

"So aside from sex," I said, trying to bring us back, "have you renounced pleasure and enjoyment? I sat next to you at lunch, and it looked like you were really enjoying the wonderful food. What is the role for you of enjoying the pleasures of life?"

"I love food. Without food, my body can't survive. You also," he said, turning to the Archbishop, "can't just think **God, God, God.** I cannot just think about **compassion, compassion, compassion.** Compassion will not fill my stomach. But, you see, each meal we have to develop the ability to consume the meal without attachment."

"Huh?" the Archbishop asked, not quite following how the Dalai Lama was using the

Buddhist term **attachment**, and perhaps also not quite following how anyone could not be attached to one's food.

"Not eating out of greed," the Dalai Lama explained. "Eating only for the survival of the body. One must think about the deeper value of nourishing the body."

At one of our meals the Dalai Lama had showed me his bowl of Tibetan rice and yogurt pudding and said, "This is typical Tibetan monk's food—I love this." He was eating with relish. There was something deeply relieving about knowing that holiness didn't require a rejection of the simple joys of life, like a good meal and especially pudding.

I felt pretty sure that he had gotten some significant amount of pleasure out of eating that dessert. He was clearly experiencing some joy through his senses. I wondered about the boundary between enjoyment and greed. Was it the second or third helping, and therefore a matter of portion size, or was it a matter of attitude toward each bite? Jinpa shared with me a well-known Tibetan Buddhist prayer that often is said before a meal: "Viewing this meal as a medicine, I shall enjoy it without greed or anger, not out of gluttony nor out of pride, not to fatten myself, but only to nourish my body." Perhaps the Dalai Lama was saying that eating to nourish the body did not require one to deny the enjoyment and satisfaction of the experience.

"So now to your question," the Dalai Lama said. "When we speak of experiencing happiness, we need to know that there are actually two different kinds. The first is the enjoyment of pleasure through our senses. Here, sex, the example I cited, is one such experience. But we can also experience happiness at the deeper level through our mind, such as through love, compassion, and generosity. What characterizes happiness at this deeper level is the sense of fulfillment that you experience. While the joy of the senses is brief, the joy at this deeper level is much longer lasting. It is true joy.

"A believer develops this deeper level of joy through faith in God, which brings inner strength, inner peace. For a nonbeliever or a nontheist like me, we must develop this deeper level of joy through training the mind. This kind of joy or happiness comes from within.

Then the pleasures of the senses become less important.

"Over the last several years, I have discussed with scientists this distinction between the sensory level of pleasure and pain and the deeper level of mental happiness and suffering. Now if we look at today's materialistic life people seem mainly concerned with sensory experiences. So that's why their satisfaction is very limited and brief, since their experience of happiness is so dependent on external stimuli. For example, so long as the music is playing, they feel happy." He tilted his head to the side with a smile as if appreciating the music. "When something good is happening, they are happy. Good food, they are happy. When these things stop, then they feel bored, restless, and unhappy. Of course this is nothing new. Even in the time of the Buddha, people would fall into the trap of thinking that sensory experience would bring them happiness.

"So when joy arises at the level of your mind and not just your senses, you can maintain a deep sense of satisfaction for a much longer period of time—even for twenty-four hours.

"So I always say to people, you have to pay more attention to the mental level of joy and happiness. Not just physical pleasure, but satisfaction at the level of mind. This is true joyfulness. When you are joyful and happy at the mental level, physical pain doesn't matter very much. But if there is no joy or happiness at the mental level, too much worrying, too much fear, then even physical comforts and pleasure will not soothe your mental discomfort."

"Many of our readers," I said, "will understand what physical pleasure is, or the physical dimension of joy and happiness. They know how a good meal or a good song makes them feel. But what is this mental happiness or mental pleasure that you're talking about that lasts for twenty-four hours?"

"A genuine sense of love and affection," the Dalai Lama said.

"Do you wake up with this joy?" I asked. "Even before coffee?"

"If you develop a strong sense of concern for the well-being of all sentient beings and in particular all human beings, this will make you happy in the morning, even **before** coffee.

"This is the value of compassion, of having

compassionate feelings for others. Even, you see, ten minutes or thirty minutes of meditating on compassion, on kindness for others, and you will see its effects all day. That's the way to maintain a calm and joyous mind.

"Everyone has had the experience of being in a good mood and some trouble comes, and you feel okay. When your mood is really bad, even when your closest friend comes, you still feel unhappy."

"Did you feel that way when I came?" the Archbishop said, playfully.

"That is exactly why I came to the airport to receive you—so I could feel more unhappy . . . and make trouble for you!"

Science has a term for the unsatisfactory nature of pursuing pleasure alone: the **hedonic treadmill**, named for the Greek school of thought that believed pleasure to be the ultimate good. Throughout history, hedonism has had its advocates, back to the birth of written culture. In the Gilgamesh tale, Siduri, the female divinity of fermentation (in other words, alcohol), admonishes, "Fill your belly.

Day and night make merry. Let days be full of
joy. Dance and make music day and night . . .
These things alone are the concern of men."
Even in the deeply spiritual culture of ancient
India, the source of much of the Dalai Lama's
Tibetan tradition, there was a hedonistic school
known as Charvaka. In many ways, hedonism
is the default philosophy of most people and
certainly has become the dominant view of
consumer "shop till you drop" culture.

Yet scientists have found that the more we
experience any pleasure, the more we become
numb to its effects and take its pleasures for
granted. The first bowl of ice cream is sublime,
the second bowl tasty, and the third causes
indigestion. It is like a drug that must be taken
in ever-greater quantities to produce the same
high. But there does seem to be one thing in the
literature that powerfully and lastingly changes
our sense of well-being. It is what the Dalai
Lama and the Archbishop had been advocating
throughout our first day: our relationships, and
specifically, our expression of love and generosity to others in our life.

Richard Davidson, the neuroscientist with
whom I had lunch in San Francisco, has drawn

together the neuroimaging research into a unified theory of the happy brain. I was so fascinated by what he was saying that I could not pay attention to my spring rolls, and those spring rolls were really good, at least on the physical level.

There are four independent brain circuits that influence our lasting well-being, Davidson explained. The first is "our ability to maintain positive states." It makes sense that the ability to maintain positive states or positive emotions would directly impact one's ability to experience happiness. These two great spiritual leaders were saying that the fastest way to this state is to start with love and compassion.

The second circuit is responsible for "our ability to recover from negative states." What was most fascinating to me was that these circuits were totally independent. One could be good at maintaining positive states but easily fall into an abyss of a negative state from which one had a hard time recovering. That explained a lot in my life.

The third circuit, also independent but essential to the others, is "our ability to focus and avoid mind-wandering." This of course was

the circuit that so much of meditation exists
to develop. Whether it was focusing on one's
breath, or a mantra, or the analytic meditation
that the Dalai Lama did each morning, this
ability to focus one's attention was fundamental.

The fourth and final circuit is "our ability to
be generous." That was amazing to me: that we
had an entire brain circuit, one of four, devoted
to generosity. It is no wonder that our brains
feel so good when we help others or are helped
by others, or even witness others being helped,
which Ekman had described as the elevation
that is one dimension of joy. There was strong
and compelling research that we come factory
equipped for cooperation, compassion, and
generosity.

John Bargh, one of the world's leading experts
on the science of the unconscious, describes
it as one of three innate (and often unconscious) goals: to survive, to reproduce, and to
cooperate. In lab experiments where eighteen-
month-old children were shown dolls facing
each other, they were more cooperative than
those who were shown dolls who were facing
away from each other. This unconscious prime,
which can be turned on or off, Bargh argues,

is one interesting example that cooperation is a deep evolutionary drive that exists from our earliest development.

Perhaps more sobering, it has also hardwired us to cooperate with and be kind to those who look like our caregivers, who presumably kept us safe. We are more wary of others who look different: these are the unconscious roots of prejudice. Our empathy does not seem to extend to those who are outside our "group," which is perhaps why the Archbishop and the Dalai Lama are constantly reminding us that we are, in fact, one group—humanity. Nonetheless, the ability and desire to cooperate and to be generous to others is there in our neural circuits, and it can be harnessed personally, socially, and globally.

Our Greatest Joy

addressed the next question to the Archbishop. "The joy that you are talking about is not just a feeling. It's not something that just comes and goes. It's something much more profound. And it sounds like what you're saying is that joy is a way of approaching the world. Many people are waiting for happiness or joy. When they get a job, when they fall in love, when they get rich, then they will be happy, then they will have joy. You are talking about something that is available right now, without waiting for anything."

The Archbishop considered his response carefully. "I mean simply to say that ultimately our greatest joy is when we seek to do good for others." Was it really that straightforward? Did we just need to stimulate and satisfy our dedicated brain circuit of generosity? As if anticipating my skepticism, the Archbishop continued, "It's how we are made. I mean we're wired to be compassionate." Quite literally wired, I thought, based on Davidson's research.

"We are wired to be caring for the other and generous to one another. We shrivel when we are not able to interact. I mean that is part of the reason why solitary confinement is such a horrendous punishment. We depend on the other in order for us to be fully who we are. I didn't know that I was going to come so soon to the concept that we have at home, the concept of Ubuntu. It says: A person is a person through other persons.

"Ubuntu says when I have a small piece of bread, it is for my benefit that I share it with you. Because, after all, none of us came into the world on our own. We needed two people to bring us into the world. And the Bible that we Jews and Christians share tells a beautiful story. God says, 'It is not good for Adam to be alone.' Well, you could have said, 'No, I'm sorry, he's not alone. I mean, there are trees, there are animals, and there are the birds. How can you say he's alone?'

"And you realize that in a very real sense we're meant for a very profound complementarity. It is the nature of things. You don't have to be a believer in anything. I mean I could not speak as I am speaking without having learned it from other human beings. I could not walk as a human being. I could not think as a human being, except through learning it from other human beings. I learned to be a human being from other human beings. We belong in this delicate network. It is actually quite profound.

"Unfortunately, in our world we tend to be blind to our connection until times of great disaster. We find we start caring about people in Timbuktu, whom we've never met and we're probably never going to meet this side of death. And yet we pour out our hearts. We give resources to help them because we realize that we are bound up together. We are bound up and can be human only together."

I was deeply moved by what the Archbishop was saying, yet I could hear the skepticism that some readers would have, that I had had. Most people do not walk around thinking about how they can help others. Whether we like it or not, most people are waking up in the morning wondering how they are going to manage to do their job, make enough money to pay the bills, and take care of their families and other responsibilities. "Nice guys finish last" is a phrase that speaks to our deep ambivalence about kindness and compassion in the West. Success in our society is measured by money, power, fame, and influence.

These men had all of these except the first, but neither would go hungry. For spiritual leaders, ignoring money was fine, but what about for those who lived and died in the almighty marketplace? Most people are not aspiring to spiritual greatness or enlightenment but to pay for their children's education and make it through retirement without running out of money. I chuckled at the memory of visiting the house of some friends outside of Las Vegas. It was a beautiful home, actually more like a Persian estate, with multiple buildings with fountains and flowing channels of water. It was reminiscent of the great structures of Islamic civilization. I was there for a discussion of the Archbishop's legacy, an

and witnessed the beauty ar

place, he had smiled and s

wrong—I do want to be ri

"As you just mentioned," the Dal

added, getting quite animated, "people think

about money or fame or power. From the point

of view of one's own personal happiness, these

are shortsighted. The reality, as the Archbishop

mentioned, is that human beings are social ani-

mals. One individual, no matter how power-

ful, how clever, cannot survive without other

human beings. So the best way to fulfill your

wishes, to reach your goals, is to help others, to

make more friends.

"How do we create more friends?" he now

asked rhetorically. "Trust. How do you develop

trust? It's simple: You show your genuine sense

of concern for their well-being. Then trust will

come. But if behind an artificial smile, or a big

banquet, is a self-centered attitude deep inside

of you, then there will never be trust. If you are

thinking how to exploit, how to take advantage

of them, then you can never develop trust in

others. Without trust, there is no friendship.

We human beings are social animals, as we've

and we need friends. Genuine friends. friends for money, friends for power are arti- ficial friends."

The Archbishop jumped in. "This God is community, fellowship. Being created by this God, we are created in order to flourish. And we flourish in community. When we become self-centered, turning in on ourselves, as sure as anything, we are going to find one day a deep, deep, **deep** frustration."

We are left with a paradox. If one of the fundamental secrets of joy is going beyond our own self-centeredness, then is it foolish selfishness (as the Dalai Lama would say) and self-defeating to focus on our own joy and happiness? The Archbishop had already said that we could not pursue joy and happiness in their own right, so is it not a mistake to focus on them at all?

Research suggests that cultivating your own joy and happiness has benefits not just for you, but also for others in your life. When we are able to move beyond our own pain and suffering, we are more available to others; pain causes

us to be extremely self-focused. Whether the
pain is physical or mental, it seems to consume
all of our focus and leave very little attention
for others. In his book with the Dalai Lama,
psychiatrist Howard Cutler summarized these
findings: "In fact, survey after survey has shown
that it is **unhappy** people who tend to be most
self-focused and are socially withdrawn, brood-
ing, and even antagonistic. Happy people, in
contrast, are generally found to be more socia-
ble, flexible, and creative, and are able to tol-
erate life's daily frustrations more easily than
unhappy people. And, most important, they
are found to be more loving and forgiving than
unhappy people."

Still some might wonder what our own joy
has to do with countering injustice and inequality. What does our happiness have to do with
addressing the suffering of the world? In short,
the more we heal our own pain, the more we
can turn to the pain of others. But in a surprising way, what the Archbishop and the Dalai
Lama were saying is that the way we heal our
own pain is actually by turning to the pain of
others. It is a virtuous cycle. The more we turn
toward others, the more joy we experience,

and the more joy we experience, the more we can bring joy to others. The goal is not just to create joy for ourselves but, as the Archbishop poetically phrased it, "to be a reservoir of joy, an oasis of peace, a pool of serenity that can ripple out to all those around you." As we will see, joy is in fact quite contagious. As is love, compassion, and generosity.

So being more joyful is not just about having more fun. We're talking about a more empathic, more empowered, even more spiritual state of mind that is totally engaged with the world. When the Archbishop and I were working on creating a training course for peace ambassadors and activists who go into conflict regions, he explained how peace must come from within. We cannot bring peace if we do not have inner peace. Similarly, we cannot hope to make the world a better, happier place if we do not also aspire for this in our own lives. I was eager to hear about how we deal with the inevitable obstacles to joy, but I knew that would need to wait for the next day. There was time for only one brief question before lunch.

I asked the Dalai Lama what it was like to wake up with joy, and he shared his experience each morning. "I think if you are an intensely religious believer, as soon as you wake up, you thank God for another day. And you try to do God's will. For a nontheist like myself, but who is a Buddhist, as soon as I wake up, I remember Buddha's teaching: the importance of kindness and compassion, wishing something good for others, or at least to reduce their suffering. Then I remember that everything is interrelated, the teaching of interdependence. So then I set my intention for the day: that this day should be meaningful. Meaningful means, if possible, serve and help others. If not possible, then at least not to harm others. That's a meaningful day."

Lunch: The Meeting of Two Mischievous People Is Wonderful

The Dalai Lama's audience room had been transformed into a dining room. At the far end was an ornate golden Buddha encased in a colorful wooden box. The walls were hung with **thangkas**, brightly painted silk scrolls that depicted images of the Buddha and other Buddhist figures. They were traditionally hung on the walls of monasteries for brief periods of time to inspire meditative practice. They were used to encourage practitioners along the path of enlightenment.

The windows were covered with white lace curtains and the table was set for lunch with

ın flat bread and boxed juice
whole setting was simple,
ᴗnic, and the meal was typical
ᴗod from the Dalai Lama's kitchen.
ᴗe were noodles and vegetables and **momos**,
the famed Tibetan steamed dumplings.

The Dalai Lama and Archbishop Tutu sat across from each other. As I sat next to the Dalai Lama I could feel in his posture and his body language the power of a leader. I remembered how strongly and tenderly he had held my hand the first time we met. His kindness did not in any way diminish his power, a valuable reminder that compassion is a feature of strength, not weakness, a point they would make throughout our conversations.

When the Dalai Lama greets you, he takes your hand and then rubs it tenderly, as a grandparent might. He looks into your eyes, feels deeply what you are feeling, and touches his forehead to yours. Whatever feeling, elation or anguish, is in your heart and reflected on your face, it is mirrored in his. But then when he meets the next person, those emotions are gone and he is wholly available for the next encounter and the next moment. Perhaps that is what it means to be fully present, available for each moment and each person we encounter, untethered by the ruminating memories of the past and not lured by the anticipatory worry about the future.

The lunch began by returning to the theme of birthdays, aging, and mortality.

"I went to see a German specialist for knees," the Dalai Lama said. "He found my physical condition very good. And then he told me my knees were the problem. He said you are not eighteen years old but eighty years old, so nothing much can be done. I really felt that was a great teaching. It is very important to think about impermanence. He reminds me I'm eighty years old. That's wonderful. But, my friend, you are even older than me."

"Are you showing off?" the Archbishop said.

"My own kitchen made this," the Dalai Lama said as he offered a piece of bread to his honored guest.

"You put your fingers on the bread and think I should eat it?" Archbishop responded. "I like this one," Archbishop Tutu said, passing over the multigrain for the white bread, glancing over at his American doctor with a smile.

"The media at the airport said, 'You must be very happy to have Archbishop Tutu visiting,'" the Dalai Lama said. "I told them, 'Yes, indeed, I am very happy. I am receiving one of my very good friends. Firstly, on the human level, he is a very good human being. Secondly, he is a religious leader, a serious practitioner who respects different religious traditions. Then thirdly, and most importantly, he is my very, very close friend.'"

"You are just flattering me."

"So then I told them that you often used to describe me as a mischievous person and so I said I also consider you a mischievous person. The meeting of two mischievous people is wonderful. So, very happy reunion." They both laughed.

Now the Archbishop crossed himself and said a prayer before eating his bread.

"Is it okay? Temperature is okay?" the Dalai Lama asked. It did not matter that he was a great spiritual leader, the former head of the Tibetan nation, and the reincarnation of the Bodhisattva of Compassion to the devout; at this moment, he was the host, and he was concerned with whether his guests were happy with the meal.

"Thank you very much," the Archbishop said. "Thank you for welcoming us and thank you for the lunch and thank you for putting all those people along the road to welcome us." He laughed. "The soup is delicious."

I have never seen Archbishop Tutu miss an opportunity to thank someone or appreciate what he has been given. He will often stop an entire production or an event to acknowledge all that are present.

"This soup **is** beautiful," the Archbishop said, fending off the monks who were trying to serve him more food. Everyone else was almost through with their meals, and he was still sipping his soup. "It's lovely. Please, please, this is all I'm going to have. I'm going later on to the dessert—I mean—the fruit salad." Then seeing that ice cream was now being offered, he laughed. "Yes, okay, maybe a little ice cream." He was swaying his head from side to side, balancing his health on the one side and his sweet tooth on the other. The Archbishop is a big fan of ice cream, especially rum raisin, and when he stayed with Rachel and me, his office kindly told us his food preferences: chicken instead of fish, rum and Coke—now given up for those pesky health reasons—and rum raisin ice cream. Rum raisin ice cream was not an easy flavor to find outside of the holidays, but we finally found a gallon container in the deep freezer of an ice cream warehouse. The Archbishop had three well-enjoyed bites for one dessert, and we ate the rest of the gallon for months.

The conversation transitioned to the topics of bringing together their two religious traditions, the great challenge of religious conflict, and the need for tolerance. The Dalai Lama began by saying it's not possible for everyone to be a Christian or a Buddhist. "There's no other choice but for followers of the world's religions to accept the reality of other faiths. We have to live together. In order to live happily, we must respect each other's traditions. I really admire other traditions."

"Kofi Annan, when he was in his last year, set up a commission," the Archbishop added. "They called it the High Level Panel, a rather pompous title. We were from all traditions, and despite our diversity, we produced a unanimous report. We concluded, 'There is nothing wrong with faiths. The problem is the faithful.'"

"That's true, that's true," the Dalai Lama agreed.

I asked what we must do about intolerance and fanaticism, which was flaring all around the world.

"Education and wider contact are really the only solutions," the Dalai Lama replied. "I have gone to make pilgrimages to holy sites all over the world—such as Fátima in Portugal, the Wailing Wall and Dome of the Rock in Jerusalem. One time I was in Barcelona, Spain, and I met a Christian monk who had spent five years in the mountains living as a hermit—with very few hot meals. I asked him what his practice was, and he said the practice of love. When he answered, there was something very special in his eyes. This is really the practice at the core of all the world's religions—love. I didn't think to myself when I met this holy man: 'Unfortunately he's not a Buddhist,' or 'It's too bad he's a Christian.'"

"I often say to people, 'Do you really think that . . .'" the Archbishop began. But the Dalai Lama had turned to one of the monks who was serving food. The Archbishop pretended to scold him: "Are you listening?"

The Dalai Lama, who had missed the Archbishop's comment, launched in with, "So, that shows, really . . ."

The Archbishop continued to pretend that he was offended. "You see? He's not listening."

"Unless you use the stick, I will not listen," the Dalai Lama said, laughing.

"But I thought you were nonviolent!"

"Now, please, you speak more. I should concentrate on eating. This is my last meal of the day." In the Buddhist monastic tradition, the Dalai Lama eats only two meals a day, breakfast and lunch.

"Okay. As I was saying, do you really think that when—I didn't say **if**; I said **when**—the Dalai Lama arrives in heaven, that God will say, 'Oh, Dalai Lama, you've been so wonderful. What a pity you are not a Christian. You'll have to go to the warmer place.' Everybody sees just how entirely ridiculous it is." The Archbishop paused and then, in a very intimate moment of friendship said, "I think one of the best things that ever happened to me was meeting you."

The Dalai Lama smiled and then started to tell another story.

"I thought you were going to try to eat!" the Archbishop said.

The Dalai Lama chortled and went back to his dessert.

"Yes, but you have been a wonderful influence in the world," the Archbishop continued. "There are many, many people that you have helped to become good people, and people of different religions, people of different faiths. They can see, they can sense—because I don't think it is what you say, although, yes, what you say is okay . . . sort of acceptable. Scientists also think you are clever, but it is really who you are. I think everywhere in the world you go, people are aware that you are authentic. You're not putting it on. You live what you teach, and you have helped very, very, very many people recover a belief in their faiths, a belief also in goodness. You are popular not just with old people but also with young people. I've said that you and Nelson Mandela are the only people that I can think of who are not pop stars and who could fill Central Park as you do. I mean when people know that you are going to come and speak, they come in droves. So the thing we say, about our world being a secular world and all of that, is only partly true."

The Dalai Lama waved his hands, dismissing his rank or specialness. "I always consider myself personally one of the seven billion human beings. Nothing special. So, on that level, I have tried to make people aware that the ultimate source of happiness is simply a healthy body and a warm heart."

As he spoke, I wondered, why this is so difficult for us to believe and to act on? It should be obvious that we are the same, but often we feel separate. There is so much isolation and alienation. Certainly I had grown up feeling this way in New York City, which at the time was the most populated place in the world.

"Everybody wants a happy life—and our individual happy life depends on a happy humanity. So we have to think about humanity, discover a sense of oneness of all seven billion human beings.

"Tea or coffee?" the Dalai Lama said, once again returning from the spiritual teacher to the host.

"I've got juice, thank you," the Archbishop

replied. "You were raised with a very special status in Tibet. You must have come to this recognition of oneness over time."

"Yes, I have grown in my wisdom from study and experience. When I first went to Peking, now Beijing, to meet Chinese leaders, and also in 1956 when I came to India and met some Indian leaders, there was too much formality, so I felt nervous. So now, when I meet people, I do it on a human-to-human level, no need for formality. I really hate formality. When we are born, there is no formality. When we die, there is no formality. When we enter hospital, there is no formality. So formality is just artificial. It just creates additional barriers. So irrespective of our beliefs, we are all the same human beings. We all want a happy life." I couldn't help wondering if the Dalai Lama's dislike of formality had to do with having spent his childhood in a gilded cage.

"Was it only when you went into exile," I asked, "that the formality ended?"

"Yes, that's right. So sometimes I say, Since I became a refugee, I have been liberated from the prison of formality. So I became much closer to reality. That's much better. I often tease my

Japanese friends that there is too much formality in their cultural etiquette. Sometimes when
we discuss something, they always respond like
this." The Dalai Lama vigorously nodded his
head. "So whether they agree or disagree, I cannot tell. The worst thing is the formal lunches.
I always tease them that the meal looks like
decoration, not like food. Everything is very
beautiful, but very small portions! I don't care
about formality, so I ask them, more rice, more
rice. Too much formality, then you are left
with a very little portion, which is maybe good
for a bird." He was scooping up the last bits of
dessert.

"Everybody may want to be happy," I offered,
"but the challenge is a lot of people don't know
how. You were talking about the importance
of being warmhearted, but a lot of people are
shy or have a hard time opening up to other
people. They get scared. They're afraid of rejection. You've spoken about when you approach
people with trust, then it inspires trust in them
as well."

"That's right. Genuine friendship is entirely
based on trust," the Dalai Lama explained. "If
you really feel a sense of concern for the well-

being of others, then trust will come. That's the basis of friendship. We are social animals. We need friends. I think, from the time of our birth till our death, friends are very important.

"Scientists have found that we need love to survive. Our mothers show tremendous love and affection to us when we are born. Many scientists say that after birth, there are a number of weeks when the mother's physical touch is the key factor to developing the brain properly. After birth, if the child is isolated without the mother or physical touch, it can be very harmful. This is nothing to do with religion. This is biology. We need love."

The Dalai Lama had first heard about this research in the 1980s from the late biologist Robert Livingston, who later became his biology "tutor." Child neurologist and neuroscientist Tallie Baram has conducted one of the more recent examples of this important field of research. She found that a mother's caress triggers activity that improves cognition and resilience to stress in a baby's developing brain. The mother's touch could literally prevent the release of stress hormones that have been shown to lead to the disintegration of dendritic spines, branchlike structures on the neurons that are important to the sending and receiving of messages and the encoding of memory.

"My mother was a twin," I said. "And she was born prematurely, at just two and half pounds, and she was in an incubator for two months without any human touch."

"Did it affect her?" Archbishop Tutu asked.

"I think it affected her very profoundly."

"Now they have—what do they call it?" Archbishop Tutu said. "A kangaroo pouch. My wife Leah and I are patrons of a children's hospital in Cape Town, and one day we were visiting there, and this massive guy was carrying around the minutest baby tied to his chest so the baby could feel his heartbeat, and they said those babies have been shown to do much better."

Mpho asked if I still had the picture of my own twin daughters just after they were born prematurely, when they were in the neonatal intensive care unit. One of our daughters had had a prolapsed cord, which was blocking her from descending through the birth canal, and her heartbeat and oxygen level were plummeting. The obstetrician, as she was trying to use a vacuum extractor on our daughter's head, had told Rachel that she had one more push to get the baby out or they would have to do an emergency cesarean. Eliana was already in the birth canal, so a cesarean was no guarantee of a safe delivery.

As a doctor, Rachel knew, as I did, that every second counted, as Eliana's oxygen level was getting dangerously low. I've never witnessed anything like the strength Rachel had exhibited as she threw herself headlong into the pain and wrenched every ounce of maternal will from her body to push our daughter out. Eliana was born blue, unresponsive, and not breathing. Her Apgar score was one—out of ten—which meant she was barely alive.

She was rushed to the crash cart, where the doctors tried to revive her, and told Rachel to speak to her baby, the voice of the mother having an almost magical healing effect, even in the high-risk operating room. We waited for the longest moments of our lives as the doctors tried to bring her around, preparing to intubate her. And then, in a moment of unspeakable joy and relief, Eliana sputtered, took her first breath, and began to cry with life. The rest of us, including the obstetrician, were weeping tears of joy.

After Eliana's traumatic birth, the twins were taken to the neonatal intensive care unit at the hospital. When I walked in shortly after, they were lying side by side, holding hands.

The importance of love for our survival, which the Dalai Lama was describing, was not abstract to me, having witnessed the mother love that saved our daughter's life and that allows us all to survive. "Oh, lovely," the Archbishop said, imagining the image.

"It's biology," said the Dalai Lama. "All mammals, including humans, have a special bond with their mother. Without the mother's care, the youngster will die. That's a fact."

"Even if they don't die, they can grow into a Hitler because they have this huge sense of lack," the Archbishop said.

"I think when Hitler was very young," the Dalai Lama countered, "he also was the same as the other children." This was the first time they disagreed in more than mischievous play. "I think his mother showed affection to him, or he would have died." Family members recount that Klara Hitler was indeed a devoted mother, although Hitler's father apparently was allegedly abusive. "So," the Dalai Lama continued, "even today these terrorists also received maximum affection from their mothers. So even these terrorists, deep inside . . ."

"I think I have to take issue with you on that," the Archbishop responded. "The people who go around becoming bullies are people who have a massive sense of insecurity, who want to prove that they are somebody, often because they did not get enough love."

"I think, yes, circumstances, environment, education all matter," the Dalai Lama replied. "Especially today; there is not much focus on inner values in education. Then, instead of inner values, we become self-centered—always thinking: **I, I, I.** A self-centered attitude brings a sense of insecurity and fear. Distrust. Too much fear brings frustration. Too much frustration brings anger. So that's the psychology, the system of mind, of emotion, which creates a chain reaction. With a self-centered attitude, you become distanced from others, then distrust, then feel insecure, then fear, then anxiety, then frustration, then anger, then violence."

It was fascinating to hear the Dalai Lama

describe the process of mind that leads to fear, alienation, and ultimately to violence. I pointed out that so often our parenting in the West is too focused on our children, and their needs alone, rather than helping them to learn to care for others. The Dalai Lama responded, "Yes, there is too much self-centeredness also among parents—'my children, my children.' That's biased love. We need unbiased love toward entire humanity, entire sentient beings, irrespective of what their attitude is toward us. So your enemies are still human brothers and sisters, so they also deserve our love, our respect, our affection. That's unbiased love. You might have to resist your enemies' actions, but you can love them as brothers and sisters. Only we human beings can do this with our human intelligence. Other animals cannot do this."

Having known the fierce and focused love of parenthood, I wondered if it was truly possible to love others with that same love. Could we really extend that circle of care to many others and not just our own family? A monastic could focus all their love on humanity, but a parent has a child to raise. I imagined that what the Dalai Lama was saying might be an aspiration for humanity, but was it a realistic one? Perhaps we would not be able to love other children as much as we love our own, but maybe we could extend that love beyond its typical boundaries. I wondered what the Archbishop, who was also a father, might say, but by now everyone had finished lunch.

We would return to the elasticity of love and compassion later in the week, but tomorrow we would begin discussing the obstacles to joy, from stress and anxiety to adversity and illness, and how we might be able to experience joy even in the face of these inevitable challenges.

Days 2 and 3

The Obstacles to Joy

You Are a Masterpiece
in the Making

I t is very simple," the Dalai Lama began. "Everyone knows that physical pain is bad and tries to avoid it. We do this not only by curing diseases, but also by trying to prevent them and by trying to keep our physical immunity strong. Mental pain is equally bad, so we should try to alleviate it as well. The way to do this is to develop mental immunity."

We had started our second day of dialogues and were turning to the obstacles to joy. The subject of the dialogues was how to discover joy in the face of suffering, and we knew we'd need two full days to discuss all of the ways that we suffer. As the Dalai Lama had said the

day before, so much of our unhappiness origi-
nates within our own mind and heart—in how
we react to events in our life.

"Mental immunity," the Dalai Lama explained, "is just learning to avoid the destructive emotions and to develop the positive ones.
First, we must understand the mind—there
are so many different states of mind—the di-
verse thoughts and emotions we experience on
a daily basis. Some of these thoughts and emotions are harmful, even toxic, while others are
healthy and healing. The former disturb our
mind and cause much mental pain. The latter
bring us true joyfulness.

"When we understand this reality, it is much
easier to deal with the mind and to take preventive measures. This is how we develop mental immunity. And just as a healthy immune
system and healthy constitution protects your
body against potentially hazardous viruses and
bacteria, mental immunity creates a healthy
disposition of the mind so that it will be less
susceptible to negative thoughts and feelings.

"Think about it this way. If your health is
strong, when viruses come they will not make
you sick. If your overall health is weak, even

small viruses will be very dangerous for you. Similarly, if your mental health is sound, then when disturbances come, you will have some distress but quickly recover. If your mental health is not good, then small disturbances, small problems will cause you much pain and suffering. You will have much fear and worry, much sadness and despair, and much anger and aggravation.

"People would like to be able to take a pill that makes their fear and anxiety go away and makes them immediately feel peaceful. This is impossible. One must develop the mind over time and cultivate mental immunity. Often people ask me for the quickest and best solution to a problem. Again, this is impossible. You can have quickest or you can have best solution, but not both. The best solution to our suffering is mental immunity, but it takes time to develop.

"One time I was talking with Al Gore, the American vice president. He said that he had lots of problems, lots of difficulties that were causing him a great deal of anxiety. I said to him that we human beings have the ability to make a distinction between the rational level and the emotional level. At the rational level, we accept that this is a serious problem that we have to deal with, but at the deeper, emotional level, we are able to keep calm. Like the ocean has many waves on the surface but deep down it is quite calm. This is possible if we know how to develop mental immunity."

"Yes," the Archbishop replied, "you have answered very well. You always answer well, but you have done this one quite well. The only thing I think is that people sometimes get quite annoyed with themselves unnecessarily, especially when they have thoughts and feelings that are really quite natural.

"Basically," the Archbishop continued, "I think we've got to accept ourselves as we are. And then hope to grow in much the way the Dalai Lama described. I mean getting to know what the things are that trigger us. These are things that you can train, you can change, but we ought not to be ashamed of ourselves. We are human, and sometimes it is a good thing that we recognize that we have human emotions. Now the thing is being able to say, when is it appropriate?"

Throughout the week of dialogues, the Archbishop said many times that we should not berate ourselves for our negative thoughts and emotions, that they are natural and unavoidable. They are only made more intense, he argued, by the glue of guilt and shame when we think we should not have them. The Dalai Lama agreed that human emotions are natural, but he did argue about whether they are unavoidable. Mental immunity, he explained, is the way to avoid them.

For months after our time in Dharamsala I wrestled with this seeming disagreement: Is it possible to truly prevent negative thoughts and emotions, to develop what the Dalai Lama was calling "mental immunity"? Or are these thoughts and emotions inevitable, and should we, as the Archbishop was suggesting, just accept them and forgive ourselves for having them?

Finally, after many discussions with psychological experts, it became clear that each position was valid and simply reflected a different stage in the cycle of emotional life. Through self-inquiry and meditation, we can discover the nature of our mind and learn to soothe our emotional reactivity. This will leave us less vulnerable to the destructive emotions and thought patterns that cause us so much suffering. This is the process of developing mental immunity.

The Archbishop was simply reminding us that even with this immunity, there will be times when we will have negative or destructive emotions, and when this does happen, the last thing we want to do is judge ourselves harshly.

In other words, the Dalai Lama was saying that if we eat healthy, take our vitamins, and get enough rest, we can stay healthy, and the Archbishop was saying, "Yes, even so, there will be times when we will catch a cold, and we should not make it worse by beating up on ourselves."

So how do we deal with these obstacles to joy—the inevitable sources of suffering, both internal and external—that cause so much pain and anguish in our lives, when they do arise? These range from the everyday troubles of stress, frustration, and worry to the life-defining experiences of adversity, illness, and ultimately having to face death. We cannot control the inevitability of these occurrences, but both men agreed that we could influence their effect in our life by adjusting the attitude we take toward them.

The first step is to accept the reality of suffering. The Buddha is supposed to have said, "I have taught one thing and one thing only: suffering and the cessation of suffering." The first Noble Truth of Buddhism is that life is filled with suffering. The Sanskrit word for suffering is **dukkha** (not to be confused with the nutty and very tasty Egyptian condiment **dukka**).

Dukkha can be translated as "stress," "anxiety," "suffering," or "dissatisfaction." It is often described as the mental and physical suffering that occurs in life, illness, and aging. It is also described as the stress and anxiety that arise from the attempt to control what is fundamentally impermanent and unable to be controlled. We try to control the moment, which results in our feeling that what is happening should not be happening. So much of what causes heartache is our wanting things to be different than they are. "I think, in many cases," the Dalai Lama explained, "you develop some sort of unhappiness, some discontent, which leads to frustration and anger."

While stress and frustration may sound like superficial problems or complaints, the Buddha identified them as the core of so much of our unnecessary, or created, suffering. I was reminded of what the Dalai Lama had said on our first day: We cannot end natural disasters or the suffering they cause, but so much of the rest of our suffering we can.

Dukkha, or suffering, is the opposite of **sukha,** which means happiness, ease, or comfort. Both words are said to have originated from the ancient Aryans who brought the Sanskrit language to India. These Aryans were a nomadic people who traveled by horse- or ox-drawn carts, and the words literally mean "having a bad (or good) axle." Was it a bumpy ride (**dukkha**), or a smooth ride (**sukha**)? Not a bad metaphor for life. What is suffering but a bumpy ride? Every life is rutted and no one can avoid some inevitable bumps, but so much is determined by our own perception of the ride. Our mind is the axle that often determines whether we experience the ride as bumpy or smooth.

This point was brought home to me in a rather literal way when I went to Dharamsala in January, several months before the dialogues, with Peggy Callahan. Peggy was responsible for filming the week in Dharamsala, and we went to prepare for the April visit. Our return flight from the cloud-covered Dharamsala airport was canceled, so we embarked on a bumpy and winding expedition to the nearest airport, holding tightly to the hand straps in the car as we bounced up and down and were tossed from side to side. We tried hard not to get carsick, and distracted ourselves by telling each other humorous stories from our travels—stretching each story as long as possible during the bone-shaking six-hour journey.

"We have perceptions about our experience, and we judge them: 'This is good.' 'This is bad.' 'This is neutral,'" the Dalai Lama explained. "Then we have responses: fear, frustration, anger. We realize that these are just different aspects of mind. They are not the actual reality. Similarly, fearlessness, kindness, love, and forgiveness are also aspects of mind. It is very useful to know the system of emotion and to understand how our mind works.

"When a fear or frustration comes, we have to think, what is causing it? In most cases, fear is simply a mental projection. When I was young and living in the Potala, there was an area that was very dark, and there were stories about ghosts there. So when I was passing through this area, I would feel something. This was completely a mental projection."

"No," the Archbishop said with a frightened face. "There were ghosts there, man."

The Dalai Lama laughed and said, "When a mad dog approaches, barking and gnashing its teeth, then you need fear. That's not a mental projection. So you have to analyze the causes of the fear. With frustration, often you see someone, and you have a mental projection even when his or her face is neutral. Similarly, when you see someone's actions, you have a mental projection even when their behavior is neutral. So you have to ask yourself if your frustration is based on something real. Even if someone criticizes you or attacks you, then you have to think: Why did this happen? This person is not your enemy from birth. Certain circumstances caused the person to be negative toward you. There may be many causes, but usually your own attitude is an important contributing factor that cannot be ignored. You realize that this happened because you have done something in the past that this person didn't like. So then when you realize your own part in the other person's criticizing or attacking you, the intensity of your frustration and anger automatically reduces. Then you also realize that basic human nature is good, is compassionate, and that the person does not want to harm you. So therefore you see their emotion is due to some misunderstanding or misinformation. You see that this person's actions are due to their own destructive emotions. You can develop a sense of concern, compassion, even feel sorry for their pain and suffering: How sad that this person is out of control, or having such a negative feeling. Instead of frustration and anger you feel sorry for the other person and concern for them."

I nodded my head and said, "But sometimes our frustration is not dependent on other people but on circumstances beyond our control. For example, we can't control canceled flights."

"When I was young and very eager to go do something," the Dalai Lama said, "then they would announce that there was a delay or cancellation of the flight, I would feel angry and sometimes angry toward the pilot or toward the airline.

"Before there was air service from Dharamsala to Delhi, I would go to the city of Jammu, about four hours' drive, to fly. So one morning, all the passengers were on the airplane when they announced that the flight had been canceled and that everyone should please leave the airplane. Later I was told that the pilot did not come because he was drinking too much the night before. So everyone was complaining, and I felt frustrated, too.

"Now when an announcement comes that my flight is canceled or postponed, which does happen quite a lot here, I take it as a good opportunity to sit and do my practice, to sit and meditate. So now I feel less frustration."

I was reminded of a flight that I had been on with Rachel; our then two-year-old son, Jesse; and my mother to Hawaii. We did not have very much money and had booked seats on the cheapest airline we could find. They had only two planes that they would shuttle back and forth to Hawaii and other holiday destinations. We were almost halfway over the Pacific from California to Oahu when I felt a sudden jerk, like someone had shoved the plane from the side. Then the plane made a sweeping turn and sometime later the crew made an announcement that we were heading back to

San Francisco. I remember being very angry and frustrated.

We had to spend the whole day waiting for another plane, so we tried to begin our vacation in California, taking Jesse to the zoo. It was fun, but I felt angry that our Hawaiian holiday was being cut short. When we finally returned to the airport and got ready to board, I overheard the pilot reveal to another member of the crew the reason for turning around.

Apparently one of the bolts had come loose in one of the engines. The pilot casually mentioned, in the way of people who are used to calmly handling high-risk situations, that if they had not shut off the engine at the moment that they did, it would have sheared off and the airplane would have crashed into the ocean. Suddenly a delayed flight and a day at the zoo didn't sound so bad after all.

"I used to feel very frustrated and angry," the Archbishop said, "when we would be rushing to a very important meeting, and we would be stuck in traffic because there was an accident up ahead. You were grinding your teeth and looking for somebody to kick. But growing older I said, well, this is an opportunity for

being quiet. And then you would try to uphold
all the people that were involved. I mean there's
not very much you can do, so grinding your
teeth and getting heated up doesn't help. So
why not use the old things that they tell you?
Count to ten. One, two, three . . . ah!" The
Archbishop pretended to lose his temper despite
his trying to count to ten.

"I think it takes time to learn to be laid-back,"
he continued. "You know, it's not something
that just comes ready-made for you. No one
ought to feel annoyed with themselves. It just
adds to the frustration. I mean, we are human
beings, fallible human beings. And as the Dalai
Lama points out, there was a time . . . I mean,
we see him serene and calm. Yet there were
times when he, too, felt annoyed and perhaps
there still are. It's like muscles that have to be
exercised to be strong. Sometimes we get too
angry with ourselves thinking that we ought
to be perfect from the word **go**. But this being
on earth is a time for us to learn to be good,
to learn to be more loving, to learn to be more
compassionate. And you learn, not theoretically." The Archbishop was pointing his index
fingers at his head. "You learn when something

happens that tests you." And then he was pretending to be speaking as God might. "'**Hello,**
you said you wanted to be more compassionate.' '**Hello,** you wanted to be a little more
laid-back.'

"We get very angry with ourselves. We think
we ought to be supermen and superwomen
from the start. The Dalai Lama's serenity didn't
come fully formed. It was through the practice
of prayer and meditation that the gentleness, the compassion grew, his being patient
and accepting—within reasonable limits.
Accepting circumstances as they are, because
if there are circumstances that you cannot
change, then it's no use beating your head
against a brick wall; that just gives you a head-
ache. This is a vale of growth and development."

I was struck by the phrase "a vale of growth
and development," which seemed to echo the
famous Christian notion that life is a vale, or val-
ley, of tears, from which we are freed only when
we enter heaven. This expression is often said to
be based on Psalm 84:6, which has the beautiful
wording: "Who passing through the vale of tears
makes it a well." Indeed, we can use our tears,
our stress and frustration, as a well from which

we can draw the life-giving waters of our emotional and spiritual growth.

"It's similar to how we learn how to be a parent," the Archbishop said as he concluded our discussion. "You learn how to react to a child who is really frustrating you. You are better with your third child than you were with your first child. And so I would say to everyone: You are made for perfection, but you are not yet perfect. You are a masterpiece in the making."

Fear, Stress, and Anxiety: I Would Be Very Nervous

We all have fears," the Archbishop explained. "Fear and anxiety are mechanisms that have helped us to survive. You know, if you did not feel fear when you saw a lion over there and you just walked merrily by, in next to no time there would be no you. God has given us these things because God knew that we needed them. Otherwise, we would be fearless, but then we'd also be very stupid, and we would not be around very long. The problem is when the fear is exaggerated or when it is provoked by something that is really quite insignificant."

When I asked the Archbishop how he man-

aged the fear during the dark days of apartheid, when he received frequent death threats,
he said, "Well, one did not do silly things like
stand in front of a lit window at night, but
one had to say to God, 'If I'm doing your
work, you better jolly well protect me.'" I have
always been impressed with how the Archbishop has been willing to admit his fears and
frailties.

We so rarely hear about the doubts, fears, and
worries of leaders, as leadership itself seems to
require an air of confidence that rarely allows
the admission of weakness or vulnerability.
I was once told an amazing story by former
Time magazine editor Rick Stengel, who had
worked with Nelson Mandela on his autobi-
ography, **Long Walk to Freedom.** Mandela
was flying in a small propeller plane with his
bodyguard, Mike. The great leader was hidden
behind the morning paper when he noticed
that one propeller was not working. He leaned
over and calmly told Mike, who informed the
pilots. They were well aware of the problem and
explained that emergency landing procedures
were in place. When Mike explained the situation to Mandela, he nodded calmly and went

back to reading his paper. Apparently, Mike, a tough guy, was trembling with fear but only calmed by the image of Mandela, who looked unbothered by the fact that they might at any moment fall out of the sky. When they had gotten into the back of the bulletproof BMW that met them at the airport, Stengel asked him about the flight. To which, Mandela leaned in, eyes wide, and said, "Man, I was **terrified** up there." Even if leadership requires a show of strength during moments of crisis, our humanity is defined equally, or perhaps even more, by our weakness and vulnerability, a fact that the Archbishop often says reminds us of our need for one another.

One of my favorite quotes that we included in Mandela's book **Notes to the Future** was on courage: "I learned that courage was not the absence of fear, but the triumph over it. I felt fear more times than I can remember, but I hid it behind a mask of boldness. The brave man is not he who does not feel afraid, but he who conquers that fear." Archbishop Tutu said something very similar when we were working on **God Has a Dream.** He said, "Courage is not the absence of fear, but the ability to act despite it." The English word **courage** comes from the French word **coeur,** or heart; courage is indeed the triumph of our heart's love and commitment over our mind's reasonable murmurings to keep us safe.

As the Archbishop had said, it is when this natural fear gets exaggerated that we experience stress, worry, and anxiety. Many of us suffer from this general state of unease, during which we have floating fears and worries that attach to any experience or relationship. It is very hard to be joyful with stress and anxiety; we have a continual feeling of being overwhelmed and not being able to handle our work commitments, our family commitments, or the digital devices that are constantly reminding us of all the things that we are missing. Juggling so many things at the same time, we can feel like we are always one step behind.

Jinpa pointed out that modern society has prioritized independence to such an extent that we are left on our own to try to manage lives that are increasingly out of control. He explained the life that the Dalai Lama and his people had in Tibet before the Chinese invasion. In the remote village of Taktser in the Amdo province, the Dalai Lama's family house, like the others in the village, was located on a plateau, overlooking rolling grasslands filled with nomads and yaks. The Dalai Lama was one of sixteen children, nine of whom died in infancy. The nearest town was three hours away by mule. The boy, then called Lhamo Thondup, slept in the kitchen, closest to the stove. Life could not have been easy for him and his family, so it was a surprise to me when Jinpa explained that life would have been much less stressful in a traditional village.

For much of human history, whether in Tibet, or Africa, or anywhere in between, there were fears and worries, some of them major, like whether there would be enough food for the winter. But these concerns were made more manageable by having a close and connected life. While survival certainly is the greatest stressor of all—for which our stress response evolved—there is something different about the constant pressures and pulls of modern life. Although there would no doubt have been times of great stress and anxiety at the loss of crops or even the loss of a child, the daily rhythms would have been far less frenzied and unfocused. "There is a wisdom that has been lost," Jinpa said. "Our opportunities are so much greater now, but so, too, are our anxieties." I thought of the journey, both physical and psychological, that Jinpa had undertaken: from life in a Buddhist monastery that was largely unchanged for thousands of years to the family life he now lives in Montreal.

But if stress and anxiety are inevitable parts of modern life, how can we begin to confront these ever-present irritants? How do we make the ride smoother? How do we minimize the worry we experience?

"Stress and anxiety often come from too much expectation and too much ambition," the Dalai Lama said. "Then when we don't fulfill that expectation or achieve that ambition, we experience frustration. Right from the beginning, it is a self-centered attitude. I want this. I want that. Often we are not being realistic about our own ability or about objective reality. When we have a clear picture about our own capacity, we can be realistic about our effort. Then there is a much greater chance of achieving our goals.

But unrealistic effort only brings disaster. So in many cases our stress is caused by our expectations and our ambition."

What is too much ambition? I wondered. For someone raised in America, where ambition is a virtue in and of itself, the marriage of initiative and persistence, I was struck by his answer. Could it be that all of the getting and grasping that we see as our major ambition in modern life might be misguided? And perhaps the belief that more is better might be a recipe for stress and frustration, and ultimately dissatisfaction?

Perhaps it is a question of priorities. What is it that is really worth pursuing? What is it we truly need? According to the Archbishop and the Dalai Lama, when we see how little we really need—love and connection—then all the getting and grasping that we thought was so essential to our well-being takes its rightful place and no longer becomes the focus or the obsession of our lives. We must try to be conscious about how we live and not get swept away by the modern trance, the relentless march, the anxious accelerator. The Dalai Lama was urging us to be more realistic so we can come to some sense of inner peace now, rather than always chasing after our expectations and ambition for the next.

Symptoms of chronic stress are feelings of fragmentation and of chasing after time—of not being able to be present. What we are looking for is a settled, joyful state of being, and we need to give this state space. The Archbishop once told me that people often think he needs time to pray and reflect because he is a religious leader. He said those who must live in the marketplace—business-people, professionals, and workers—need it even more.

As chronic stress becomes a global epidemic, our stress response is being studied intensively to see if we can unwind its mysteries. It turns out that our perspective has a surprising amount of influence over the body's stress response. When we turn a **threat** into a **challenge**, our body responds very differently.

Psychologist Elissa Epel is one of the leading researchers on stress, and she explained to me how stress is supposed to work. Our stress response evolved to save us from attack or danger, like a hungry lion or a falling avalanche.

Cortisol and adrenalin course into our blood. This causes our pupils to dilate so we can see more clearly, our heart and breathing to speed up so we can respond faster, and the blood to divert from our organs to our large muscles so we can fight or flee. This stress response evolved as a rare and temporary experience, but for many in our modern world, it is constantly activated. Epel and her colleague, Nobel Prize–winning molecular biologist Elizabeth Blackburn, have found that constant stress actually wears down our telomeres, the caps on our DNA that protect our cells from illness and aging. It is not just stress but our thought patterns in general that impact our telomeres, which has led Epel and Blackburn to conclude that our cells are actually "listening to our thoughts."

The problem is not the existence of stressors, which cannot be avoided; stress is simply the brain's way of signaling that something is important. The problem—or perhaps the opportunity—is how we respond to this stress.

Epel and Blackburn explain that it is not the stress alone that damages our telomeres. It is our response to the stress that is most important. They encourage us to develop **stress**

resilience. This involves turning what is called "threat stress," or the perception that a stressful event is a threat that will harm us, into what is called "challenge stress," or the perception that a stressful event is a challenge that will help us grow. The remedy they offer is quite straightforward. One simply notices the fight-or-flight stress response in one's body—the beating heart, the pulsing blood or tingling feeling in our hands and face, the rapid breathing—then remembers that these are natural responses to stress and that our body is just preparing to rise to the challenge.

What determines whether we see something or someone as a threat? The Archbishop and the Dalai Lama were saying that so much of our stress is dependent on seeing ourselves as separate from others, which perhaps returns to the loss of our sense of communal connection, of Ubuntu. I had once asked the Archbishop how he handled worry and insomnia, and he said that he thought about people all around the world who also were awake and unable to sleep. Thinking about others and remembering that he was not alone lessened his distress and his worries, as he would say a prayer for them.

"I would give teachings when I was young," the Dalai Lama explained, describing one of the experiences that would cause him to experience stress and anxiety. "I would be very nervous because I did not see myself as the same as the people in the audience. Then after 1959, when I left Tibet, I started thinking, These people are just like me, same human being. If we think we are something special or not special enough, then fear, nervousness, stress, and anxiety arise. We are the same."

"What the Dalai Lama and I are offering," the Archbishop added, "is a way of handling your worries: thinking about others. You can think about others who are in a similar situation or perhaps even in a worse situation, but who have survived, even thrived. It does help quite a lot to see yourself as part of a greater whole." Once again, the path of joy was connection and the path of sorrow was separation. When we see others as separate, they become a threat. When we see others as part of us, as connected, as interdependent, then there is no challenge we cannot face—together.

"When I meet someone," the Dalai Lama said, returning to what was becoming an important theme, "I always try to relate to the person on the basic human level. On that level, I know that, just like me, he or she wishes to find happiness, to have fewer problems and less difficulty in their life. Whether I am speaking with one person, or whether I am giving a talk to a large group of people, I always see myself first and foremost as just another fellow human. That way, there is in fact no need for introduction.

If, on the other hand, I relate to others from the perspective of myself as someone different— a Buddhist, a Tibetan, and so on—I will then create walls to keep me apart from others. And if I relate to others, thinking that I am the Dalai Lama, I will create the basis for my own separation and loneliness. After all, there is only one Dalai Lama in the entire world. In contrast, if I see myself primarily in terms of myself as a fellow human, I will then have more than seven billion people who I can feel deep connection with. And this is wonderful, isn't it? What do you need to fear or worry about when you have seven billion other people who are with you?"

Frustration and Anger:
I Would Shout

More than a decade before coming to Dharamsala, I was driving with the Archbishop in Jacksonville, Florida—in traffic. You could say that this was, in fact, one of my major motivations for wanting to work with him. To understand: How does a deeply spiritual and moral leader drive in traffic?

We had left the house, where we had earlier recorded an interview sitting by the alligator pond, dangling our feet precariously close to the hungry water. We stopped off at the Boston Market restaurant chain for a quick lunch, where he had gone out of his way to greet and say hello to all of the employees, who were in

awe of their celebrity customer who was order-
ing chicken and mashed potatoes. We were
on our way to the university where he was a
guest lecturer, and I was interviewing him as
we drove, trying to use every precious moment
of our time together to gather his pearls of
wisdom. We were talking about many high-
minded philosophies and theologies, but what
I really wanted to know was how all his spiritual practice and beliefs affected his day-to-day
interactions, like driving in traffic.

All of a sudden a car cut across the lanes in
front of us and the Archbishop had to swerve
out of the way to avoid hitting the other car.
"There are some truly amazing drivers on the
road!" the Archbishop said with exasperation
and a head-shaking chuckle.

I asked him what went through his head at
moments like this, and he said that perhaps the
driver was on his way to the hospital because
his wife was giving birth, or a relative was sick.

There it was. He reacted with the inevitable
and uncontrollable surprise, which is one of our
instinctual responses, but then instead of taking the low road of anger, he took the high
road of humor, acceptance, and even compas-

sion. And it was gone: no fuming, no lingering frustration, no raised blood pressure.

We often think of fear and anger as two quite separate emotions, so I was surprised to hear the Dalai Lama connect them. "Where there is fear, frustration will come. Frustration brings anger. So, you see, fear and anger are very close." The Dalai Lama's perspective, I later learned, is supported by our basic biology. Fear and anger are two poles of our natural response, as we prepare to flee (fear) or to fight (anger).

The Dalai Lama was responding to one of the students at the Tibetan Children's Village, where we went later in the week to celebrate his birthday. One of the older students had asked, "Your Holiness, how do you control your anger in your daily life?"

The Archbishop started to cackle—not just laughing, but practically doubling over, presumably enjoying immensely the challenge that anger poses even to holy men.

"When I used to get angry, I would shout," the Dalai Lama said, admitting that even the

Bodhisattva of Compassion can lose his cool. The children were laughing, too. "I have a story: Around 1956 or '57, when I was in my early twenties, I had an old car, which belonged to the 13th Dalai Lama." It was one of the very few cars in Lhasa at the time and had been carried in pieces to the capital and reassembled, since there were no drivable roads in Tibet at the time, other than short stretches in and around Lhasa.

"One of the people who used to drive the car would also repair it when it broke down, which was quite often. One day he was under the car repairing it when I came by to see him. As he came out from under the car, he banged his head on the fender. This made him lose his temper. He was so mad that he banged his head against the car again and again. Bang, bang, bang." The Dalai Lama pretended to hit his head into the imaginary fender, to the delight of the children. "That is anger. What use is it? The very reason he lost his temper is that he hit his head and then he hits his head on purpose, inflicting more pain on himself. It's foolish. When anger develops, think, what is the cause? And then also think, what will be the result of my anger, my angry face, or my shouting? Then you will realize that anger is not helpful."

Neuropsychiatrist Daniel Siegel explains that when we get very angry, we can "flip our lid," so to speak, losing the benefit of our critical-thinking cortex. As a result, the prefrontal cortex, which is important for emotion regulation and moral judgment, loses its ability to control our emotional limbic system. The Dalai Lama's driver had flipped his lid, and as a result he acted in a rather silly way, causing himself even more pain. This scene is comical because it is so common. We've all been there. So what is the alternative to "losing it"?

The Dalai Lama then made the subtle and profound connection between fear and anger, explaining how fear underlies anger. Typically frustration and anger come from being hurt. The driver hitting his head was an obvious example. In addition to physical pain, we can also experience emotional pain, which may be even more common. We want something that we did not get, like respect or kindness, or we get something that we did not want, like disrespect or criticism. Underlying this anger, the Dalai Lama was saying, is a fear that we will not get what we need, that we are not loved, that we are not respected, that we will not be included.

One way out of anger, then, is to ask, What is the hurt that has caused our anger, what is the fear that we have? Psychologists often call anger a secondary emotion, because it comes as a defense to feeling threatened. When we can acknowledge and express the fear—how we are feeling threatened—then we are often able to soothe the anger.

But we need to be willing to admit our vulnerability. We are often ashamed of these fears and hurts, thinking that if we were invulnerable, we would never experience pain, but this, as the Archbishop said, is not the nature of being human. If we can have compassion for ourselves, and acknowledge how we feel afraid, hurt, or threatened, we can have compassion for others—possibly even for those who have evoked our anger.

When you set yourself goals, and you encounter obstacles, you will naturally feel frustrated," the Archbishop said. "Or when you are trying to do your best and those with whom you are working, or should be working, aren't as cooperative as you had hoped, or at home with your family when something you do is misconstrued, this inevitably leads to frustration and anger. When people impugn your intentions, and you know that you have noble intentions. It's really quite painful. You grind your teeth and you say, there they go again.

"Or, on a larger scale, at home when we were involved in the apartheid struggle, and there were those amongst us who used methods that were not acceptable, like 'necklacing,' where they would set somebody alight with a car tire filled with gasoline around their neck and kill them, and you wanted to say, We don't need this, it just makes it easier for them to criticize us and our movement.

"Or in a personal way, when you have to deal with physical ailments, and you wish maybe that you had a great deal more energy than you in fact have. One is reminded of one's humanity and one's fragility."

"One time I was in Jerusalem," the Dalai Lama said, "and I met with a teacher who used to tell his students, When you are irritated or

angry with someone, you should remember
that they are made in the image of God. Some
of the students in the class were Palestinians,
and they had to cross through Israeli check-
points. They told him that when they would
get nervous and irritated, they would think
that these soldiers were made in the image
of God, and they would relax and feel better.
At the physical level one has to act accord-
ingly, but at the mental level one can remain
calm and relaxed. This is how you train the
mind."

Yet certainly anger must have a place, I
thought. Sometimes it serves a role in protect-
ing us or others from hurt or harm. What,
I wondered, was the role of righteous anger?
The Archbishop, during the killings that often
marred the peaceful protests against apartheid,
would raise a fist and a rant, calling down fire
and brimstone against the evildoers of injustice. His biography, by his longtime press secretary John Allen, is called **Rabble-Rouser for
Peace,** which succinctly describes the paradox
of the Archbishop's struggle for freedom. He
was not afraid of anger and righteous indigna-

tion in pursuit of peace, justice, and equality in his homeland.

The Archbishop simply and succinctly explained the power and limits of this use of anger. "Righteous anger is usually not about oneself. It is about those whom one sees being harmed and whom one wants to help." In short, righteous anger is a tool of justice, a scythe of compassion, more than a reactive emotion. Although it may have its roots deep in our fight-or-flight desire to protect those in our family or group who are threatened, it is a chosen response and not simply an uncontrollable reaction. And it is not about one's own besieged self-image, or one's feelings of separation, but of one's collective responsibility, and one's feeling of deep, empowering connection.

"Now medical scientists say," the Dalai Lama continued, "that constant fear, constant anger, constant hatred harms our immune system. Everybody tries to take care of his or her health. So they need both a healthy body and a healthy mind. A healthy mind is a calm mind. Fear and anger are destroyers of a calm mind. Then you realize that anger is no use in solving problems. It will not help. It creates more problems. Then eventually through training of our mind—and using reasoning—we can transform our emotions."

The Dalai Lama added, "Clear, like that," as if fear and anger, these fundamental parts of the human experience, these sources of so much negative emotion, so much suffering, could be banished with the wave of a rational mind. I knew what he was describing was a lifelong practice, in which we have to continually wrestle with the fear and anger mechanisms of our mammalian brain. Otherwise we are prone to lose it more often than we would like to admit.

Paul Ekman told me an astonishing story over dinner one night about how the Dalai Lama had healed him of his anger issues. Ekman is not a Buddhist and was not that interested in meeting the Dalai Lama, but his daughter was a fan, and when Ekman heard that scientists invited to the biannual Mind and Life conference with the Dalai Lama could bring a guest, he agreed to attend.

Ekman explained that he used to be a very timid and quiet child but became what is popularly called a "rage-aholic" after experiencing his father's belligerence and abuse and his mother's suicide. Ekman would have what he and other emotion clinicians call "regrettable incidents," flying into a rage several times a week. When he went to see the Dalai Lama, something very strange happened.

The Dalai Lama took Ekman's hands, looked into his eyes lovingly, and suddenly, Ekman said, it felt like all the anger drained out of his body. He did not have another regrettable incident for over six months, and although they did return, they were much less frequent. Ekman does not know what happened to him, but said that perhaps the Dalai Lama's deep compassion helped heal some lingering hurt and reactivity. The Dalai Lama has asked Ekman to map the emotional landscape, to help others avoid the rocky terrain of negative emotions and find their way more easily to the promised land of compassion and contentment.

The Dalai Lama had said earlier that if we can discover our role in creating the situations that upset us, we are able to reduce our feelings of frustration and anger. Also, when we are able to recognize that the other person has their own fears and hurts, their own fragile and human perspective, then we have a chance of escaping from the normal reflex of anger.

"And so finally, sometimes it is a matter of timing," the Dalai Lama said, concluding our first morning session as we were about to break for tea. "Too much tiredness can lead us to feel frustration and anger. In my own case, when I encounter some difficult situation in the morning, my mind is calm, and it is much easier. When the same situation happens in the late evening, and I am a little bit tired, then I feel annoyed. So your basic physical condition makes a difference, whether your body is fresh, whether your mind is fresh. So this also shows how much depends on your own perception and your limited subjective view."

Next we had planned to discuss sadness and grief, feelings that so many try to avoid. I was very surprised to hear them explain how the royal road to joy would lead right through these emotions.

Sadness and Grief:
The Hard Times Knit
Us More Closely Together

The very first day of the Truth and Reconciliation Commission," the Archbishop began, "when one of the witnesses came to tell us about his experiences—it was at the end of a long and grueling day—and he was trying to tell us how they had tortured him. Then there was a point in trying to recall what they had done to him that he found it difficult to speak. He had now developed a speech impediment. I don't know what it was, the recalling or the speech impediment, but the witness was not able to go on. And he started a sentence and then put his hand up to his eyes and started weeping. And I joined him.

"At the end of it I said to my colleagues, 'I told you I am not fit to be chairing this. And lo and behold, I was right. I've made a public spectacle of myself.' I'm a crybaby. I cry easily. . . . I suppose I love easily, too.

"And so I think we shouldn't think we are superwomen and supermen. To hold down emotions in a controlled environment, as it were, is not wise. I would say go ahead and even maybe shout out your sadness and pain. This can bring you back to normal. It's locking them up and pretending that they are not there that causes them to fester and become a wound. I've not read this in a book. It's just how I have handled them."

Sadness is seemingly the most direct challenge to joy, but as the Archbishop argued strongly, it often leads us most directly to empathy and compassion and to recognizing our need for one another.

Sadness is a very powerful and enduring emotion. In one study it was found that sadness lasted many times longer than more fleeting emotions like fear and anger: While fear lasted on average thirty minutes, sadness often lasted up to a hundred and twenty hours, or almost five days. While the evolutionary value of our fight (anger) and flight (fear) responses are clear, the value of sadness seems harder to understand.

New studies conducted by psychology researcher Joseph Forgas show that mild sadness can actually have a number of benefits that could reflect its value. In his experiments, people who were in a sad mood had better judgment and memory, and were more motivated, more sensitive to social norms, and more generous than the happier control group. People who are in a so-called negative state of sadness were more discerning about their situation, better able to remember details, and more motivated to change their situation. What is particularly interesting is that brief sadness might generate more empathy or generosity. Participants in the study played a game, part of which involved deciding how much money to give themselves and how much to give others. The sad participants gave significantly more to the other participants.

While depression certainly collapses our circle of concern inward, the periodic feeling of sadness might widen it. Forgas concluded that sadness may have some benefit in our lives, which may be why people are drawn to music, art, and literature that makes them feel sad. He urges us to embrace all of our emotions, because they no doubt play a necessary role in our lives.

Sadness is in many ways the emotion that causes us to reach out to one another in support and solidarity. The Archbishop expressed it quite wonderfully when he explained, "We don't really get close to others if our relationship is made up of unending hunky-dory-ness. It is the hard times, the painful times, the sadness and the grief that knit us more closely together." A funeral is perhaps the most obvious example of this weaving of our relationships and community together, but even tears are a signal to others that we need comfort and kindness, that we are vulnerable and need help.

We try so hard to separate joy and sorrow into their own boxes, but the Archbishop and the Dalai Lama tell us that they are inevitably fastened together. Neither advocate the kind of fleeting happiness, often called hedonic happiness, that requires only positive states and banishes feelings like sadness to emotional exile. The kind of happiness that they describe is often called eudemonic happiness and is characterized by self-understanding, meaning, growth, and acceptance, including life's inevitable suffering, sadness, and grief.

often receive questions," the Dalai Lama said, "from those whose dear friend, or parent, or even child has passed away. They ask me, 'What should I do?'

"I share with them from my own experience. My beloved main teacher, who gave me my monk's ordination, died, and I was really grief-stricken. While he was alive I always felt like he was a solid rock behind me that I could lean on. I really felt very, very sad and full of grief when he passed away.

"The way through the sadness and grief that comes from great loss is to use it as motivation and to generate a deeper sense of purpose. When my teacher passed away, I used to think that now I have even more responsibility to fulfill his wishes, so my sadness translated into more enthusiasm, more determination. I have told those who had lost their dear friend or family member, It is very sad, but this sadness should translate into more determination to fulfill their wishes. If the one you have lost could see you, and you are determined and full of hope, they would be happy. With the great sadness of the loss, one can live an even more meaningful life.

"Sadness and grief are, of course, natural human responses to loss, but if your focus remains on the loved one you have just lost, the experience is less likely to lead to despair. In contrast, if your focus while grieving remains mostly on yourself—'What am I going to do now? How can I cope?'—then there is a greater danger of going down the path of despair and depression. So, again, so much depends on how we respond to our experience of loss and sadness."

The Dalai Lama mentioned the famous Buddhist story of the woman who had lost her child and was inconsolable in her grief, carrying her dead child throughout the land, begging for someone to help heal her child. When she came to the Buddha, she begged him to help her. He told her he could help her if she would collect mustard seeds for the medicine. She eagerly agreed, but then the Buddha explained that the mustard seeds needed to come from a house that had not been touched by death. When the woman visited each house in search of the mustard seeds that might heal her son, she discovered that there was no house that had not suffered the loss of a parent, or a spouse, or a child. Seeing that her suffering was not unique, she was able to bury her child in the forest and release her grief.

My friend Gordon Wheeler, who is a psychologist, explains that grief is the reminder of the depth of our love. Without love, there is no grief. So when we feel our grief, uncomfortable and aching as it may be, it is actually a reminder of the beauty of that love, now lost. I'll never forget calling Gordon while I was traveling, and hearing him say that he was out to dinner by himself after the loss of a dear friend "so he could feel his grief." He knew that in the blinking and buzzing world of our lives, it is so easy to delete the past and move on to the next moment. To linger in the longing, the loss, the yearning is a way of feeling the rich and embroidered texture of life, the torn cloth of our world that is endlessly being ripped and rewoven.

Despair: The World Is
in Such Turmoil

I t was time to ask the question that people from around the world most wanted me to ask, a question not about joy but about sorrow, and not about theirs but about others. "People all over the world wanted to know how they could possibly live with joy in a world so filled with sorrow and suffering. A woman named Dawn, who sent in a question, asked it this way: 'The world is in such turmoil—war, starvation, terrorism, pollution, genocide. My heart hurts for these issues. How do I find joy in the midst of such large world problems?'"

"You're the elder," the Dalai Lama said, gesturing to the Archbishop.

"You show your humanity," the Archbishop began, "by how you see yourself not as apart from others but from your connection to others. I have frequently wept about the things such as the ones you have mentioned.

"God created us and said, Go now, my child. You have freedom. And God has such an incredible reverence for that freedom that God would much rather we went freely to hell than compel us to come to heaven.

"Yes, we're capable of the most awful atrocities. We can give a catalog. And God weeps until there are those who say I do want to try to do something. It is good also to remember that we have a fantastic capacity for goodness. And then you look again. And you see those doctors and nurses from other parts of the world who go into those situations. I mean, you think of, say, Doctors Without Borders. Why do they go there? I mean, they could stay in France or wherever and have a wonderful practice. But they don't. They go off to some of the most poverty-stricken places.

"You've seen it with Ebola. People go into a hugely dangerous situation. Coming from countries where they don't have Ebola. And they have no reason to go to Sierra Leone or wherever. They are just showing us what we are all capable of being. And by proxy we link ourselves to those and try as much as we can to enter into who we are: people of compassion.

"What can you do to help change that situation? You might not be able to do a great deal, but start where you are and do what you can where you are. And yes, be appalled. It would be awful if we looked on all of that horrendousness and we said, Ah, it doesn't really matter. It's so wonderful that we can be distressed. That's part of the greatness of who we are—that you are distressed about someone who is not family in any conventional way. And yet you feel distressed, equally. It's incredible just how compassionate and generous people can be.

"When a disaster such as 9/11 happens, we realize we are family. We **are** family. Those people in the Twin Towers are our sisters and brothers. And even more startlingly, the people who were piloting those planes, they are our sisters and brothers. You have a tsunami happen, and have you seen the outpouring of love and compassion and caring? I mean, you don't know the victims from a brass farthing. And people just gave and gave. Because that's actually who we **really** are.

"After 9/11 you would have expected that those who hated America would have been gloating. But there were very, very, very few people gloating. People were deeply, deeply distressed.

"Had the American president not hit back, we might have had a different world. We will have a different world of course, eventually. But just look at any tragedy. When miners are trapped in Russia, people don't say, I can't speak Russian, or, I don't even know where that place is on the map. There is a compassion that just springs up."

The Archbishop's and the Dalai Lama's conviction that we would have a different world, eventually, was striking. Several months after the interviews I was visiting with the Archbishop in South Africa when terrorist attacks took place in Paris. So many people were despairing at humanity's obvious inhumanity. When I asked him what he would say to those who were caught in such despair, he replied, "Yes, we do have setbacks, but you must keep everything in perspective. The world is getting better. Think about the rights of women or how slavery was considered morally justified a few hundred years ago. It takes time. We are growing and learning how to be compassionate, how to be caring, how to be human."

Almost a month later to the day, the world came together in Paris and ratified climate change accords that overcame national differences and economic greed to give our world a better chance of survival. The Archbishop often liked to quote one of his heroes, Dr. Martin Luther King Jr., who in turn was quoting one of his heroes, an abolitionist minister named Theodore Parker, who said: "The arc of the moral universe is long, but it bends toward justice."

"Perhaps here I may mention something from my own experience," the Dalai Lama said. "March 10, 2008." Every year, the Tibetan exile community commemorates March 10 as Tibetan Uprising Day, remembering the 1959 protest against Chinese occupation that ultimately led to the crackdown against the Tibetan freedom movement and the Dalai Lama's flight into exile. In 2008, leading up to the Beijing Olympics, that day had turned violent, starting in the Tibetan capital city of Lhasa and then spreading throughout Tibet and cities around the world.

"As usual we had a gathering to commemorate the tenth of March. After the meeting was over, I received a message from Lhasa that some of the local people had started demonstrations. When I heard this I was very concerned and quite anxious. I could not do anything. I felt helpless. I knew if they really carried out demonstrations, it would actually result only in more suffering, more problems. And this is exactly what happened, with the violent crackdown and the death and imprisonment of so many Tibetans who had participated in the protests. Over the next few days, during my meditation, I actually visualized some of those Chinese local authorities and did one of our practices, called **tonglen,** literally meaning 'giving and taking.' I tried to take on their fear, anger, suspicion, and to give them my love, my forgiveness. Of course, this would have no physical effect on the ground. It would not change the situation. But you see, mentally it was very, very helpful to keep a calm mind. It was a good opportunity to practice forgiveness and compassion. So I think that every person has this same sort of opportunity, this same capacity."

"I do at times get very angry with God," the Archbishop then added, laughing.

"Some of my friends," the Dalai Lama said, "when they are really facing some trouble, sometimes they complain at the Buddha—so similar idea."

"Yes," the Archbishop continued, "I usually would go to my chapel if I had something that really upset me. I would lambast God. The prophet Jeremiah would say to God, 'You misled me. You called me to be a prophet, and I said I don't want to be a prophet. And you said, no, I will be with you. All you have made me say to these people—people I love very much—is to condemn them.' And, yes, that is how I do it. Jeremiah is my favorite prophet in the Bible for precisely this honesty that he had. You can go to God and speak all you have, pouring it out in that fashion." I wondered how many times the Archbishop, like Jeremiah, had told God he did not want to be a prophet.

"I weep when something has happened where I may not be able to assist. I acknowledge that it is something I can do very little about.

"I remember one of the times that I was quite despairing. Chris Hani was one of our most incredible young leaders. There was no doubt he was going to succeed Nelson Mandela. But then he was assassinated just before Easter, leading up to our first democratic elections.

"I was at the cathedral in Cape Town when I heard. I was stunned, as were most South Africans. I got back home to Bishopscourt. Leah said to me that there have been many calls about Chris Hani. I broke down, and Leah held me, like I was a baby. I think it helped because later on I had to go and preach at his funeral. And we had a huge crowd of people who were very, very angry. I knew how they felt, because I had been through the same sort of thing. And I could appeal to them not from a superior position but from a position of one who was with them and who had felt the same anguish and pain.

"It is also good to recognize—speaking from our struggle against apartheid—how incredibly noble people are. You know human beings are basically good. You know that's where we have to start. That everything else is an aberration. Anything that swerves away from that is the exception—even when now and again they can be very frustrating. People are remarkably, remarkably, remarkably good, incredible in their generosity. And we had the opportunity of seeing this, especially during the Truth and Reconciliation Commission in South Africa. It was amazing to listen to people who had suffered, not only black people, you know—white people, too. Not only South Africans, but Americans.

"There was a family whose daughter had been killed, brutally killed, who came and said they supported the granting of amnesty to those who had killed their daughter so gruesomely. The parents had even opened a nonprofit to help people in the township where their daughter had been murdered, and they had even employed the men who had killed their daughter and whose amnesty they had supported.

"We've always got to be recognizing that despite the aberrations, the fundamental thing about humanity, about humankind, about people, is that they are good, they were made good, and they really want to be good.

"Yes, there are many, many things that can depress us. But there also are very many things that are fantastic about our world. Unfortunately the media do not report on these because they are not seen as news."

"I think you are right," the Dalai Lama said. "When bad things happen they become news, and it is easy to feel like our basic human nature is to kill or to rape or to be corrupt. Then we can feel that there is not much hope for our future.

"All these things happen, but they are unusual, which is why they become news. There are millions and millions of children who are loved by their parents every day. Then in school their teachers care for them. Okay, maybe there are some bad teachers, but most of them really are kind and caring. Then in the hospital, every day millions of people receive immense caring. But this is so common that none of it becomes news. We take it for granted.

"When we look at the news, we must keep this more holistic view. Yes, this or that terrible thing has happened. No doubt, there are very negative things, but at the same time there are many more positive things happening in our world. We must have a sense of proportion and a wider perspective. Then we will not feel despair when we see these sad things."

Neither man was asking us to look at the world through rose-colored glasses or to not see the world with anything but a searingly honest view. The Archbishop even discouraged people from being optimistic.

"You've spoken, Archbishop, very powerfully, about how hope is not the same as optimism. Could you tell us a little bit about the distinction you make?"

"Hope," the Archbishop said, "is quite different from optimism, which is more superficial and liable to become pessimism when the circumstances change. Hope is something much deeper.

"I mentioned earlier about Chris Hani, whose assassination occurred at a very critical point in the negotiations for a new, democratic South Africa. We were on the edge of a precipice. It was so serious that the then president, the white president of South Africa, F. W. de Klerk, asked Nelson Mandela to address the nation.

"That incident could have caused the collapse of the negotiations, but it didn't, in fact.

We were fortunate that we had someone like Nelson Mandela.

"Now, if you had been an optimist, you would have said, Well, the assassination of Chris Hani is really the end of everything. What made people want to go on going on—holding on by the skin of their teeth—was not optimism but hope—dogged, inextinguishable hope.

"I say to people that I'm not an optimist, because that, in a sense, is something that depends on feelings more than the actual reality. We feel optimistic, or we feel pessimistic. Now, hope is different in that it is based not on the ephemerality of feelings but on the firm ground of conviction. I believe with a steadfast faith that there can never be a situation that is utterly, totally hopeless. Hope is deeper and very, very close to unshakable. It's in the pit of your tummy. It's not in your head. It's all here," he said, pointing to his abdomen.

"Despair can come from deep grief, but it can also be a defense against the risks of bitter disappointment and shattering heartbreak. Resignation and cynicism are easier, more self-soothing postures that do not require the raw vulnerability and tragic risk of hope. To choose hope is to step firmly forward into the howling wind, baring one's chest to the elements, knowing that, in time, the storm will pass."

As the Archbishop was explaining, hope is the antidote to despair. Yet hope requires faith, even if that faith is in nothing more than human nature or the very persistence of life to find a way. Hope is also nurtured by relationship, by community, whether that community is a literal one or one fashioned from the long memory of human striving whose membership includes Gandhi, King, Mandela, and countless others. Despair turns us inward. Hope sends us into the arms of others.

And then the Archbishop turned to me and made it so personal yet so universal.

"In many ways it's the same kind of thing as love. Why did you propose to Rachel? What made you think it was going to last? You know you didn't have evidence. A lot of people were as madly in love as you were with her early on. And a few years later, they divorced. But you knew in the depth of your being, this is she for me, as she also said, this is he for me. And, well," he said with a laugh, "you turned out to be right."

Loneliness: No Need
for Introduction

"Throughout society today people feel great loneliness," the Dalai Lama said as we began our discussion after tea.

We were talking about loneliness and alienation and some troubling recent statistics. A study by sociologist Lynn Smith-Lovin had found that the number of close friends people report having has reduced from three to two. While we might have hundreds of Facebook friends, our true, close friends are decreasing. Perhaps most concerning of all, one in ten people said they had no close friendships at all.

"Actually, in America and in India also," the Dalai Lama continued, "people in the big cities are very busy, and although they may see each other's faces or even know each other for several years, they have practically no human connection. So when something happens, people feel lonely because they have no one they can turn to for help or support."

Having grown up in Manhattan, surrounded by seven million New Yorkers, I knew exactly what the Dalai Lama was saying. As a boy, I never really met the people who lived on our apartment floor. I would occasionally hear their doors close with an empty metallic clang, and locks turn behind them. If we did see them while waiting for the elevator, few words were spoken and eyes were averted. I was always bewildered by this willful avoidance and finally concluded that it must have been a defense against the crush of so many people crowded together.

"In rural areas, farmers have had a stronger sense of community," the Dalai Lama explained. "So, when someone or some family is facing a problem, you have the feeling that you can ask your neighbors for help. Even in big cities with millions of people, we still have the responsibility for each other whether we know each other or not."

I thought of the locked doors on our apartment building floor. How could we have responsibility for people we did not even know? Those closed doors, and the unseen people behind them, were like a constant reminder that we were not connected. Now, as the Dalai Lama was speaking, I wondered if the averted eyes of my childhood, waiting for the elevator or in the subway, were perhaps the shame of being physically close and emotionally distant.

"We are same human beings," the Dalai Lama said, returning to one of his most profound refrains. "No need for introduction. Same human face, when we see one another we immediately know this is a human brother or sister. Whether you know them or not, you can smile and say hello." I thought of the times that I had smiled and spoken with warmth to the person waiting for an elevator or standing in a subway. Yes, sometimes my bid for human connection was met with confusion, since it was not the social expectation, but most often there was a relieved smile, as if we had broken a trance and were once again acknowledging our human bond.

"Our whole society has a materialistic culture," the Dalai Lama said. "In the materialistic way of life, there's no concept of friendship, no concept of love, just work, twenty-four hours a day, like a machine. So in modern society, we eventually also become part of that large moving machine."

The Dalai Lama was naming a deep pain in the chest of modern life, but one that was so common we had forgotten that it was not normal. I thought of what the Archbishop had said of Ubuntu, how we are who we are through one another, how our humanity is bound up in one another.

The Dalai Lama had explained that in Buddhism there is the recognition of our interdependence on every level—socially, personally, subatomically. The Dalai Lama had often emphasized that we are born and die totally dependent on others, and that the independence that we think we experience in between is a myth.

"If we stress secondary level of differences—my nation, my religion, my color—then we notice the differences. Like this moment now in Africa, there is too much emphasis on this nation or that nation. They should think that we are same Africans. Furthermore, we are same human beings. Same with religion: Shiite and Sunni, or Christian and Muslim. We are same human beings. These differences between religions are personal matters. When we relate to others from the place of compassion it goes to the first level, the human level, not the secondary level of difference. Then you can even have compassion for your enemy.

"So, we all have the same potential for affection. And now scientists are discovering that our basic human nature is compassionate. The problem is that children go to schools where they are not taught to nurture these deeper human values, so their basic human potential becomes dormant."

"Perhaps our synagogues, our temples, and our churches," Archbishop Tutu added, "are not as welcoming as they should be. I really think that we do need for these fellowships to do a great deal more to have those who are lonely come and share. Not in an aggressive way, or in order, as it were, to increase their records or their ranks, but really just keenly interested in one person who comes and gets what they did not have before—warmth and fellowship. There are programs that set out to break down that loneliness."

We often are alone without feeling lonely and feel lonely when we are not alone, as when we are in a crowd of strangers or at a party of people we do not know. Clearly the psychological experience of loneliness is quite different from the physical experience of being alone. We can feel joy when we are alone but not when we are lonely. After our tea break, the dialogue returned to this topic.

"Your Holiness, we finished our last session talking about loneliness, and I wanted to come back to the subject for one more question. Monks spend a lot of time alone. So what is the difference between being alone and being lonely?"

The Dalai Lama turned to the Archbishop to see if he wanted to answer.

"No, I've not been a monk, man. You start."

"Monks separate themselves from the material world, not just physically but mentally. According to his religion," he said, pointing to the Archbishop, "Christian monks are always thinking they're in the light of God, dedicated to serving God. We cannot touch God directly, so the only way is serving God's children, humanity. So we are never really lonely.

"Much depends on your attitude. If you are filled with negative judgment and anger, then you will feel separate from other people. You will feel lonely. But if you have an open heart and are filled with trust and friendship, even if you are physically alone, even living a hermit's life, you will never feel lonely."

"It is ironic, isn't it?" I offered, remembering Lama Tenzin, who told us, while we bought doughnuts on our way to Dharamsala, that he had a desire to live in a cave for the traditional length of over three years. "You can spend three years, three months, and three days in a cave and not be lonely, but you can be lonely in the middle of a crowd."

"That's right," the Dalai Lama replied. "There are at least seven billion people and the number of sentient beings is limitless. If you are always thinking about the seven billion human beings, you will never experience loneliness.

"The only thing that will bring happiness is affection and warmheartedness. This really brings inner strength and self-confidence, reduces fear, develops trust, and trust brings friendship. We are social animals, and cooperation is necessary for our survival, but cooperation is entirely based on trust. When there is trust, people are brought together—whole nations are brought together. When you have a more compassionate mind and cultivate warmheartedness, the whole atmosphere around you becomes more positive and friendlier. You see friends everywhere. If you feel fear and distrust, then other people will distance themselves. They will also feel cautious, suspicious, and distrustful. Then comes the feeling of loneliness.

"When someone is warmhearted, they are always completely relaxed. If you live with fear and consider yourself as something special, then automatically, emotionally, you are distanced from others. You then create the basis for feelings of alienation from others and loneliness. So, I never consider, even when giving a talk to a large crowd, that I am something special, I am 'His Holiness the Dalai Lama,'" he said, mocking his venerated status. "I always emphasize that when I meet people, we are all the same human beings. A thousand people—same human being. Ten thousand or a hundred thousand—same human being—mentally, emotionally, and physically. Then, you see, no barrier. Then my mind remains completely calm and relaxed. If too much emphasis on myself, and I start to think I'm something special, then more anxiety, more nervousness.

"The paradox is that although the drive behind excessive self-focus is to seek greater happiness for yourself, it ends up doing exactly the opposite. When you focus too much on yourself, you become disconnected and alienated from others. In the end, you also become alienated from yourself, since the need for connection with others is such a fundamental part of who we are as human beings.

"This excessive self-focus is also bad for your health. Too much fear and distrust, too much focus on yourself leads to stress and high blood pressure. Many years ago, I was at a gathering of medical scientists and researchers at

Columbia University in New York. One of the medical scientists said in his presentation that those people who disproportionately use the first-person pronouns—**I, I, I, me, me, me, and mine, mine, mine**—have a significantly greater risk of having a heart attack. He didn't explain why, but I felt this must be true. This is a deep insight. With too much self-focus your vision becomes narrow, and with this even a small problem appears out of proportion and unbearable.

"Also, fear and distrust come from too much focus on yourself. This will cause you to always remain separate from your human brothers and sisters. This brings loneliness and difficulty communicating with other people. After all, you are part of the community, so you have to deal with them. Your interests and your future depend on other people. If you isolate yourself from them, how can you be a happy person? You just have more worry and more stress. Sometimes I say that too much self-centeredness closes our inner door, and it becomes hard to communicate with other people. When we are concerned with the well-being of other human beings, that inner door opens, and we are able to communicate very easily with other people."

The Dalai Lama was saying that when one is thinking about others with kindness and compassion, one is never lonely. Openheartedness—warmheartedness—is the antidote to loneliness. It has often amazed me that one day I can walk down the street feeling judgmental and critical of others, and I will feel separate and lonely, and the next day I can walk down the same street with more openhearted acceptance and compassion and suddenly everyone seems warm and friendly. It is almost as if my inner state of mind and heart changes the physical and social world around me completely.

This focus on the importance of warmheartedness echoes the research of social psychologists Chen-Bo Zhong and Shira Gabriel, who have found that when people are feeling lonely or socially rejected, they literally seek warmth, like sipping hot soup. What the Dalai Lama and the Archbishop were saying is that we can generate that warmth simply by opening our hearts and turning our attention and our concern to other people.

"Archbishop, did you want to add anything?

I know you haven't been a monastic, but you do spend a lot of time in prayer and meditation on your own."

"Certainly in our sort of prayer," the Archbishop explained, "it is never the alone speaking to the alone. Our concept of God is of a God who is one, but who is a fellowship, a community, the Trinity. And we are made in the image of this God. When you become a Christian, you are incorporated into a fellowship. So even when you go into retreat, you are not alone."

"It's similar to what the Dalai Lama is saying," I said. "If you connect, even if that fellowship is seven billion people, then you don't feel lonely."

"Yes, yes," the Archbishop replied. "It's something of an oxymoron to be lonely. But I can very well understand when you feel alienated, when you are not on the same wavelength, as it were. And one wants to enter into that sense of being in solidarity. I don't think we help people by making them feel guilty. We want to try to be as welcoming as we possibly can and say that the experience they have is something that many other people also have. Feeling lonely is not something that we do deliberately. I don't think you set out to say, I want to feel lonely. It's just there. It happens and for very many reasons.

"You want to make the person feel really as they are, special. And accepted as they are and help to open them. I can very well understand the incredible anguish and pain that someone must feel who is cooped up in a room because they are scared of going out and being rejected. And you just hope and pray that they will find a fellowship of people who will embrace and welcome them. It's wonderful to see people who were closed down open up like a beautiful flower in the warmth and acceptance of those around them."

What I had learned from our dialogue was that we did not have to wait for others to open their hearts to us. By opening our heart to them, we could feel connected to them, whether on a mountaintop or in the middle of Manhattan.

Envy: That Guy Goes Past Yet Again in His Mercedes-Benz

It is not that you wake up in the morning and you say, Now, I'm going to be envious. It just rises spontaneously," the Archbishop began, once again arguing for the naturalness of our emotions and for self-compassion. "I mean you get up, and you're trying to be a good person and that guy goes past yet again, for the third time this week, in his Mercedes-Benz or some other very nice car. You have been trying not to feel jealous each time he passes with his car, but this feeling just comes up."

Comparison is indeed human—even beyond human; it is natural throughout the animal world. As the Dalai Lama would point out, even dogs that are eating together peacefully can suddenly start comparing the size of their portion to another's, and a fight can break out with barking and the gnashing of teeth. But it is for humans that envy can become a source of great dissatisfaction. There is a Tibetan Buddhist teaching that says what causes suffering in life is a general pattern of how we relate to others: "Envy toward the above, competitiveness toward the equal, and contempt toward the lower."

Fairness seems to be hardwired into our genes, and so we are very uncomfortable with inequality of any sort. Primatologist Frans de Waal has a video of an experiment with capuchin monkeys, our distant relatives who are often used in psychological tests as proxies for humans. In the video, which has gone wildly viral, one of the small-headed, long-limbed gray monkeys gives the experimenter a rock and then receives a cucumber slice as payment. The monkey is quite happy to do this over and over, until he sees his neighbor perform the same rock-giving task but receive a grape. In the world of capuchin monkeys, a grape is a better, sweeter food than a cucumber. Perhaps for humans, too. After the first monkey sees his neighbor getting a grape, he performs the rock-giving task yet again, although even more eagerly this time, his head now perking up in expectation at his grape reward. However, as required in this experiment of social comparisons, the experimenter gives the first monkey another cucumber instead of a grape.

The capuchin looks at the cucumber in his hand, pulling his head back in seeming disbelief, and then throws the cucumber back at the experimenter. In uncontrollable rage, the monkey grabs the bars of the cage and shakes them. This video became popular during the time of the Wall Street protests in the United States because it so succinctly and poignantly revealed how our fundamental instincts for fairness work and why inequality is stressful and damaging to a society.

The Archbishop and the Dalai Lama spoke frequently through the week of dialogues about the need to address inequality on the societal level. Yet however much we address these large global imbalances, as the Archbishop has pointed out, there will always be people who have more than we do, or who are more successful, or who are more talented or smarter or better-looking.

Usually, we don't actually compare ourselves to the hedge fund billionaire or to the genius scientist or to the supermodel. We tend to compare ourselves to those who are in our social circle. As the old saying goes, "If you want to be poor, find some rich friends. If you want to be rich, find some poor friends." Keeping up with the Joneses happens within a peer group.

Jinpa told me that in the 1990s the United States gave green cards to about a thousand Tibetans in India as part of a special program for refugees. When these Tibetans started sending dollars back to their families, their neighbors started to get jealous because suddenly these families had more disposable income and could renovate their homes or buy their children motorbikes. It's not that those families who had no one in the States had become poorer; it's that their neighbors with family in the States had suddenly become richer.

According to the happiness research, "upward comparisons" are particularly corrosive to our well-being. Envy doesn't leave room for joy.

The Tibetan word for envy is **trakdok**, which means "heavy or constricted shoulders," and indeed the feeling of envy leaves one with a pinched feeling of discontent and resentment, tinged with guilt. Buddhism sees envy as so corrosive that it compares it to a venomous snake that poisons us. In the Judeo-Christian tradition, one of the Ten Commandments forbids "coveting" thy neighbor's house.

The Archbishop and the Dalai Lama were in disagreement about how to respond to envy, with the Archbishop coming down on the side of acceptance and self-forgiveness. "I mean, you don't really have a great deal of control over it. I think, far too frequently, we are too hard on ourselves. We forget that many of these things affect all of us universally. I would hope that we could help people dissipate the guilt that they also tend to have, because almost everybody, when they are feeling envious, also has guilt attached to it. I would say the thing that we want to be saying to God's children out there is, For goodness' sake, there are things about us that we do not control."

The Archbishop then went on to offer a powerful remedy for envy: gratitude. "I think that one of the best ways you can begin to counter it is that old one of counting your blessings. That might sound very old, old, old, old, old, grandfather-style, but yes, it does help. You know you might not have as big a house as that person, but you know what? You're not living in a shack. So being thankful for the things that you do in fact have can help."

And then he offered another remedy: motivation. "Certainly with envy, it can also be a spur, you know? It can help you say, I haven't got a car or a house like that guy, so why don't I aim to work to try and get something like that?" As the Archbishop and the Dalai Lama had said, these external goals will not bring us true joy or lasting happiness, but motivation to improve our situation is certainly better than envy of someone else's.

And then the Archbishop offered his final and most effective remedy: reframing. "The very best is being able to ask yourself, 'Why do I want to have a house that has seven rooms when there are only two or three of us? Why do I want to have it?' And you can turn it on its head and look at how we are in such a mess with climate change because of our galloping consumption, which for the environment has been nothing less than disastrous. So you buy the small electric car instead, and you say, no I don't need or want that big luxury car. So instead of it being your enemy, now it's your ally."

Jinpa translated what the Archbishop had said for the Dalai Lama.

"That's exactly what I said," the Archbishop said, and laughed.

"Fortunately, you do not understand Tibetan," the Dalai Lama shot back with a quick smile. And then I saw him do what each of them did throughout the dialogues when they would come to a point of disagreement: reaffirm the relationship and compliment the other. It made me think of relationship scientists John Gottman and Julie Schwartz Gottman's observation that in successful conflict there is a "softened start-up," or a delicate entry into the area of disagreement.

"So I think, from my viewpoint, my spiritual brother's explanation is wonderful, wonderful. You see, at the moment that envy or jealousy develops, you no longer can maintain your peace of mind. So jealousy actually destroys your peace of mind. Then that jealousy can become corrosive to the relationship. Even with your good friend, if you develop some sort of jealousy, it will be very harmful to your friendship. Even with husband and wife, if some kind of jealousy develops, it will be very harmful to the marriage. We can see it even with dogs that are eating in a happy atmosphere peacefully, but if one becomes jealous of what another has—conflict, fighting.

"It is important to cultivate any emotion that brings joyfulness and peace of mind. Any sort of emotion that disturbs this happiness and peace of mind, we must learn to avoid right from the beginning.

"I think it is a mistake just to consider all of these negative emotions, like anger or jealousy, as normal parts of our mind, something we cannot do much about. Too many negative emotions destroy our own peace of mind, our health, and create trouble in our family, with our friends, and in our community.

"Often envy comes because we are too focused on material possessions and not on our true inner values. When we focus on experience or knowledge, there is much less envy. But most important is to develop a sense of concern for others' well-being. If you have genuine kindness or compassion, then when someone gets something or has more success you are able to rejoice in their good fortune. For a person who is committed to compassion practice and a genuine sense of concern for others' well-being, then you will rejoice in others' good fortune because you will be happy that what that person aspires for is being obtained."

The Dalai Lama was describing the Buddhist concept of **mudita,** which is often translated as "sympathetic joy" and described as the antidote to envy. Mudita is so important in Buddhism that it is considered one of the Four Immeasurables, qualities we can cultivate infinitely. The other three are loving-kindness, compassion, and equanimity.

Jinpa had explained how mudita works: If someone has something that we want, say, a bigger house, we can consciously take joy in their good fortune by telling ourselves: "Good for him. Just like me, he, too, wants to be happy. He, too, wants to be successful. He, too, wants to support his family. May he be happy. I congratulate him and want him to have more success." Mudita recognizes that life is not a zero-sum game, that there is not just one slice of cake in which someone else's taking more means we get less. Mudita sees joy as limitless.

As mentioned earlier, mudita is also the opposite feeling to schadenfreude, the German word for the feeling of satisfaction or pleasure in hearing of others' misfortune. Schadenfreude sees us in a constant struggle of one against all others, and if someone else succeeds or accomplishes something, then we are somehow diminished, less successful, less acceptable, less lovable. Schadenfreude is a natural outgrowth of envy. Mudita is a natural outgrowth of compassion.

Mudita is based on the recognition of our interdependence, or Ubuntu. The Archbishop explains that in African villages, one would ask in greeting, "How are we?" This understanding sees that someone else's achievements or happiness is in a very real way our own. The Archbishop frequently marvels at the extraordinary beauty and talent that we humans have. "Look how beautiful you all are," he will say to a gathered crowd. Unfortunately, however, most of us want to cut others down to our self-perceived size, and we see ourselves as so terribly small and weak. When we remember our interdependence, we discover we are so incredibly large and strong.

"There is an old story from the time of the Buddha," the Dalai Lama said. "One day a king invited the Buddha and his monks for lunch. On his way to the palace, the Buddha passed by a beggar who was praising the king and smiling as he spoke of the beauty of the palace. After the king's servants served a long meal, with many courses, to the Buddha and his gathering of monks, the time came for making the dedication. The Buddha chanted a prayer to dedicate the merit, or the good karma, of the meal. However, instead of dedicating the merit of the host, the king who made the generous offering of the meal to the Buddha and his assembly, which was the custom, the Buddha chose the beggar standing outside. Shocked, one of his senior monks asked the Buddha why he chose the beggar for his dedication prayer. The Buddha replied that the king was filled with pride in showing off his kingdom, while the beggar, who had nothing, was able to rejoice in the king's good fortune. For this reason the beggar had created more merit than the king. Even today in Thailand they maintain this tradition of dedicating the merit of the offering of a meal. During my visit to Thailand in the early 1970s I had the honor to participate in one such lunch, where one of the senior monks said prayers and offered the dedication. So rejoicing in others' good fortune really brings a lot of positive benefits."

"How," I asked the Dalai Lama, "do people cultivate mudita?"

"Firstly, we should recognize our shared humanity. These are our human brothers and sisters, who have the same right and the same desire to have a happy life. This is not a spiritual thing. It is simply common sense. We are part of the same society. We are part of the same humanity. When humanity is happy, we will be happy. When humanity is peaceful, our own lives are peaceful. Just like if your family is happy, you are better off.

"If we have a strong sense of 'I and they,' it is hard to practice mudita. We must develop the sense of 'we.' Once you're able to develop that sense of common humanity and the oneness of humanity, then naturally you will want all others to be free from suffering and enjoy happiness. The desire for happiness is a natural instinct shared by everyone. It is simply a sense of concern once again for others' well-being."

"Obviously, envy is not a virtue," the Archbishop said, cautious once again that our self-development might lead to self-reproach. "Yet I would hope we would not make someone feel guilty, at least initially, about something that springs up spontaneously. You can't do very much about that feeling, but you can counter it."

"Like physical illness," the Dalai Lama insisted. "Preventive measures are the best way. Yes, if some disease has already developed, then there's no other choice but to take medicine. So similarly, once a person develops a strong negative emotion, like anger or jealousy, it is very difficult to counter it at that moment. So the best thing is to cultivate your mind through practice so that you can learn to prevent it from arising in the first place. For example, the major source of anger is frustration and dissatisfaction. At the moment when an emotion like anger is full-blown, even if we try to use our experience and our knowledge to reduce it, we will find it is very difficult to stop. At that point it is like a flood. During monsoon season, it is too late to stop the flooding. We need to start early in the spring and investigate what is causing the flooding and try to build flood walls to prevent disaster.

"Similarly, for our mental health also, the earlier we start practicing preventive measures, the easier and more effective they are. When we are already sick it is hard to remember our doctor's advice. I think no doctor would say, If you have more anger, you will be healthier. Does your doctor say that?"

"No," the Archbishop agreed.

"Doctors always advise us to relax. Relax means calm mind. Not too much agitation, which will destroy your relaxation. Also, too much attachment will destroy your peace of mind," the Dalai Lama said, returning again to envy and jealousy. "You can have a nice house with a nice bedroom and a nice bath, and play relaxing music, but if you are full of anger, full of jealousy, full of attachment, you will never be able to relax. In contrast, you may be sitting on a rock with nothing, but if your mind is completely peaceful, then you can be relaxed."

Jinpa told me that there is a memorable

verse in a well-known Tibetan text by the first
Panchen Lama. This is a beautiful prayer that
Jinpa uses to cultivate mudita:

> **As for suffering I do not wish even the
> slightest;
> as for happiness I am never satisfied.
> In this, there is no difference between
> others and me.
> Bless me so I may take joy in others'
> happiness.**

Suffering and Adversity: Passing through Difficulties

"There is a Tibetan saying that adversities can turn into good opportunities," the Dalai Lama explained in response to my question about how it is possible to experience joy even at times of suffering and adversity. "Even a tragic situation can become an opportunity. There's another Tibetan saying that it is actually the painful experiences that shine the light on the nature of happiness. They do this by bringing joyful experiences into sharp relief.

"You can see this in an entire generation that has experienced great difficulties like you, Archbishop," the Dalai Lama said. "When you got your freedom, you really felt joyous. Now

the new generation, who are born after, they
don't know the true joy of freedom, and complain more."

I remembered seeing the lines of people who
had waited for hours and hours to vote in the
first democratic election in South Africa in
1994. The lines snaked on for miles. I remember wondering at the time, as U.S. voter turn-
out was hovering under forty percent, how long
that sense of joy and appreciation for the right
to vote would last and whether there was any
way to revive it in America among those who
have never been denied the right to vote.

"I think in Europe, too," the Dalai Lama
continued, "the older generation really went
through great hardships. They were hardened
and strengthened by those painful experiences.
So this shows that the Tibetan saying is really
true. The suffering is what makes you appreciate the joy."

As the Dalai Lama was speaking, I could
not help thinking of how we try so hard, with
our natural parental instinct, to save our children from pain and suffering, but when we do,
we rob them of their ability to grow and learn
from adversity. I recalled psychologist and Aus-

chwitz survivor Edith Eva Eger saying that the spoiled, pampered children were the first to die at Auschwitz. They kept waiting for others to come save them, and when no one came, they gave up. They had not learned how to save themselves.

"Many people think of suffering as a problem," the Dalai Lama said. "Actually, it is an opportunity destiny has given to you. In spite of difficulties and suffering, you can remain firm and maintain your composure."

I understood what the Dalai Lama was saying, but how do we actually embrace our suffering and see it as an opportunity while we are in the middle of it? Certainly this was easier said than done. Jinpa had mentioned that in the Tibetan spiritual teaching known as the Seven-Point Mind Training, three categories of people are identified as being special objects of focus because these are the most challenging: your family members, your teachers, and your enemies. "Three objects, three poisons, and three roots of virtue." Jinpa explained the meaning of this cryptic and intriguing phrase: "Often it is our day-to-day interaction with these three objects that give rise to the three poisons of attachment, anger, and delusion, which are at the heart of so much suffering. Through spiritual training we have the opportunity to transform our engagement with our family, teachers, and adversaries into the development of the three roots of virtue—nonattachment, compassion, and wisdom."

"Many Tibetans," the Dalai Lama said, "spent years in Chinese gulags, work camps where they were tortured and forced to do hard labor. This, some of them told me, was a good time to test the real person, and their inner strength. Some lost hope; some kept going. Education had very little to do with who survived. In the end, it was their inner spirit, or warmhearted-ness, that made the real difference."

I had expected the Dalai Lama to say that it was their fierce resolve and determination that had made the difference. It was fascinating to hear that it was what he called inner spirit, or warmheartedness, that had allowed some to endure the hardships of the gulags.

The Archbishop now responded to the Dalai Lama with a question, echoing the one I had asked at the beginning of our discussion. We had been clear from the beginning that this book was to be about joy in the face of life's inevitable suffering and not some abstract or aspirational theory of joy. We wanted readers to know how to maintain joy at the most trying moments of our life, not just when all was, to quote the Archbishop, "hunky-dory-ness."

"He is asking, How do we help people who really want to be joyful, who really want to see the world become a better place? They look at the world and they see the horrendous problems there are. And they face quite extraordinary adversity in their own lives. Why are you joyful even when you see these problems and have faced such challenges? There are very, very many people in the world who do want to be good, who want to be joyful, who want to be like you. I mean, how do they get to have this calm in the midst of it all? And yes, I think that you are the most eloquent statement. But they want us now to translate that statement into language that they can understand."

And then as if inspired to answer his own question, the Archbishop continued, "This is what we want to tell them. We say that you will be surprised by the joy the minute you stop being too self-regarding. Of course, you have to be somewhat self-regarding, because the Lord that I follow said—taking it from the scripture— **'love thy neighbor as**—'"

"'You,'" the Dalai Lama said, finishing the famous teaching.

"Yes," the Archbishop said. "Thyself. Love others as you love yourself."

"Yes, yes." The Dalai Lama was nodding his head in agreement.

The Archbishop translated the scripture into contemporary phrasing. "You must long for the best for that other as you would want the best for you."

"That's right," the Dalai Lama said.

"They look on you and they see you as a wonderful guru, or teacher, and not just a teacher but an embodiment. And they long to be able to have the same calm and joy, even when they have all of the many, many, many frustrations, like you have encountered."

"This I think merits discussion," the Dalai Lama said. "You see, in reality like our physical body, where growth takes time, our mental development also takes time—minute by minute, day by day, month by month, year by year, decade by decade. Perhaps I will share a story from my own life.

"When I was sixteen, I lost my freedom in two senses. The previous Dalai Lama had not taken on political responsibility until he was eighteen, but in my case, the people asked me to become head of the government early because the situation was very serious, as the Chinese military had already invaded the eastern part of Tibet. When the Chinese authorities reached Lhasa, things became even more delicate, and I lost my freedom in a second way, as they severely restricted my actions.

"This political responsibility also greatly damaged my studies. As I carried out my **geshe** examinations at the major monastic universities around Lhasa in central Tibet, the Tibetan soldiers had to stand guard on the mountainside nearby. Then my final examination was to be in the courtyard of the central temple in Lhasa. There were some worries about the Chinese military, and some Tibetan officials wanted to change the location because they thought it was too dangerous, but I said I did not think it was necessary. But during the debate I had a lot of anxiety and worry, not just for my safety but also for that of my people.

"So then at age twenty-four, when I escaped to India in March 1959, I lost my own country. In one way, this made me very sad, particularly when I think of the serious question of whether the Tibetan nation, with its unique cultural heritage, will actually survive or not. The Tibetan civilization has existed for ten thousand years, and in some areas of the Tibetan plateau, human habitation existed for as many as thirty thousand years. And today's situation of Tibet is the most serious crisis in the entire history of the nation. During the Cultural Revolution, some Chinese officials made a pledge that within fifteen years the Tibetan language must be eliminated. So they burned books, such as the three-hundred-volume Tibetan canon of scriptures translated from India, as well as several thousand volumes written by Tibetans themselves. I was told that the books would burn for one or two weeks. Our statues and our monasteries were being destroyed. So it was a very, very serious situation.

"And when we came to India as refugees in 1959, we were strangers in a new place. As the

Tibetan saying goes: 'The only things that were familiar to us were the sky and the earth.' But we received immense help from the Indian government and some international organizations, including some Christian organizations, who rebuilt the Tibetan community so that we could keep our culture, our language, and our knowledge alive. So a lot of difficulties, a lot of problems, but when you carry out the work, and the more difficulties you encounter, then when you see some results, the greater the joy. Isn't it?" The Dalai Lama was now turning to the Archbishop for confirmation.

"Yes," the Archbishop said, still clearly moved by the suffering that the Dalai Lama had encountered.

"You see, if there are no difficulties and you are always relaxed, then you complain more," the Dalai Lama said, now laughing at the irony that we could experience more joy in the face of great adversity than when life is seemingly easy and uneventful.

The Archbishop was laughing, too. Joy, it seemed, was a strange alchemy of mind over matter. The path to joy, like with sadness, did not lead away from suffering and adversity but through it. As the Archbishop had said, nothing beautiful comes without some suffering. Jinpa shared how the Dalai Lama often viewed his exile as an opportunity. "His Holiness often says that when you become a refugee you get closer to life," Jinpa said, speaking no doubt from his own experience as well, "because there is no room for pretense. In this way, you get closer to truth."

"Archbishop," I said, "maybe we could turn to you for a moment. The Dalai Lama is saying that you actually feel more joy after you've succeeded in the face of opposition . . ." I stopped as I saw the Archbishop gazing at the Dalai Lama with a sense of amazement.

"I'm really actually very humbled listening to His Holiness," the Archbishop said, "because I've frequently mentioned to people the fact of his serenity and his calm and joyfulness. We would probably have said 'in spite of' the adversity, but it seems like he's saying 'because of' the adversity that this has evolved for him." The Archbishop was holding the Dalai Lama's hand, patting and rubbing his palm affectionately.

"It just increases my own personal admira-

tion for him. It almost seems perverse, but one
wants to say thank goodness that the Chinese
invaded Tibet. Yes, because I don't think that
we would have had the same contact; we certainly would not have had the same friendship."
And then, seeing the ironic humor in history,
the Archbishop started to cackle. "You probably would not have got a Nobel Peace Prize."
The Dalai Lama was now also laughing as they
poked fun at these esteemed prizes, as if to say
that we can never know what, in the end, will
come of our suffering and adversity, what is
good and what is bad.

Certainly, he was not saying that the Peace
Prize or their friendship would somehow jus-
tify the suffering of millions that the Chinese
invasion had caused, but in a bizarre way, perverse really, as the Archbishop had said, the
Dalai Lama would never have become a global
spiritual leader without being chased out of his
cloistered kingdom.

It reminded one of the famous Chinese story
about the farmer whose horse runs away. His
neighbors are quick to comment on his bad
luck. The farmer responds that no one can know
what is good and what is bad. When the horse

comes back with a wild stallion, the neighbors are quick to comment, this time talking about the farmer's good luck. Again, the farmer replies that no one can know what is good and what is bad. When the farmer's son breaks his leg trying to tame the wild stallion, the neighbors now are certain of the farmer's bad luck. Again, the farmer says that no one knows. When war breaks out, all the able-bodied young men are conscripted into battle except the farmer's son, who was spared because of his broken leg.

"But to come to your question," the Archbishop said, "I was thinking as the Dalai Lama was speaking, about something that was personal, although perhaps you could extrapolate it more generally. I'm thinking of Nelson Mandela. As we said, Nelson Mandela, when he went to prison, was a very angry young man, or youngish man. He was the commander in chief of the military wing of the ANC, as we said. He believed firmly that the enemy had to be decimated, and he and his comrades had been found guilty in a travesty of justice. That is the guy who went in, aggressive and angry. He comes onto Robben Island and is mistreated, as most of them were. Today when people go and they see his cell, there's a bed. They didn't have a bed. They were sleeping on the floor, no mattress, just a thin little thing." The Archbishop was pinching his thumb and forefinger to emphasize the discomfort, the pain, and the suffering that he endured, even in sleep.

"These were sophisticated, educated people. What do they do? What are they made to do? They are made to go and dig in a quarry. And they are wearing very inadequate clothing. Nelson Mandela and all of them wore shorts, even in winter. They were made to do almost senseless work, breaking rocks and sewing post office bags. He was a highly qualified lawyer. There he's sitting and sewing."

During a visit to Robben Island with Ahmed Kathrada, one of Mandela's colleagues and fellow prisoners, he showed us in the cafeteria the different rations that were given to the prisoners—based on their race—a daily reminder of the obsessive racial fascism that they were fighting: "Six ounces of meat for coloreds/Asiatics and five ounces for Bantus (blacks); one ounce of jam or syrup for coloreds/Asiatics and none for Bantus."

"I mean, it must have frustrated him to no

end, made him very, very angry. God was good and said, You're going to stay here twenty-seven years. And after those twenty-seven years he emerges on the other side as someone of immense magnanimity, because in an extraordinary way his suffering helped to grow him. Where they thought it was going to break him, it helped him. It helped him to see the point of view of the other. Twenty-seven years later, he comes out kind, caring, ready to trust his erstwhile enemy."

"So how did he do it?" I asked. "I mean, why do you think he was able to see his suffering as ennobling rather than embittering?"

"He didn't see it. It happened."

"So why did it happen for him? Because for others it has not."

"Yes, of course, some people it would embitter." The Archbishop had once explained to me that suffering can either embitter us or ennoble us and that the difference lies in whether we are able to find meaning in our suffering. Without meaning, when suffering seems senseless, we can easily become embittered. But when we can find a shred of meaning or redemption in our suffering, it can ennoble us, as it did for Nelson Mandela.

"One has learned in very many instances," he continued, "that for us to grow in generosity of spirit we have to undergo in some way or other a diminishing, a frustration. You may not always think of it as being so. There are very few lives that just move smoothly from beginning to end. They have to be refined."

"What is it that needs to be refined?"

"Our almost natural response is, When I'm hit, I hit back. When you have been refined, you want to find out what it is that impelled this other one to do what he did. And so you put yourself in the shoes of the other. So it is almost an axiom that generosity of spirit seems to require that one will have had setbacks to remove the dross.

"Removing the dross," the Archbishop continued, "and learning, yes, to put yourself in the shoes of the other. And it seems almost without fail that generosity of spirit requires that we will have experienced if not suffering, then at least frustrations, things that seem to want to stop us from moving in the particular direction that we have chosen. You don't move easily, straight-forwardly like this. There are things that force you off course, and you have to come back." The Archbishop was gesturing with his delicate and frail right hand, which was paralyzed by polio as a child, a vivid example of the suffering that he had experienced at a very young age.

"It is probably something like your muscle," he concluded. "I mean, if you want a good muscle tone, you know, you work against it, offering it resistance, and it will grow. If you are limp, it won't grow. You can't expand the volume of your chest just by sitting. You have to walk up mountains. There's a measure of going against, as it were, your nature. Your natural longing is to want to sit still. But if you do that and become a sofa cabbage or a couch potato, it's going to show. So what is true physi-cally is, in a wonderful way, true spiritually as well. Deep down we grow in kindness when our kindness is tested."

"Absolutely, absolutely." The Dalai Lama was agreeing, swaying back and forth, from side to side, looking down thoughtfully, fingertips touching.

"This reminds me of my friend who told me

about being sent to a Chinese gulag at the time I escaped from Tibet. The night I fled from the palace of Norbulingka, I went to a chapel to pay my respects, knowing that it was likely the last time I would ever see it again. My friend, who was already a senior monk at Namgyal Monastery, was there at the chapel. Lopon-la, as he is affectionately known by his fellow monks, did not know it was me, because my visit was top secret, and I could not tell him. Then as soon as I had left the palace, the Chinese bombardment started. They arrested many people and about one hundred and thirty were sent to a very remote area, like during Stalin's rule, when people were sent to Siberia. After eighteen years of hard labor, Lopon-la was able to come to India, and he told me what had happened during his time in the work camp.

"They had no shoes, even during the very coldest of days. Sometimes it was so cold that when you spit, it would land as ice. They were always hungry. One day he was so hungry that he tried to eat the body of one of the other prisoners that had died, but the flesh of the dead person was frozen and too hard to bite.

"Throughout the whole time, they tortured

the prisoners. There is Soviet-style torture and Japanese-style torture and Chinese-style torture, and at this camp they combined them all into an immensely cruel kind of torture.

"When he left the camp, only twenty people had survived. He told me that during those eighteen years he faced some real dangers. I thought, of course, he was talking about dangers to his life."

"He told me he was in danger of losing . . . his compassion for his Chinese guards."

I could hear a gasp in the room at this extraordinary statement, that the greatest danger for this man had been the risk of losing his compassion, losing his heart, losing his humanity.

"Now he is still alive, age ninety-seven, and his mind is still in very good shape, sharp and healthy. So as you mentioned, his spirituality and his experience reinforced his ability for compassion, his human qualities. There are a number of cases where Tibetans who spent many years of hard labor in Chinese gulags told me that it was their best period for spiritual practice, for developing patience and compassion. One of my personal physicians, Dr. Tenzin Choedrak, who years later managed to come to India, was quite clever. In the gulag, he was prevented from having the rosary and was forced to read Chairman Mao's Red Book. So he used the syllables of the words as his rosary and recited Buddhist prayers, but in the eyes of the Chinese guards, he was very seriously studying Mao's book!

"So, like in Nelson Mandela's case, when you are imprisoned, as you said, it's normal to experience great difficulties. But these experiences can, with the right way of thinking, lead you to have great inner strength. So I think that this is something very useful, particularly when we're passing through difficulties."

I was quite struck by the Dalai Lama's phrase of "passing through difficulties." We often feel that suffering will engulf us, or that the suffering will never end, but if we can realize that it, too, will pass, or as the Buddhists say, that it is impermanent, we can survive them more easily, and perhaps appreciate what we have to learn from them, find the meaning in them, so that we come out the other side, not embittered but ennobled. The depth of our suffering can also result in the height of our joy.

Shantideva, the Buddhist monk and scholar,

described the virtues of suffering. Because of the shock suffering causes us, our arrogance falls away. Suffering also gives rise to compassion for all others who are suffering, and, because of our experience of suffering, we avoid actions that will bring suffering to others. Lopon-la and Dr. Choedrak would have known these teachings by Shantideva and may have clung to them during the years of hardship and seemingly endless suffering, making meaning out of what must have at times felt like meaningless agony.

The Dalai Lama and the Archbishop were emphasizing that some degree of tolerance and acceptance is essential, as is realizing that these sorrows happen to all people, not just to us, and not because we have done anything wrong. The year before our dialogues, my father fell down a flight of stairs and suffered a traumatic brain injury. The doctors explained that with a broken bone, we know exactly how long it will take to heal, but with the brain we never know how it will heal and if it will heal completely. For more than a month he was in the intensive care unit and neuro rehab, in varying states of delirium, as we worried whether he would ever return to his former self, to his great mind and heart. I will never forget the first telephone call I received from him from the hospital, since we did not know if he would ever be able to communicate consciously again. When my brother was visiting with my dad, he said, "I'm so sorry you've had this terrible experience." My father replied, "Oh, no, not at all. It's all part of my curriculum."

Illness and Fear of Death:
I Prefer to Go to Hell

The trip was bookended by funerals. We had to change the flight itinerary to India and back twice because dear friends of Archbishop Tutu had died. Although these were funerals for men who had lived good long lives, it was a fitting reminder of death, and of the limited time each of us has. Certainly illness and mortality are two of the great verities and sources of suffering in our lives.

"Be careful—lots of my friends are dying," the Archbishop said when we had just arrived at the airport, wagging a finger at the Dalai Lama. Then he went on to say what a great man Philip Potter, one of the deceased, had been.

"He was the first black general secretary of the World Council of Churches," he explained. But with the Archbishop, sanctity and levity, death and life were close bedfellows, so even as he was honoring his friend he began to tell a joke.

"He was a very formidable man, much taller than you and me. Yesterday I was looking at his coffin. It was a massive thing. Both of us would have gone in there. And I would have gone to heaven, and where would you have gone?"

"Most probably hell," the Dalai Lama replied.

The conversation about death and who was going to heaven and hell was one of the jokes that they played with throughout the week, making fun of their traditions and conflicting pieties.

I asked them to make the subject of illness and death more personal. "How do you think about your own deaths? You're both in your eighties, and it's a reality, or at least a possibility—hopefully far in the future."

"Quite polite," the Dalai Lama said, and laughed.

"Well, he doesn't mind too much," the Archbishop cut in, pointing at the Dalai Lama, "because for him there's reincarnation."

"With reincarnation," the Dalai Lama responded, "I'm not really sure where I will be born, so much uncertainty. But you are quite sure you are going to heaven."

"Since the Chinese say they are going to decide where you are reincarnated," the Archbishop responded, "you must be nice to them."

The Archbishop then looked down as if focusing inwardly on the seriousness of the question—his own mortality. "I should say that for a very long time, the thought of my demise was something that brought a great deal of anxiety.

"I know I've had a number of near-fatal illnesses. As a child, I had polio, and they say that my father went off to buy the wood for making my coffin and my mother went off to get herself black clothes because they thought I was at the end. In my teenage years I developed tuberculosis and went to a TB hospital, where I noticed that almost all of the patients who started to hemorrhage, coughing up blood, ended up being pushed out on a trolley to the mortuary. I must've been about fifteen or so when I began coughing, coughing up blood, too. I was sitting down with this receptacle in front of me and each time I coughed, blood just came out that way. I said, 'God, if you want, if this is curtains for me, then it's okay.' I have to admit that I was surprised at the calm and the peace that came over me. Well, of course, you know that they didn't wheel me out on a trolley to the mortuary. Many years later, I met up with Archbishop Trevor Huddleston, who used to come when I was in hospital and visit me weekly for months on end. So it was many years after, when we were both archbishops, that he said he was told by the doctor, 'Your young friend'—meaning me—'is not going to make it.' Well, I guess I seem to have made it for a bit since then."

I have often thought about the strength that the Archbishop gained from facing illness and death so early in life. Illness is one of the most common sources of suffering and adversity that people face, and yet even here, as with my father, people can find meaning and spiritual growth in it. In many ways, it's probably the most common motivation for people to reevaluate and transform their lives. It's almost a cliché that people with serious or life-threatening illnesses start to savor each moment and to be more fully alive. I worked on a book many years ago with a physician who cared for seriously ill and dying patients. He made a powerful distinction between healing and curing: Curing involves the resolution of the illness but was not always possible. Healing, he said, was coming to wholeness and could happen whether or not the illness was curable.

The Archbishop explained how he was planning to be cremated, to conserve space, and wanted a simple funeral to encourage others in his country to avoid the expensive caskets and ceremonies that are traditional. Even in death, moral leaders teach by their choices. Then the Archbishop looked at me, and said with a commonsense finality, "Death is a fact of life. You are going to die." The Archbishop continued, "It's actually a wonderful thing to do what they call a living will, where you are giving instructions for when the end comes. It's not being morbid. You're saying this is a fact of life. I've conducted a number of funerals myself, and I have come to the stage where I'm saying, 'By the way, this is where you are going. That could so easily be you now.' Yes, of course, there is a kind of nostalgia for the things that you have had that you will miss. I will miss my family. I will miss the person who has been my partner for these sixty years. There are many things that I will miss. But in this Christian tradition to which I belong, I will be entering into a fuller life.

"It is wonderful. I mean, imagine if we didn't die. Our poor world would not be able to carry the burden. It's not able to carry the burden of seven billion as it is. I mean, I have had a beginning, I've had a middle, and I'll have an end. There is a lovely symmetry about it. Symmetry." He laughed as he lingered over the word and repeated it.

"If we didn't die, imagine the number of people that would be in the world now. I hope that the things I believe about heaven are really true: that I will meet my loved ones, my parents, my older brother, whom I didn't know because he died in infancy. I will meet many wonderful stalwarts. I want to meet St. Augustine. I want to meet St. Thomas Aquinas and people who have taught us so much about praying.

"Because God is God, because God is infinite, because none of us who are creatures will ever fathom the infinitude that is God, heaven is going to be forever a place of new discovery." The Archbishop's eyes were transfixed, his gaze distant. "I would say, 'Oh, God, you're so beautiful.' And I will call, I will call, 'Come, come and see,' and this other one will say, 'Have you seen just how beautiful God is?'"

The Archbishop fell silent.

Perhaps death and the fear of death is truly the greatest challenge to joy. Well, when we are dead, it does not really matter, but it is the fear of its approaching, of the suffering that often precedes it, and ultimately the fear of the oblivion and the loss of our personhood that frighten us. Many psychologists say that the fear of death lies behind all other fears, and many historians of religion argue that religion arose to try to solve the mystery of death. Modern life keeps that fear at bay, as we don't interact with the very old or the very sick, and illness, frailty, and death get tucked away behind institutional walls from our everyday lives.

After a few moments the Dalai Lama began speaking.

"I think, for thousands of years, the human mind has been curious about death, and many traditions have many ideas and concepts of what will happen next. Heaven, as you mentioned, is a beautiful understanding. Shintoism in Japan also has the idea that after death you automatically go to heaven where all your ancestors are living.

"When many people think about death, they are very, very afraid. Usually I tell them that you should accept that death is part of our life. There's a beginning and there's an end, as you mentioned. So once we accept that it is normal and that sooner or later it will come, our attitude changes. Some people are embarrassed when asked about their age or pretend that they are still young. This is silly—deceiving oneself. We should be realistic."

"Yes, yes," the Archbishop agreed.

"If a person is sick," the Dalai Lama said, "it is much better to accept that you have some kind of illness and get medical treatment, rather than saying nothing is wrong and deceiving yourself."

While the Archbishop was in Dharamsala we had arranged for him to see Yeshi Dhonden, one of the Dalai Lama's doctors. Rachel is an integrative physician and was interested to know if this revered healer might have helpful recommendations for the Archbishop, whose prostate cancer was back.

In an amazing coincidence, Dr. Dhonden had helped cure my mother of blood cancer while he was visiting New York many years ago, when I was still in high school. When I was in Dharamsala in January preparing for the visit, I was told that Dr. Dhonden had died, but I had just heard that he was still alive at almost ninety. I was excited to meet him, to thank him for helping to save my mother's life, and to see if he might be able to help the Archbishop.

He came into the Archbishop's bedroom at the hotel, his bald head and large ears making him look a little like an only slightly taller Yoda from the Star Wars movies. His face was impassive, and his hands had a powerful delicacy while they took the Archbishop's pulse. The Archbishop was lying on his king-sized bed. Through the windows, the valleys of Dharamsala plunged down in steep hillsides of oaks and evergreens, ending with a vista of the vast plains below.

Through a translator, Dr. Dhonden began to describe health issues that the Archbishop had experienced decades ago and that had led to his current prostate cancer. The Archbishop looked

surprised as Rachel, who was familiar with
many traditional medical systems, explained
what Dr. Dhonden was saying in a way that
made sense to a modern medical understanding of the body.

After a fifteen- or twenty-minute exam, Dr.
Dhonden pointed to the can of Coke Zero on
the bedside table. The Archbishop has given
up the rum and Cokes he used to favor, but
he is still quite fond of his Coke Zero, having
agreed to the diet soda to cut down on his sugar
consumption. According to Dr. Dhonden, the
Coke Zero was still not helping his health and
should be removed from his diet.

When this was translated to the Archbishop,
he got out of his bed rather spryly, and jokingly
waved his hands, saying, "I think it's time for
you to go."

Rachel assured the Archbishop that while
she had been trying to get him to kick his
Coke Zero habit for years, at eighty-four he
was allowed to eat and drink what he pleased.
Dr. Dhonden made some additional recommendations, photos were taken together of the
famous doctor and famous patient, and then
the good doctor left.

"As a Buddhist practitioner," the Dalai Lama said, "I take seriously the contemplation of the Buddha's first teaching, about the inevitability of suffering and the transient nature of our existence. Also, the Buddha's last teaching at the time of his death ends with the truth of impermanence, reminding us how it is the nature of all things that come into existence to have an end. The Buddha said nothing lasts.

"So it is important that in our daily meditation practice we continue to think about our own mortality. There are two levels of impermanence. At the grosser level, life keeps changing and things cease to exist, including us. At the more subtle level, in every single moment everything is changing, something science is able to show us happening, even at the atomic and subatomic level. Our body is constantly changing, as is our mind. Everything is in a constant state of change—nothing remains static, and nothing remains permanent. In fact, as the Buddha reminds us, the very causes that have given rise to something, such as our life, have created the mechanism, or the seed, for that thing's eventual end. Recognizing this truth is an important part of the contemplation on impermanence.

"Then I ask why impermanence happens. The answer is because of interdependence—nothing exists independently. So this kind of contemplation is part of my usual daily meditation practice. This practice is actually to help one prepare for death, the intermediate state, and then rebirth, so in order to carry out the practice effectively, you should reflect on these things and visualize the process of death.

"Finally, I think you mentioned that we old people should prepare for death, and it is important to make space for the future, for younger generations. What is important to remember is that sooner or later death comes and to make our life meaningful while we're alive. I think maximum lifespan is about a hundred years. Compared to human history, a hundred years is quite short. So if we utilize that short period to create more problems on this planet, our life would be meaningless. If we could live for a million years, **then** maybe it would be worthwhile to create some problems. But our life is short. Now you see, we are guests here on this planet, visitors who have come for a short time, so we need to use our days wisely, to make our world a little better for everyone."

Jinpa explained that there is a profound teaching by an ancient Tibetan master: The true measure of spiritual development is how one confronts one's own mortality. The best way is when one is able to approach death with joy; next best way is without fear; third best way is at least not to have regrets.

"So earlier I was explaining about the night that we fled from Norbulingka," the Dalai Lama said, now turning to his own experiences of facing the fear of death. "For me, that was the most frightening night of my life, the night of the 17th of March, 1959. At that time, my life really was in danger. I still remember the alertness of mind I felt as I stepped out of the Norbulingka Palace in disguise, dressed in a Tibetan layman's clothes. All my efforts to calm down the situation in Lhasa had failed. A huge crowd of Tibetans had gathered outside the Norbulingka Palace, wanting to block any attempts on the part of the Chinese military to take me away. I had tried my best, but both sides, the Chinese and the Tibetans, were deeply entrenched in their positions. Of course, the Tibetan side was deeply devout and was trying to protect me." The Dalai Lama paused and looked reflective as he recalled the devotion of his people and their self-sacrifice for his safety.

This spontaneous gathering of Tibetans outside Norbulingka Palace was the culmination of days of uprising against the Communist Chinese occupation by the Tibetan people that first began on March 10, 1959. This time, the public had come to prevent the Chinese authorities from taking the Dalai Lama away from Norbulingka Palace, supposedly for his own personal safety. Something had to happen. The situation was explosive and the Dalai Lama knew that it could only lead to a massacre.

"So that night, the 17th of March 1959, the plan for my escape was executed. We went at night and in disguise along a road that followed a river. On the other side of the river was the Chinese military barracks. We could see the guards. No one in our party was allowed to use flashlights, and we tried to minimize the sound of the horses' hoofs. But still there was danger. If they saw us and opened fire, we were finished.

"Yet as a Buddhist practitioner, I thought of

Shantideva's somewhat stern advice: If there is a way to overcome the situation, then instead of feeling too much sadness, too much fear, or too much anger, make an effort to change the situation. If there's nothing you can do to overcome the situation, then there is no need for fear or sadness or anger. So I told myself, at that moment, that even if something were to happen to me, it would still be okay.

"You face the facts, the reality. And making an attempt to escape was the best response in the face of that reality. Actually, fear is part of human nature; it's a natural response that arises in the face of a danger. But with courage, when in fact real dangers come, you can be more fearless, more realistic. On the other hand, if you let your imagination run wild, then you exacerbate the situation further and then bring more fear.

"Many people on this planet worry about going to hell, but this is not much use. There is no need to be afraid. While we remain on the earth worrying about hell, about death, about all the things that could go wrong, we will have lots of anxiety, and we will never find joy and happiness. If you are truly afraid of hell, you need to live your life with some purpose, especially through helping others.

"So," the Dalai Lama finally said, slapping the Archbishop on the wrist playfully. "I prefer to go to hell than to heaven. I can solve more problems in hell. I can help more people there."

Meditation: Now I'll Tell You a Secret Thing

We arrived at the Dalai Lama's complex early in the morning as the sun was still waking up. We went through the vigilant security, which reminded us that not all were as loving toward the Dalai Lama as he was toward them. I had decided to see the pat down, not unlike those we are often subjected to at airports, as a brief massage rather than as an intrusion of my personal space or as an accusation of my potential danger. I was already learning how much one's perspective shaped one's reality.

We crossed the brief distance to the Dalai Lama's private residence. We were later told that some of the people who had worked with the Dalai Lama for thirty years had never been inside. This was his retreat, one of the few places where this very public man could experience solitude, and it was a great privilege to be welcomed into his inner sanctum.

From the outside, the Dalai Lama's home is a yellow-painted concrete structure with a green roof, like so many in Dharamsala. The double doors and walls have plenty of glass to let in the high altitude light. On the roof is a balcony where the Dalai Lama can take a morning constitutional and look out at his beloved greenhouse filled with purple, pink, and white delphiniums and marigolds, bursting like tiny suns. Beyond he can see a panoramic vista down to the lush green Indian plains, and in the other direction the towering glacial Dhauladhar Mountains cloaked in white snow year-round. While far less grand than the Potala of his youth, his residence has a modest elegance and warmth that the endless thousand-room palace, with its empty, ghost-haunted rooms, must have lacked.

. . .

We followed the Dalai Lama and the Archbishop into the house as the now-brightening light streamed in through the glass window panels. The curtains were held back with ties, and the ceiling was painted black and red. The hallway was hung with brightly colored **thangkas**, and the hall was narrowed by bookshelves piled high with golden-spined sacred texts.

"Now this is my—how do you say—living room, a prayer room," the Dalai Lama explained. It seemed fitting that his living room was his prayer room, since so much of his life is spent in prayer and meditation. As we entered the room we saw a large, glassed-in altar with a statue of a somewhat emaciated Buddha. Along the sides of the case were traditional Tibetan sacred texts, which looked like rectangular blocks. This altar was similar to a breakfront in a Western home that might be filled with silver or porcelain objects. On a ledge was a tablet displaying the face of a clock, which chimed out the hours.

As we entered the room, we saw a much larger altar, which was also encased in glass. "Now, this statue," the Dalai Lama said, introduc-

ing the Archbishop to the standing Buddha at
the center, "is from the seventh century. Am I
right?" the Dalai Lama asked, turning to Jinpa.
"Right, seventh century," Jinpa confirmed.

"He was a member of the monastery where
this statue once stood," the Dalai Lama said,
pointing to Jinpa. Known as "Kyirong Jowo,"
literally the brother from Kyirong, this statue
of the Buddha is revered as one of the most
precious religious treasures of the Tibetan people. It was clothed in a traditional Tibetan robe
and crowned with a golden, jeweled coronet.
It was surrounded by dozens of smaller statues of the Buddha and other sacred figures and
was framed by white and purple orchids. The
statue was beautifully carved sandalwood, and
its face was painted gold. The eyes were wide-
set, the eyebrows thin, the lips curving, the
whole face serene. The statue's right hand was
extended, palm up, in a gentle gesture of welcome, acceptance, and generosity.

"**Wonderful,**" the Archbishop said.

"Originally, there were two similar statues, both carved from the same single piece
of sandalwood. And since the time of the
5th Dalai Lama, one was housed in the Potala

Palace," the Dalai Lama explained. The Great Fifth, as he is often called, lived in the seventeenth century and united central Tibet, ending its many civil wars. He is the Charlemagne of Tibet—well, maybe the Charlemagne and the pope combined. "While one statue was in the Potala," he said, "this statue was in western Tibet. They were like two brothers, twins. So eventually when the Chinese army destroyed the Potala, that one was killed." It might have been a misspoken word, but his personification of the statue and its death did seem quite poignant. "Then the monks in western Tibet smuggled this one out of Tibet and into India. So then there was a question of whether it should go with the monks of that monastery to south India, where they were resettled, or stay here with me. I made some investigations in the mysterious way—divinations—which I think you also have in African culture. So then this statue, how do you say?"

He spoke in Tibetan to Jinpa, who then translated: "The divination revealed that the statue preferred to stay with the one who is more famous."

Everyone laughed.

"Now I'll tell you a secret thing, something quite unique. Each morning, you see, I pray to this statue. Then I see his facial expression changing." The Dalai Lama had a mischievous look, and it was hard to know whether he was pulling the Archbishop's leg.

"Really?" the Archbishop said, trying not to sound too incredulous. The Dalai Lama rocked his head from side to side as if to say, Maybe it does, maybe it doesn't. Then the Archbishop asked, "Does it smile?"

"Yes, it is smiling like you, really," the Dalai Lama said as he leaned in and touched foreheads with the Archbishop. Then, wagging a finger at him, he added quickly, "Oh, but not like your eyes, so big and round." The Dalai Lama's eyes went wide with an expression that could be surprise, fear, or anger. "Okay, now our session."

But as he walked to his chair he stopped at another altar in the center of the room. On the round table was a very lifelike crucifix, carved out of white marble, with black nails sticking out of the palms of the hands. There was also a statue of the Madonna. "Now this is a black Madonna from Mexico." The statue was of

Mary wearing a golden robe and crown and holding a golden orb of the world. On her lap was a small baby Jesus.

"Mary is the symbol of love," the Dalai Lama said, gesturing at the statue with the same open palm of the sandalwood Buddha. "It's wonderful."

There was also a deep blue globe nested in a golden stand, a sacred symbol perhaps of another kind, and a tangible reminder of the Buddhist understanding of interdependence. The Dalai Lama's prayer practice and concern, like the Archbishop's, enveloped the whole world.

The Dalai Lama showed the Archbishop over to a heavily cushioned beige chair with a high-winged back. The Archbishop wore a navy blue Tibetan shirt with the button in the corner, near the shoulder, which made the shirt seem like a pouch into which he had been snugly fit. A skilled tailor, Lama Tenzin's father had specially made it for him as a gift. The Archbishop sat down, his small frame practically disappearing into the large chair.

The rest of us began to sit down on the floor, and the Dalai Lama asked whether we wanted chairs, but we said we were quite happy.

"Originally I also used to sit on the floor," the Dalai Lama said. "But I started to have this problem with my knees. So now I prefer like this." He gestured to a wide chair draped in a red velvety fabric. He pulled his robes up a little and sat down. Behind him a yellow, red, and green **thangka** hung on the wall. In front of him was a low wooden table with a stack of Buddhist texts, shaped like horizontal literary blocks. Two long thin lamps, sentinels on either side of the table, likely lit the table and the long Tibetan scriptures in the early mornings when the Dalai Lama began his practice. A pot of pink tulips and a gold-colored bowl for ceremonial rice throwing added some color. Finally, two slender tablets also stood on the crowded table, one to display the weather and the other to listen to BBC News.

"Because of our program, today I started my meditation at 2:30."

"Hmm," the Archbishop said, perhaps still marveling at this very early rising.

"Then, as usual, shower and then continue with my meditation practice. Now, you feel okay? Temperature is okay?" The Dalai Lama was extending his hands with concern.

The Archbishop smiled and gave him the thumbs-up. "Thank you," the Archbishop said as they settled in beside each other.

"This part is a clear light of death meditation," the Dalai Lama said, as if he were about to lead us into a meditation focusing on the breath and not the wasting away of our bodily form. "We are training our mind by going through quite a detailed process for what we will experience at the time of death."

"Mmhmm," the Archbishop said with wide eyes, as if he had just been invited to warm up for the spiritual Olympics with a short marathon.

"According to Buddhist Vajrayana psychology, there are different levels of consciousness," the Dalai Lama said, referring to the esoteric Buddhist tradition, which aims to help the practitioner discover ultimate truth. "There's a dissolution that occurs as the grosser levels of our bodily and mental states come to an end, and when more and more subtle levels become manifest. Then at the innermost or most subtle level, this state of clear light arises at the moment of dying. Not death. Dying. Physical feeling completely ceases. Breathing ceases.

Heart ceases, it's no longer beating. Brain also ceases its functioning. Still subtle, very subtle levels of consciousness remain, getting ready for another destination of life."

The consciousness at the moment of death that the Dalai Lama was describing is free of duality and content and abides in the form of pure luminosity. (In a popular Hollywood comedy, **Caddyshack**, there is a scene where Bill Murray's character, Carl, describes a tall tale about carrying golf clubs for the 12th Dalai Lama on a glacier. Carl asked for a tip after the game, and the Dalai Lama is said to have responded, "Oh, there won't be any money, but when you die, on your deathbed, you will receive total consciousness." Perhaps the screenwriters were onto something and knew about the clear light of death meditation.)

"So, in Buddhist thought," the Dalai Lama explained, "we speak of death, intermediate state, and rebirth. In my case, I undertake this kind of meditation five times in a day, so on a daily basis, I kind of go through death and rebirth—five times I leave and five times I come back. So I suppose," said the Dalai Lama, "when I actually die, I should be well prepared!"

With these words, his twinkling eyes and mischievous smile became thoughtful and tender. "But I don't know. When actual death comes, I hope I will have the ability to apply this practice effectively. I don't know. So I need **your** prayers."

"The Chinese say you will not decide who your reincarnation will be," the Archbishop said, returning to a source of humor throughout the week. For the Archbishop, one did not want to miss the opportunity to link prayer to politics and meditation to activism—or a good joke. Certainly the declaration that the Chinese government (which does not sanction or accept religion) would choose the next reincarnation of the Dalai Lama was fodder for another good laugh.

"I prefer, after my death," the Dalai Lama said with a laugh, "that **you** search for my reincarnation, that you carry the investigation rather than an antireligious, atheistic, Communist government."

"Yes," the Archbishop said after a pause, perhaps wondering how he would carry on the investigation to find the next Dalai Lama.

"I usually say—" the Dalai Lama continued,

"half-joking, half-serious—first Chinese Communist Party should accept the theory of rebirth, then they should recognize Chairman Mao Tse Tung's reincarnation, then Deng Xiaoping's reincarnation, then they have a right to be involved with the Dalai Lama's reincarnation."

"Yes," the Archbishop mused. "I was very interested because they claim to be atheists and all of that, but they say they will decide whether you are going to be reincarnated. That is quite something." The Archbishop was chuckling and shaking his head at the absurdity of the Chinese government trying to restrict the Dalai Lama's movements even in the next life.

Then words fell away, dialogue and jokes settled into quiet contemplation.

The Dalai Lama took off his glasses. His beautiful face was so familiar and yet suddenly quite different. His face looked long and oval, from his wide balding scalp, over his triangular eyebrows and slightly opened eyes, to his straight, broad nose, and peaked cheeks that looked chiseled now and weathered like the cliff face of a Himalayan summit, then to his straight and pursed lips, and ending with his soft, rounded chin. He looked down, as if the shades of his mind had been drawn, and now he was concerned only with the inward journey.

The Dalai Lama scratched his temple, and I felt relieved that he was not some austere ascetic who would deny his itches and aches. He wrapped his cloak more tightly around his shoulders and settled into quiet, his hands resting in his lap.

At first my mind started racing, and I was having a hard time staying focused, thinking about the questions I would ask, the video camera that was filming, the other people in the room, and if everything was as it should be and everyone had what they needed. Then as I watched the Dalai Lama's face, my own mirror neuron system seemed to resonate with the mind-state that I was witnessing. Mirror neurons allow us to imitate others and experience their internal states, and therefore may play an important role in empathy. I started to experience a tingling in my forehead and then a sharpening of focus as various parts of my brain started to quiet and calm, as if the activity began to center on what spiritual adepts have called the third eye, or what neuroscientists call the middle prefrontal cortex.

Daniel Siegel had explained to me that the neural integration created by this crucial area of the brain links many disparate areas and is the locus of everything from emotional regulation to morality. Meditation, he and other scientists have proposed, helps with these processes. He explained that the integrative fibers of the discerning middle prefrontal cortex seem to reach out and soothe the more reactive emotional structures of the brain. We inherited the reactivity of this part of our brain, and particularly the sensitive amygdala, from our skittish fight-or-flight ancestors. Yet so much of the inner journey means freeing ourselves from this evolutionary response so that we do not flip our lid or lose our higher reasoning when facing stressful situations.

The real secret of freedom may simply be extending this brief space between stimulus and response. Meditation seems to elongate this pause and help expand our ability to choose our response. For example, can we expand the momentary pause between our spouse's annoyed words and our angry or hurt reaction? Can we change the channel on the mental broadcasting system from self-righteous indignation—how dare she or he speak to me like that—to compassionate understanding—she or he must be very tired. I will never forget seeing the Archbishop do exactly this—pause and choose his response—during a pointed challenge I had made some years ago.

We had been engaged in two full, exhausting days of interviews, hoping to create a legacy project around his pioneering work with the Truth and Reconciliation Commission in South Africa. We were many hours into the dialogue with a film crew, and he was visibly tired and frankly a little cranky. It was not easy work to try to describe systematically the process of truth, forgiveness, and reconciliation that he had used so effectively but often instinctively to heal his country.

At one particularly tense moment I had asked him about his decision to return to South Africa from England, an event that had profound implications for the anti-apartheid movement and the freeing of his country but also had quite painful consequences for his wife, Leah, and their children. Not only were they leaving a country where they were free and equal citizens to return to an oppressive and racist society, but also they were choosing to break up their family as well. The apartheid government had created Bantu education for blacks and other nonwhites, an educational system that had the specific goal of educating its students for menial jobs. It was the purposeful mental subjugation of generations of students. This would never be tolerable for the Archbishop and Leah, and they knew they would need to send their children away to a boarding school in Swaziland.

This had been one of the most difficult moments in their marriage, and it had almost broken them. Certainly it had caused Leah enormous pain. After saying that few marital disputes are vindicated by history, I asked the Archbishop if he had ever apologized to Leah for the pain his decision had caused. He defended his decision, with the true righteousness of the cause and perhaps a little of the entitlement of a man of his generation. I pushed him hard about why he had not apologized for the anguish it had caused Leah, even if the decision had been the right one.

As my verbal assault became more pointed and challenging, I saw his head draw back in reaction and perhaps some defensiveness. Most of us might have argued more adamantly or attacked back in such a disagreement, but it was as if I could see the Archbishop—in a split-second pause—collect his consciousness, reflect on his options, and choose his response, one that was thoughtful and engaged rather than reactive and rejecting. It was one of the most profound examples of what a prayerful and meditative life can give us—that pause, the freedom to respond instead of react. A few weeks later he wrote to me that he had discussed the experience with Leah and had apologized. She told him that she had forgiven him long ago. Marriages, even the best ones—perhaps especially the best ones—are an ongoing process of spoken and unspoken forgiveness.

The Archbishop cradled his right hand in his left. He hung his head in concentration.

The goal was meditation, but I've never been quite sure where meditation ends and prayer begins, or where prayer ends and meditation begins. I have heard it said that prayer is when we speak to God, and meditation is when God answers. Whether it is God answering or some wiser part of our own intelligence, I am not sure it mattered to me, as I was just trying to quiet the inner noise and listen through the thick and enveloping silence.

After the Dalai Lama ended the meditation, it was the Archbishop's turn to share his spiritual practice. The Archbishop begins his day with prayer and meditation in the small closet-sized upstairs chapel in his home in Cape Town. Before becoming the archbishop of Cape Town, he and his family lived in Soweto, the former black township outside of Johannesburg that was so central to the antiapartheid struggle and the site of the Soweto Uprising. There he had a slightly larger semidetached chapel with a stained glass window and actual pews. It was a lovely cloistered space, and we had spent some beautiful moments of quiet together in there. It felt like being in the spiritual headquarters of the anti-apartheid struggle, where the Archbishop had turned to God so many times in anguish and uncertainty and found direction.

As the Archbishop and Mpho got the bread and wine ready, the Dalai Lama said, "A Buddhist monk does not take wine or any alcohol—in principle, that is. But today, with you, I will take a little." He added, "Don't worry, you can rest assured, I will not be drunk."

"I still won't let you drink and drive," the Archbishop replied.

"This is the first time we get to pray together," the Dalai Lama said. "One Buddhist, one Christian, brothers. I mentioned to you that since 1975 I have been making pilgrimages to different religious traditions. Sometimes it takes a major disaster for followers of all different faiths to come together and see that we are the same, human brothers and sisters. I consider what we are doing today to be part of the same kind of pilgrimage. When I look at this statue of Jesus Christ, I am really moved. I think this teacher has brought immense inspiration to millions of people. Now it is time for your meditation."

The Archbishop and Mpho handed out the

small prayer booklets and led the Eucharist, also called Holy Communion. This rite is considered to be a reenactment of the Last Supper, which was a celebration of the Jewish Passover meal. Jesus is believed to have said that his followers should eat the bread and drink the wine as a remembrance of him, and for many Christians the bread is transformed into Christ's body and the wine into his blood. The Eucharist celebrates Jesus's sacrifice of himself. I had joined the Archbishop for Eucharist many times, usually as the only Jew, a point that the Archbishop enjoyed pointing out, often adding that I was there to make sure the Eucharist was "kosher." As a non-Christian, I did not actually receive Communion, so it was a surprise to see the Archbishop and the Dalai Lama break convention in both of their traditions.

Many Christian denominations forbid those who are not Christians, or even other Christians who are not of their specific denomination (those with whom they are not in full communion), from sharing in the Eucharist. In other words, like so many religious traditions it defines who is part of the group and who is not. This is one of the greatest challenges that humanity faces: removing the barriers between who we see as "us" and who we see as "other." The latest brain scan research suggests that we have a rather binary understanding of self and other and that our empathy circuits do not activate unless we see the other person as part of our own group. So many wars have been fought and so much injustice has been perpetrated because we've banished others from our group and therefore our circle of concern. I remember the Archbishop starkly pointing out this fact during the Iraq War, when the tallies of American and Iraqi casualties were reported and valued differently by the media in the United States. In the Archbishop's tally these were all God's children, indivisible and valued equally.

The Archbishop and the Dalai Lama are truly two of the most inclusive religious figures in the world, and throughout the week the theme underlying their teachings was about transcending our narrow definitions and finding love and compassion for all of humanity. The sharing of traditions that we were engaged in that morning was a reminder to put aside our own narrow beliefs of self and other, ours and theirs, Christian and Buddhist, Hindu and

Jew, believer and atheist. In the land of Gandhi that we were in, I thought of his totemic words when asked if he was a Hindu: "Yes I am. I am also a Christian, a Muslim, a Buddhist, and a Jew." We were looking for human truth, and we would drink from the cup of wisdom from whatever source it came.

"Is it English?" the Dalai Lama asked as he took the booklet.

"It's English, yes. Do you want to read in Xhosa?" the Archbishop said, referring to his African mother tongue, clicking as he said the word.

"That one I don't know."

"For your sake we will use English."

"Thank you, thank you," the Dalai Lama said.

"But the language of heaven is Xhosa. When you get up there, they are going to have to find a translator for you."

"There is a connection," the Dalai Lama said. "You see, historians say that the first human beings came from Africa—our real ancestors. So God's creation began in Africa."

"Not very far from my home," the Archbishop replied, "the site that they say is the Cradle of

Humankind. So although you look like you look, you are an African!"

"The European, the Asian, the Arab, the American . . ." the Dalai Lama began.

"They are all African," the Archbishop finished. "We are all African. Some of us were farther away from the heat and their complexions changed. Now we want to be quiet."

"Yes. First, you should be quiet. Then we will follow," the Dalai Lama said, one last tease before sanctity descended, although I often felt like, for these two men, holiness and lightheartedness were indivisible.

The Dalai Lama now sat there with his lips pursed together reverentially. As the service began he nodded his head attentively. When we stood, he stood straight and wrapped his crimson cloak around him. His hands were pressed together, his fingers laced. I knew that each leader was used to serving as the representative of their entire tradition, and the Dalai Lama was attempting to offer his respects on behalf of the whole Tibetan Buddhist—perhaps the whole Buddhist—community.

. . .

Mpho Tutu wore a bright red dress and a matching red headscarf as well as a black cloak. She began with a prayer for all of those places where injustice exists, where there is strife, and continued to offer prayers of healing for all of those who are in need. She concluded by blessing the work that we were doing together.

We finished the prayers and affirmations of the Eucharist with the words "Peace be with you. The peace of the Lord be with you." Everyone went around to kiss and embrace one another. The Dalai Lama was behind his meditation table. I was thinking about how few embraces he must get, and went over to greet him. Mpho did, too. Then the Archbishop did as well. They held hands and bowed to each other.

Now was the time for Communion. The Archbishop lifted up a small piece of Tibetan white bread and placed it in the Dalai Lama's mouth. One could see the beaded **U-B-U-N-T-U** bracelet on the Archbishop's wrist affirming our connectedness and interdependence to one another. It was the reminder that we can be in communion with everyone.

Then Mpho approached with the glass of red wine. The Dalai Lama dipped the tip of his left ring finger into the glass and then placed the smallest drop into his mouth.

After giving everyone Communion, the Archbishop used his finger to collect all the crumbs, so not a smidgen of the symbolic body would be discarded, then poured any remaining bits into the glass of watered-down wine and drank it.

The Archbishop ended with a blessing in Xhosa, clicking repeatedly in the beautiful sound poetry of his native language, crossed himself, and then made the sign of the cross over the gathered fellowship. "I'm driving you out, go out into the world. Go in peace to love and serve the Lord. Hallelujah. Hallelujah. In the name of Christ. Amen. Hallelujah. Hallelujah."

Before we left, the Dalai Lama stopped to take some pills, which he explained were Tibetan medicines. He chewed them up, his face puckering at their bitter taste.

"That's why you are looking so handsome," the Archbishop said.

"Because of God's grace," the Dalai Lama replied.

Rachel then added, "God's grace sends the Tibetan doctor."

"In terms of physical strength, God loves the nonbeliever more than the believer!" the Dalai Lama said, laughing.

The Archbishop began to cackle, too, as he took his cane and started to walk away but then turned around: "Don't laugh at your own jokes, man."

"You taught me to do that." Then the Dalai Lama got up, wrapped his cloak around his shoulders, and took the Archbishop's arm. "Thank you very much," he said, referring to the service. "Very impressive."

"Thank you for your hospitality," the Archbishop replied.

They exited back down the dark hallway lined with **thangkas**. The bright light was streaming in through the windows at the end of the hallway now. They stepped outside and down the concrete stairs, the Archbishop moving slowly, bracing himself with the handrail.

A car was waiting, but the Archbishop and the Dalai Lama decided to walk up the path together to the conference room where the interviews were being filmed.

The Dalai Lama took the Archbishop's hand, the one that held the cane. They walked together rather nimbly.

"Have you had any problems with security here?" the Archbishop asked.

"No, no," the Dalai Lama said.

"I'm quite surprised," the Archbishop responded.

"No," the Dalai Lama said again, confirming his safety. "I usually describe myself as the longest guest of the Indian government, now fifty-six years."

"Fifty-six? But, I mean, there have not been any intruders? People who have wanted to come in here and attack you?" He was no doubt thinking of his own death threats and the actual plan to assassinate him. It was foiled by the embrace of a crowd of people that had surrounded him at the airport and prevented the would-be assassin from getting close enough.

"No, no. Twenty-four hours a day. India provides protection."

"Quite amazing, but even so, they can be quite clever. They can infiltrate the security

establishment, and you think that it is someone who is coming to protect you, and it turns
out . . ."

"Even in the White House," the Dalai Lama
said, "someone entered without much notice."

"It is wonderful that you have been able to be
secure here."

"The only danger," the Dalai Lama said, "is
an earthquake."

Days 4 and 5

The Eight Pillars of Joy

I.

Perspective: There Are Many Different Angles

As we said right at the beginning, joy is a by-product," the Archbishop began. "If you set out and say, I want to be happy, clenching your teeth with determination, this is the quickest way of missing the bus." So if joy and happiness are by-products, what exactly are they by-products of? It was time to delve deeper into the qualities of mind and heart that we needed to cultivate to catch that bus.

"We have now covered the nature of true joy and the obstacles to joy," I said as we began our fourth day of dialogues. "Now we are ready to

move on to the positive qualities that allow us
to experience more joy."

We had discussed the topic of mental immunity in reducing fear and anger and other obstacles to joy, but the Dalai Lama had explained
that mental immunity was also about filling
our mind and heart with positive thoughts
and feelings. As our dialogue progressed, we
converged on eight pillars of joy. Four were
qualities of the mind: **perspective, humility,
humor, and acceptance.** Four were qualities
of the heart: **forgiveness, gratitude, compassion, and generosity.**

On the first day, the Archbishop had touched
the fingers of his right hand to his heart to
emphasize its centrality. We would end up,
ultimately, at compassion and generosity, and
indeed both men would insist that these two
qualities were perhaps most pivotal to any lasting happiness. Yet we needed to begin with
some fundamental qualities of the mind that
would allow us to turn more easily and frequently to the compassionate and generous
response to life. As the Dalai Lama had said
at the start of our dialogues, we create most of
our suffering, so we should be able to create

more joy. The key, he had explained, was our perspective and the thoughts, feelings, and actions that come as a result.

Scientific research consistently supported so much of the dialogue that was unfolding over the week. The factors that psychologist Sonja Lyubomirsky has found to have the greatest influence on our happiness supported a number of the eight pillars. The first concerned our perspective toward life, or, as Lyubomirsky described it, our ability to reframe our situation more positively. Our capacity to experience gratitude and our choice to be kind and generous were the others.

A healthy perspective really is the foundation of joy and happiness, because the way we see the world is the way we experience the world. Changing the way we see the world in turn changes the way we feel and the way we act, which changes the world itself. Or, as the Buddha says in the Dhammapada, "With our mind we create our own world."

For every event in life," the Dalai Lama said, "there are many different angles. When you

look at the same event from a wider perspective, your sense of worry and anxiety reduces,
and you have greater joy." The Dalai Lama had
discussed the importance of a wider perspective when he was telling us about how he was
able to see the calamity of his losing his country as an opportunity. It was jaw-dropping to
hear him "reframe more positively" the last
half century of exile. He had been able to see
not only what he had lost but also what he
had gained: wider contact and new relationships, less formality and more freedom to discover the world and learn from others. He had
concluded, "So therefore, if you look from one
angle, you feel, Oh, how bad, how sad. But if
you look from another angle at that same tragedy, that same event, you see that it gives me
new opportunities."

Edith Eva Eger tells the story of visiting two
soldiers on the same day at William Beaumont
Army Medical Center at Fort Bliss. Both were
paraplegics who had lost the use of their legs
in combat. They had the same diagnosis and
the same prognosis. The first veteran, Tom,
was lying on his bed knotted into a fetal position, railing against life and decrying his fate.

The second, Chuck, was out of bed in his wheelchair, explaining that he felt as if he had been given a second chance in life. As he was wheeled through the garden, he had realized that he was closer to the flowers and could look right into his children's eyes.

Eger often quotes fellow Auschwitz survivor Viktor Frankl, who said that our perspective toward life is our final and ultimate freedom. She explains that our perspective literally has the power to keep us alive or to cause our death. One of her fellow inmates at Auschwitz was terribly ill and weak, and others in her bunk asked her how she was holding on to life. The prisoner said that she had heard that they were going to be liberated by Christmas. The woman lived against all odds, but she died on Christmas Day when they were not liberated. It's no wonder that during the week the Dalai Lama had called some thoughts and feelings toxic, even poisonous.

Jinpa explained that while changing our emotions is quite hard, changing our perspective is actually relatively easy. It is a part of our mind, over which we have influence. The way you see the world, the meaning you give to what you witness, changes the way you feel. It can be the first step of "a spiritual and neural journey that results in more and more equanimity and of our default state being increasingly more joyful," as psychologist and writer Daniel Goleman poetically put it on a pretrip call. Perspective, Jinpa argued, is nothing less than the skull key that opens all of the locks that imprison our happiness. What is this perspective shift that has such power? What is the healthy perspective that the Dalai Lama and the Archbishop bring to life, that allows them to greet life with so much joy in the face of so much sorrow?

The Dalai Lama used the terms **wider perspective** and **larger perspective**. They involve stepping back, within our own mind, to look at the bigger picture and to move beyond our limited self-awareness and our limited self-interest. Every situation we confront in life comes from the convergence of many contributing factors. The Dalai Lama had explained, "We must look at any given situation or problem from the front and from the back, from the sides, and from the top and the bottom, so from at least six different angles. This allows us to take a more complete and holistic view of reality, and if we do, our response will be more constructive."

We suffer from a perspectival myopia. As a result, we are left nearsighted, unable to see our experience in a larger way. When we confront a challenge, we often react to the situation with fear and anger. The stress can make it hard for us to step back and see other perspectives and other solutions. This is natural, the Archbishop emphasized throughout the week. But if we try, we can become less fixated, or attached, to use the Buddhist term, to one outcome and can use more skillful means to handle the situation. We see that in the most seemingly limiting circumstance we have choice and freedom, even if that freedom is ultimately the attitude we will take. How can a trauma lead to growth and transformation? How can a negative event actually become positive? We were being invited to see the blessing in the curse, the joy in the sorrow. Jinpa offered a silver-lining thought experiment to take us out of our limited perspective: Take something bad that happened in the past and then consider all the good that came out of it.

But is this simply being Pollyanna? Are we seeing the world less clearly when we view it through these rose-colored glasses? I do not think anyone would accuse the Dalai Lama or Archbishop Tutu of not seeing the struggles they have faced or the horrors of our world with keen and unflinching vision. What they are reminding us is that often what we think is reality is only part of the picture. We look at one of the calamities in our world, as the Archbishop suggested, and then we look again, and we see all those who are helping to heal those who have been harmed. This is the ability to reframe life more positively based on a broader, richer, more nuanced perspective.

With a wider perspective, we can see our situation and all those involved in a larger context and from a more neutral position. By seeing the many conditions and circumstances that have led to this event, we can recognize that our limited perspective is not the truth. As the Dalai Lama said, we can even see our own role in any conflict or misunderstanding.

By stepping back we can also see the long view, and have a clearer understanding of our actions and our problems in the larger frame of our life. This allows us to see that even though our situation may seem challenging now, from the vantage point of a month or a year or a decade these challenges will seem much more manageable. When the Archbishop was awarded the Templeton Prize in London, I had the opportunity to meet the astronomer royal of the United Kingdom, Sir Martin Rees, who explained to me that our Earth will exist for an equivalent amount of time as it has taken us to go from one-celled organisms to human beings—in other words, we are only halfway through our evolution on this planet. Thinking of our world's problems in this long sweep of planetary history really is the long view. It puts our daily concerns into a much broader perspective.

This wider perspective also leads us beyond our own self-regard. Self-centeredness is most of our default perspective. It comes quite understandably from the fact that we are at the center of our world. But as the Dalai Lama and the Archbishop demonstrate so powerfully, we also have the ability to take on the perspectives of others.

I remembered the Archbishop wondering if the person who had cut him off in traffic might be rushing to the hospital because his wife was giving birth or because a loved one was dying. "I have sometimes said to people," the Archbishop said, "when you are stuck in a traffic jam, you can deal with it in one of two ways. You can let the frustration really eat you up. Or you can look around at the other drivers and see that one might have a wife who has pancreatic cancer. It doesn't matter if you don't know exactly what they might have, but you know they are all suffering with worries and fears because they are human. And you can lift them up and bless them. You can say, Please, God, give each one of them what they need.

"The very fact of not thinking about your own frustration and pain does something. I don't know why. But it will make you feel much better. And I think it has therapeutic consequences for your own health, physical and spiritual. But what does frustration help? I mean, you feel it in the pit of your tummy, the anger.

I mean, you just get more angry, and after a while you are going to develop ulcers in the stomach from the fact that you got annoyed at sitting in a traffic jam."

Taking a "God's-eye perspective," as the Archbishop might say, allows us to transcend our limited identity and limited self-interest. One does not have to believe in God to experience this mind-altering shift in perspective. The famous Overview Effect is perhaps the most profound example. Many astronauts have reported that once they glimpsed Earth from space—a small blue ball floating in the vast expanse, lacking our human-made borders—they never looked at their personal or national interests in quite the same way again. They saw the oneness of terrestrial life and the preciousness of our planetary home.

Fundamentally, the Dalai Lama and the Archbishop were trying to shift our perspective from focusing on **I** and **me** and **mine** to **we** and **us** and **ours**. Earlier in the week the Dalai Lama had referenced a classic study that suggested the constant use of personal pronouns leads to a greater risk of heart attack. In a multi-center prospective study of coronary heart disease, health researcher Larry Scherwitz found that people who more frequently said **I**, **me**, or **mine** had a higher risk of having a heart attack and had a higher risk of their heart attack being fatal. Scherwitz found that this so-called "self-involvement" was a better predictor of death than smoking, high cholesterol levels, or high blood pressure. A more recent study conducted by researcher Johannes Zimmerman found that people who more often use first-person singular words—**I** and **me**—are more likely to be depressed than people who more often use first-person plural—**we** and **us**. This was interesting evidence that being too self-regarding really does make us unhappy.

When we have a wider perspective, we are also less likely to spend our time lost in self-referential thoughts, ruminating. Jinpa offered another thought experiment designed to take us out of our self-absorption, one that the Archbishop described using when he was in the hospital being treated for prostate cancer, and that the Dalai Lama used when he was doubled over in pain from a gallbladder infection: Think about where you are suffering in your life and then think about all the other people who are going through a similar situation. This perhaps is quite literally the birth of compassion, which means "suffering with." The incredible thing, the Dalai Lama and the Archbishop pointed out, was that this "suffering with" others reminds us that we are not alone, and actually lessens our own pain. This recognition of our interdependence begins to soften our rigid sense of self, the boundaries that separate us from others. The Dalai Lama had said earlier in the week, "If, on the other hand, I relate to others from the perspective of myself as someone different—a Buddhist, a Tibetan, and so on—I will then create walls to keep me apart from others."

We were back at the conversation that began the week, when we had just gotten off the airplane and were sitting in the lounge of the airport. The Dalai Lama had asked, "Where is Bishop Tutu's self? We can't find it." The Dalai Lama, in a traditional twist of Buddhist reasoning, said, "This is his body, but not himself. This is his mind, but not himself." Buddhists follow this line of inquiry to reduce our attachment to our identity, recognizing that the less attached we are, the less defensive and reactive we will be and the more effective and skillful we can be.

As the Dalai Lama and the Archbishop explained, the wider perspective leads to serenity and equanimity. It does not mean we don't have the strength to confront a problem, but we can confront it with creativity and compassion rather than rigidity and reactivity. When we take the perspective of others, we can empathize with them. One starts to see the interdependence that envelops us all, which reveals that how we treat others is ultimately how we treat ourselves. We also are able to recognize that we do not control all aspects of any situation. This leads to a greater sense of humility, humor, and acceptance.

2.

Humility: I Tried to Look Humble and Modest

want to respond to your comment about being at the funeral," the Dalai Lama said, referring back to the Archbishop's story about preaching at Chris Hani's funeral. "You mentioned when you spoke at the funeral that you did not consider yourself as superior, you were just one of them. That's very, very important. I always feel the same way when I give a talk. I consider myself as simply another person, just like those in the audience, same human being. So, I am just one human being talking to other human beings.

"Similarly, they should consider me as the

same human being, with the same potential for constructive emotions and destructive emotions. When we meet anyone, first and foremost we must remember that they, too, have the same desire to have a happy day, a happy month, a happy life. And all have the right to achieve it.

"Then, you see, my talk may offer them something relevant, but if I consider myself something special, or if they also consider me something different and special, then my experience will not be of much use. So it's wonderful that, in you, Archbishop, I have found a comrade who fully shares this same view."

The Dalai Lama and the Archbishop were uninterested in status and superiority. The Dalai Lama began to tell a story that was a poignant reminder that not all shared their view in the religious world.

"You have said I am a mischievous person," he said, pointing at the Archbishop. "One day, at a big interfaith meeting in Delhi, one Indian spiritual leader sat there next to me like this." The Dalai Lama sat up stiffly and made a rigid, scowling face. "He said that his seat should be higher than the others. What do you call this?" the Dalai Lama asked, tapping the base of his chair.

"The legs," the Archbishop offered.

"Yes, the legs were not long enough, so the organizers had to bring some extra bricks to make this spiritual leader's chair higher. The whole time I sat next to him, he remained immobile like a statue. Then I thought, If one of the bricks were to move, and he fell over, then we would see what would happen—"

"Did you move the brick?" the Archbishop asked.

"If I had . . ."

"I don't believe you."

"Maybe you will see some mysterious force move the brick because I will pray to God, 'Please, just topple that chair.' Then that spiritual leader will act like a real human being."

The Dalai Lama and the Archbishop were cackling.

"As I mentioned earlier I used to get nervous," the Dalai Lama continued. "When I was young and had to give some formal teachings, because I was not thinking that we are all same, I would experience anxiety. I would forget that I'm just talking as a human being to fellow humans beings. I would think of myself as something special, and that kind of thinking would make me feel isolated. It is this sense of separateness that isolates us from other people. In fact, this kind of arrogant way of thinking creates a sense of loneliness, and then anxiety.

"In 1954, just after I reached Beijing on an official visit, the Indian ambassador came to see me. Some Chinese officials were also there. The Chinese Communist officials, again, were like statues, like this—very serious and reserved. Then somehow a bowl of fruit on the table toppled over. I don't know what happened. So then those stern-looking Chinese officials got down on their knees to chase and pick up the fruit. You see? When things go smoothly, then we can pretend we are something very special. But something happens, something unexpected, then we are forced to act like normal human beings."

I began asking another question, when the Dalai Lama glanced at a clock that was displaying the wrong time and asked whether it was time for the tea break. I explained that we still had a half hour but asked the Archbishop, whose energy level we were monitoring closely, whether he needed a break.

"No."

"You're okay?" I asked again, aware that the Archbishop might push himself beyond what would be good for his health.

"He's doing very well," the Archbishop said, referring to the Dalai Lama. "He's behaving like a human being."

"So you describe me as mischievous person," the Dalai Lama joked back. "So when I'm at a very holy or formal meeting, I truly am thinking that I wish something would go wrong."

"Now people are going to know that when the Dalai Lama comes into a room, and maybe he's sitting with presidents, he's looking around and hoping that one of the chairs will break."

"So that's why," the Dalai Lama continued to explain, "when I first met President Bush, we immediately became close friends on the human level—not official level—human level. We were sitting together, when some cookies were served. Then I asked, 'Which one is the best?' And he immediately said, pointing to one, 'This one is very good.' He acted like a normal human being, so we became very close. Some other leaders, when we are meeting, there'll be some distance. Then the second time, little closer, third time, little closer." With each **time**, he was moving his head a little closer to the Archbishop.

"When I was very young, in Lhasa, I used to receive copies of the American magazine called **Life**. One issue had a picture of Princess Elizabeth, the future queen, at some very big official function. The princess was reading a message with Prince Philip by her side. The wind had blown Her Majesty's skirt like that." The Dalai Lama was puffing his robes out. "Both Princess Elizabeth and Prince Philip pretended like nothing had happened, but an American photographer took the picture. When I saw that picture I laughed. I really thought it was very funny. Sometimes, especially in formal occasions, people act as if they are different and special. But we all know that we are all the same, ordinary human beings."

"Can you explain the role that humility plays in cultivating joy?" I asked, as the Archbishop started laughing.

"They tell the story of a bishop," he began, "who was about to ordain candidates to the priesthood. They were speaking about virtues, including the virtue of humility. One of the candidates came up to the bishop and said, 'My lord, I've been looking in the library to find a book on humility.' The bishop said, 'Oh, yes, I've written the best book on the subject.'"

I thought he might also share the joke he often tells of the three bishops: These three religious leaders were standing before the altar, beating their breasts with great humility, saying how, before God, they were nothing. Shortly, one of the lowly acolytes in the church approached and started to beat his chest, professing that he, too, was nothing. When the three bishops heard him, one elbowed the other and said, "Look who thinks he's nothing."

These stories about false modesty are funny because humility is not something that one can claim to have. It is for this reason that I think that the Archbishop was laughing about the question even before I had finished asking it. He did not want to claim to be an expert on humility. Nonetheless he and the Dalai Lama were saying that humility is essential to a life of joy. And it's exactly this humility that allows these two men to be so approachable, so connected to others, and so effective in their work in the world.

"There is a Tibetan prayer," the Dalai Lama said, "which is part of the mind-training teachings. A Tibetan master says, 'Whenever I see someone, may I never feel superior. From the depth of my heart, may I be able to really appreciate the other person in front of me.'" And then he turned to the Archbishop and said, "Sometimes you tell me to act . . ."

"Like a holy man," the Archbishop finished.

"Yes, like a holy man," the Dalai Lama said, laughing as if his being a holy man was the funniest thing he had ever heard.

"Yes, yes," the Archbishop said. "I mean, people expect that you would have a presence and behave properly. Not take my cap and put it on your own head. I mean, people don't expect that from a holy man."

"But if you think you are just a normal person—one human being out of seven billion—you see there's no reason to be surprised or to feel like I should be something special. So whenever I'm with queens or kings or presidents or prime ministers or beggars I always remember that we are all the same."

"So when people treat you as His Holiness with such deference," I said, "does that make it difficult to maintain your humility?"

"No, I don't care about formality or protocol. These are artificial. Really. Bishop, you were born the same human way. There is no special way that bishops are born. And I think, when the end comes, also you will die as a normal human being."

"Yes," the Archbishop said, "but when people come into your presence they don't come as they come into my presence."

"That I think is because I come from mysterious land, Tibet. Some people call Tibet Shangri-La, so perhaps a person who spent many years in Potala is sort of mysterious. And then I think these days you see Chinese hardliners always criticize me. So that also makes more publicity. So these—" The Dalai Lama was laughing at his mysteriousness and his global fame.

The Archbishop cut him off. "You see— that's exactly what we mean. You laugh at what would normally be a source of anguish. And people say, I hope that when I have some anguish in my life, I can respond in the way that I saw the Dalai Lama respond to how the Chinese treated him. How are you able to cultivate it? How did you cultivate it? You were not born like that."

"That's true, it was through training and also the good fortune of receiving my mother's love. When I was young, I never saw my mother's angry face. She was very, very kind. But my father had a very short temper. On a few occasions I even got his blessing." The Dalai Lama made the gesture of being slapped. "When I was young," he continued, "I followed my father's way, remaining quite short-tempered. But as I got a little older, then I began to take after my mother's way. So that way I lived up to the expectation of both my parents!"

The Dalai Lama and the Archbishop were both insistent that humility is essential to any possibility of joy. When we have a wider perspective, we have a natural understanding of our place in the great sweep of all that was, is, and will be. This naturally leads to humility and the recognition that as human beings we can't solve everything or control all aspects of life. We need others. The Archbishop has poignantly said that our vulnerabilities, our frailties, and our limitations are a reminder that we need one another: We are not created for independence or self-sufficiency, but for inter-dependence and mutual support. The Dalai Lama was saying that we are all born and all die in the same way, and at these moments we are totally dependent on others, whether we are a Dalai Lama or a beggar, whether we are an Archbishop or a refugee.

With the keen insight of a longtime friend and collaborator, Daniel Goleman character-ized the Dalai Lama's attitude toward life: "The Dalai Lama seems amused by everything that is going on around him, taking pleasure in whatever is going on, but not taking any-thing too personally, and not worrying or tak-ing offense at anything that is happening." The Dalai Lama was reminding us throughout the week not to get caught up in roles, and indeed arrogance is the confusion between our tempo-rary roles and our fundamental identity. When Juan, our sound technician, wired up his remote microphone, the Dalai Lama playfully pulled on Juan's Don Quixote beard, which would start everyone giggling, most of all the Dalai Lama. He was saying: Today you are the sound technician and I am the Dalai Lama, next time maybe the roles will be reversed. Next time might be another year or another life, as the idea of reincarnation does remind us that all of our roles are temporary.

The word **humility** actually comes from the Latin word for earth or soil, **humus**—which sounds a lot like but should not be confused with the simple but delicious Middle Eastern chickpea dip, hummus. Humility literally brings us back down to earth, sometimes with a thud. The Archbishop tells the story of flying from Durban to Johannesburg during the anti-apartheid struggle. A flight attendant said that one of the passengers had asked if he would autograph a book. He recalls, "I tried to look humble and modest, although I was thinking in my heart that there were some people who recognized a good thing when they saw it." But when she handed him the book, and he took out his pen, she said, "You are Bishop Muzorewa, aren't you?"

None of us are immune to the all-too-human traits of pride or ego, but true arrogance really comes from insecurity. Needing to feel that we are bigger than others comes from a nagging fear that we are smaller. Whenever the Dalai Lama senses this danger, he looks at a bug or some other creature and reminds himself that, in some ways, this creature is better than we are, because it is innocent and free of malice. "When we realize that we are all children of God," the Archbishop has explained, "and of equal and intrinsic value, then we don't have to feel better or worse than others." The Archbishop was adamant: "No one is a divine accident." While we may not be special, we are essential. No one can fulfill our role but us in the divine plan or karmic unfolding.

"Sometimes we confuse humility with timidity," the Archbishop explained. "This gives little glory to the one who has given us our gifts. Humility is the recognition that your gifts are from God, and this lets you sit relatively loosely to those gifts. Humility allows us to celebrate the gifts of others, but it does not mean you have to deny your own gifts or shrink from using them. God uses each of us in our own way, and even if you are not the best one, you may be the one who is needed or the one who is there."

I recalled how the night before the interviews

began I had tossed and turned in bed, feeling quite insecure and nervous. I was going to have to interview these two great spiritual teachers and needed to make sure I was asking the right questions. We had one opportunity to get this right—one opportunity to capture this historic meeting and series of dialogues for the world. I was not a news anchor or journalist. Surely there were many others who were more qualified to conduct the interviews. I was attempting to do something I had never done before, and whenever we challenge ourselves, fear and doubt are inevitable. I am not sure we ever vanquish these voices. Whenever we are at the edge of our ability and experience, they always whisper in our ears, their worried words. I have come to see that these voices are actually trying to keep us safe as they warn us away from the unfamiliar and the unknown, but this does not make their daggers of self-doubt any less painful. I finally was able to fall asleep when I realized that this was not about me, or my limitations. I was simply the ambassador asking questions on behalf of all those who wanted to benefit from the wisdom of the Archbishop and the Dalai Lama—and I would not be alone during the interviews or in the writing of this book. As the Archbishop had said, whether I was the best one or not, I was the one who was there.

"We have a question from a boy named Emory," I said. "It is addressed to you, Your Holiness. He writes: 'Your quotes always lift me up and give me purpose when I am down on myself. What is the best way to keep a positive attitude when things aren't going your way?' So here is a boy who gets down on himself, the way we all do. How can we deal with the self-critical voices that we all have?"

"So many people," the Dalai Lama said, "seem to struggle with being kind to themselves. This is really sad. You see, if you don't have genuine love and kindness toward yourself, how can you extend these to others? We must remind people, as the Archbishop has said, that basic human nature is good, is positive, so this can give us some courage and self-confidence. As we said, too much focus on yourself leads to fear, insecurity, and anxiety. Remember, you are not alone. You are part of a whole generation that is the future of humanity. Then you will get a sense of courage and purpose in life.

"Now, we should also realize that the recognition of our own limitations and weaknesses can be very positive. This can be wisdom. If you realize that you are inadequate in some way, then you develop effort. If you think, everything is fine and I'm okay just as I am, then you will not try to develop further. There is a Tibetan saying that wisdom is like rainwater—both gather in the low places. There is another saying that when the spring bloom comes, where does it start? Does it start on the hilltops or down in the valleys first? Growth begins first in the low places. So similarly if you remain humble, then there is the possibility to keep learning. So I often tell people that although I'm eighty years old, I still consider myself a student."

"Really?" the Archbishop said with a wry smile.

"Really. Every day learning, learning."

"Yes, you are wonderful."

"Oh." The Dalai Lama laughed. "I expect that kind of comment from you."

The Archbishop laughed, too, trying to keep

himself humble. When we have humility, we can laugh at ourselves. It was surprising to hear the Archbishop and the Dalai Lama describe the importance of a proper sense of humor, and especially the ability to laugh at our own foibles, as essential to the cultivation of joy.

3.
Humor: Laughter,
Joking Is Much Better

One of the most stunning aspects of the week was how much of it was spent laughing. At times the Dalai Lama and the Archbishop seemed to be as much a comedy duo as two venerable spiritual teachers. It is their ability to joke, and laugh, and poke fun at the ordinary pieties that so righteously violates expectation. When a Dalai Lama and an Archbishop walk into a bar, you don't expect them to be the ones cracking the jokes. Having worked with many spiritual leaders, I'm tempted to see laughter and a sense of humor as a universal index of spiritual development. The Arch-

bishop and the Dalai Lama were certainly at
the top of that index, and they skewered hum-
bug, status, injustice, and evil, all with the
power of humor. They and everyone around
them were constantly guffawing, chortling,
giggling, and belly laughing throughout the
week, as moments of great levity were spliced
together with moments of profundity and sanctity. So often their first response to any subject,
no matter how seemingly painful, was to laugh.

It was clear that humor was central to their
joyful way of being, but why was laughter so
central?

"I worked with a Mexican shaman once," I
said, introducing the topic. "He said that laughing and crying are the same thing—laughing
just feels better. It's clear that laughter is central to the way that you are in the world.
And the Archbishop was just saying, Your Holiness, that you laugh at something that could
ordinarily be a source of anguish."

"That's right. That's right."

"Can you tell us about the role of laughter
and humor in the cultivation of joy?"

"It is much better when there is not too
much seriousness," the Dalai Lama responded.

"Laughter, joking is much better. Then we can be completely relaxed. I met some scientists in Japan, and they explained that wholehearted laughter—not artificial laughter—is very good for your heart and your health in general." When he said "artificial laughter," he pretended to smile and forced a chuckle. He was making a connection between wholehearted laughter and a warm heart, which he had already said was the key to happiness.

I once heard that laughter was the most direct line between any two people, and certainly the Dalai Lama and the Archbishop used humor to break down the social barriers that separate us. **Humor**, like **humility**, comes from the same root word for **humanity: humus**. The lowly and sustaining earth is the source for all three words. Is it any surprise that we have to have a sense of humility to be able to laugh at ourselves and that to laugh at ourselves reminds us of our shared humanity?

"I think that the scientists are right," the Dalai Lama concluded. "People who are always laughing have a sense of abandon and ease. They are less likely to have a heart attack than those people who are really serious and who have difficulty connecting with other people. Those serious people are in real danger."

"We found at home . . ." the Archbishop added, gazing down thoughtfully, remembering those painful times, "when we were conducting funerals of people who had been killed by the police, we would have hundreds and hundreds of people attending the funerals. It was a state of emergency—you were not allowed any other gatherings—so the funerals turned into political rallies. We found that one of the best ways of helping our people direct their energies in positive directions was laughter. Telling jokes, even at our expense, was such a wonderful flip to our morale. Of course some of the things that happened were just so horrendous. Like I was saying yesterday, about Chris Hani, humor helped to defuse a very, very tense situation, telling stories that made people laugh and especially to laugh at themselves.

"People were really angry and you'd have the police standing not far away—and it was an explosive situation. Anything could have gone wrong. My weaponry, if you can call it that, was almost always to use humor, and especially self-denigrating humor, where you are laughing at yourself.

"We came to a township just outside of Johannesburg, where the apartheid forces had provided weapons to one group, and they had killed quite a number of people. We were having a meeting of bishops close by, and I was part of those leading the funeral of the victims of that massacre. The people were obviously extremely angry, and I remembered a story that had been told about how at the beginning of creation, God molded us out of clay and then put us into a kiln, like you do with bricks. God put one lot in and then got busy with other things and forgot about those he had put into the kiln. And after a while he remembered and rushed to the kiln, where the whole lot was burned to cinders. They say this is how we black people came about. Everyone laughed a little. And then I said, 'Next, God put in a second lot, and this time he was overanxious and opened the oven too quickly, and this second lot that came out was underdone. And that's how white people came about.'" The Archbishop finished with a little laugh and then that cackle that climbs up the flagpole and back down.

"We tend to want to blow ourselves up, inflate ourselves because most of us have tended to have a poor self-image. When you're in a situation such as the one in South Africa where you were discriminated against, it was very easy to lose your sense of self, and humor seems to do something for people. Humor certainly did one good thing: it deflated, defused a particularly tense situation."

The Archbishop had visited Rwanda shortly after the genocide and was asked to give a talk to the Hutus and the Tutsis. How does one talk about a wound that is so fresh in the soul of a people? The Archbishop's solution, as it so often is, was to speak truth to power—through humor. He began telling a story about the big-nose people and the small-nose people and how the big-nose people were excluding the small-nose people. The people in the audience were laughing, and as they were laughing they suddenly realized what he was talking about: the ridiculousness of prejudice and hatred, whether in his country or theirs. Humor was, as he said, a very powerful weapon.

The Dalai Lama visited Belfast in northern Ireland after the Troubles. He was invited to attend a private meeting where victims and perpetrators of violence were present. The atmosphere was very tense, as the suffering was practically palpable in the air. As the meeting began, a former Protestant militant spoke of how, when he was growing up, he was told by other loyalists that what they did in opposition to the Catholics was justified because Jesus was a Protestant and not a Catholic. Knowing that Jesus was, of course, a Jew, the Dalai Lama laughed so hard that he completely changed the atmosphere. Able to laugh at the absurdity of our prejudices and our hatreds, everyone was able to communicate more honestly and compassionately with each other.

"When we learn to take ourselves slightly less seriously," the Archbishop continued, "then it is a very great help. We can see the ridiculous in us. I was helped by the fact that I came out of a family who did like to take the mickey out of others, and who were quite fond of pointing out the ridiculous, especially when someone was being a bit hoity-toity. And they had a way of puncturing your sense of self-importance.

"I mean, of course it's not a laughing matter not to know where your next meal is going to come from. It's not a laughing matter when you get up in the morning and you don't have a job. Yet it was those people who quite frequently were the ones who formed part of the crowds that used to come to the political rallies, the funerals. And they were the people who were able to laugh at themselves. And then their laughing at others would be less malicious. They weren't particularly number one in God's garden, but they were able to laugh at life in all its cruelty and uncertainty. Humor really is the saving grace.

"I have been helped by my wife, Leah, who was very—is very—good at keeping me humble. Once, we were driving, and I noticed that she was a little smugger than she normally is. And then when I looked again at the car in front of us, I saw a bumper sticker that said: 'Any woman who wants to be equal to a man has no ambition.'"

"Archbishop," I said, "humor can also be very cruel. But your humor, as I've seen over the years, is about bringing us together, not about

separating us and putting anyone down—
except maybe the Dalai Lama. But most of
the time it's about uniting. Can you two tell
us a little bit about the ways in which humor
can bring us together and show us our shared
ridiculousness?"

"Well, yes, if you are longing to bring people
together, you're not going to do so by being
acerbic. You know, it's so good to see the ridiculous in us all, really. I think we then get to see
our common humanity in many ways.

"Ultimately, I think it's about being able to
laugh at yourself and being able not to take
yourself so seriously. It's not about the belit-
tling humor that puts others down and yourself
up. It's about bringing people onto common
ground.

"If you can manage to downgrade yourself,
if you are able to laugh at yourself and get
others to laugh at you without feeling guilty
that they are laughing at you. The humor that
doesn't demean is an invitation to everyone to
join in the laughter. Even if they're laughing at
you they're joining you in a laughter that feels
wholesome."

"When you and the Dalai Lama tease each other," I added, "it does not feel demeaning at all."

"Yes, the Dalai Lama and I tease each other, but it is a statement of trust in the relationship. It's an indication that there's enough of a reservoir of goodwill that you're really saying, 'I trust you. And you trust me that I know you will not undermine me or be offended by me.'

"I'm just thinking that we're so very apt to belittle because we are also so unsure of ourselves and we think that the best way of asserting who we are is by putting you down, whereas this kind of humor says, 'Come stand next to me and let's laugh at me together, then we can laugh at you together.' It does not belittle either of us but uplifts us, allows us to recognize and laugh about our shared humanity, about our shared vulnerabilities, our shared frailties. Life is hard, you know, and laughter is how we come to terms with all the ironies and cruelties and uncertainties that we face."

Scientific research on humor is rather limited, but it does seem that there is an evolutionary role for laughter and humor in managing the anxiety and stress of the unknown. Jokes are funny precisely because they break our expectations and help us to accept the unexpected. Other people are one of the greatest sources of uncertainty in our lives, so it is not surprising that much humor is used to manage and massage these encounters. The Archbishop and the Dalai Lama are masters of using humor to connect and join together when meeting others.

Perhaps that is one of the reasons that their time together was so filled with laughter. For all the joy they felt being together, it was an unprecedented and no doubt uncertain experience to meet for a week together in Dharamsala. They had met only a half dozen times before, and these were largely brief and formal occasions. Global leaders have full schedules, and their times together are highly scripted, so an opportunity to just joke and be themselves was exceedingly rare.

"What do you say to people," I asked the Archbishop, "who say they are not funny or that they do not have a good sense of humor?"

"I reckon there are many people who think they have to be somber because it gives them gravitas, and they feel they are more likely to be respected if they are serious. But I believe very

fervently that one of the ways of getting into
the hearts of people is the capacity of making
them laugh. If you are able to laugh at yourself, then everyone knows you're not pompous.
Besides, you hardly ever knock down someone who is knocking himself down. You're not
likely to clobber someone if they've already, as
it were, self-clobbered.

"I don't think I woke up and presto I was
funny. I think it is something that you can cultivate. Like anything else, it is a skill. Yes, it
does help if you have the inclination, and especially if you can laugh at yourself, so learn to
laugh at yourself. It's really the easiest place
to begin. It's about humility. Laugh at yourself and don't be so pompous and serious. If
you start looking for the humor in life, you
will find it. You will stop asking, Why me? and
start recognizing that life happens to all of us.
It makes everything easier, including your ability to accept others and accept all that life will
bring."

4.

Acceptance: The Only Place
Where Change Can Begin

When we had visited the Tibetan Children's Village in January, we noticed a wall displaying a quote that the Dalai Lama referenced in the dialogues. It was a translation of Shantideva's famous questions that His Holiness had mentioned, only in a slightly different translation: "Why be unhappy about something if it can be remedied? And what is the use of being unhappy if it cannot be remedied?" In this short teaching is the profound essence of the Dalai Lama's approach to life. It was at the root of his stunning ability to accept the reality of his exile without, as the Archbishop put it, being morose.

Once we can see life in its wider perspective, once we are able to see our role in its drama with some degree of humility, and once we are able to laugh at ourselves, we then come to the fourth and final quality of mind, which is the ability to accept our life in all its pain, imperfection, and beauty.

Acceptance, it must be pointed out, is the opposite of resignation and defeat. The Archbishop and the Dalai Lama are two of the most tireless activists for creating a better world for all of its inhabitants, but their activism comes from a deep acceptance of what is. The Archbishop did not accept the inevitability of apartheid, but he did accept its reality.

"We are meant to live in joy," the Archbishop explained. "This does not mean that life will be easy or painless. It means that we can turn our faces to the wind and accept that this is the storm we must pass through. We cannot succeed by denying what exists. The acceptance of reality is the only place from which change can begin." The Archbishop had said that when one grows in the spiritual life, "You are able to accept anything that happens to you." You accept the inevitable frustrations and hardships as part of the warp and woof of life. The question, he had said, is not: How do we escape it? The question is: How can we use this as something positive?

The Archbishop's prayer practice involves reading quotations from the scriptures as well as quotes from the saints and spiritual masters throughout history. One of his favorites is the Christian mystic Julian of Norwich, whose **Revelations of Divine Love**, penned shortly after she recovered from a life-threatening illness in 1373, is believed to be the first book written by a woman in the English language. In it, she writes,

> . . . deeds are done which appear so evil to us and people suffer such terrible evils that it does not seem as though any good will ever come of them; and we consider this, sorrowing and grieving over it so that we cannot find peace in the blessed contemplation of God as we should do; and this is why: our reasoning powers are so blind now, so humble and so simple, that we

cannot know the high, marvelous wisdom, the might and the goodness of the Holy Trinity. And this is what he means where he says, "You shall see for yourself that all manner of things shall be well," as if he said, Pay attention to this now, faithfully and confidently, and at the end of time you will truly see it in the fullness of joy.

Acceptance—whether we believe in God or not—allows us to move into the fullness of joy. It allows us to engage with life on its own terms rather than rail against the fact that life is not as we would wish. It allows us not to struggle against the day-to-day current. The Dalai Lama had told us that stress and anxiety come from our expectations of how life should be. When we are able to accept that life is how it is, not as we think it should be, we are able to ease the ride, to go from that bumpy axle (**dukkha**), with all its suffering, stress, anxiety, and dissatisfaction, to the smooth axle (**sukha**), with its greater ease, comfort, and happiness.

So many of the causes of suffering come from our reacting to the people, places, things, and circumstances in our lives, rather than accepting them. When we react, we stay locked in judgment and criticism, anxiety and despair, even denial and addiction. It is impossible to experience joy when we are stuck this way. Acceptance is the sword that cuts through all of this resistance, allowing us to relax, to see clearly, and to respond appropriately.

Much of traditional Buddhist practice is directed toward the ability to see life accurately, beyond all the expectations, projections, and distortions that we typically bring to it. Meditative practice allows us to quiet the distracting thoughts and feelings so that we can perceive reality, and respond to it more skillfully. The ability to be present in each moment is nothing more and nothing less than the ability to accept the vulnerability, discomfort, and anxiety of everyday life.

"With a deeper understanding of reality," the Dalai Lama has explained, "you can go beyond appearances and relate to the world in a much more appropriate, effective, and realistic manner. I often give the example of how we should relate to our neighbors. Imagine that you are living next to a difficult neighbor. You can judge and criticize them. You can live in anxiety and despair that you will never have a good relationship with them. You can deny the problem or pretend that you do not have a difficult relationship with your neighbor. None of these is very helpful.

"Instead, you can accept that your relationship with your neighbor is difficult and that you would like to improve it. You may or may not succeed, but all you can do is try. You cannot control your neighbor, but you do have some control over your thoughts and feelings. Instead of anger, instead of hatred, instead of fear, you can cultivate compassion for them, you can cultivate kindness toward them, you can cultivate warmheartedness toward them. This is the only chance to improve the relationship. In time, maybe they will become less difficult. Maybe not. This you cannot control, but you will have your peace of mind. You will be able to be joyful and happy whether your neighbor becomes less difficult or not."

We come back to the beginning of our discussion and Shantideva's questions. The kind of acceptance that the Dalai Lama and the Archbishop were advocating is not passive. It is powerful. It does not deny the importance of taking life seriously and working hard to change what needs changing, to redeem what needs redemption. "You must not hate those who do harmful things," the Dalai Lama has explained. "The compassionate thing is to do what you can to stop them—for they are harming themselves as well as those who suffer from their actions."

One of the key paradoxes in Buddhism is that we need goals to be inspired, to grow, and to develop, even to become enlightened, but at the same time we must not get overly fixated or attached to these aspirations. If the goal is noble, your commitment to the goal should not be contingent on your ability to attain it, and in pursuit of our goal, we must release our rigid assumptions about how we must achieve it. Peace and equanimity come from letting go of our attachment to the goal and the method. That is the essence of acceptance.

Reflecting on this seeming paradox, of pursuing a goal yet with no attachment to its outcome, Jinpa explained to me that there is an important insight. This is a deep recognition that while each of us should do everything we can to realize the goal we seek, whether or not we succeed often depends on many factors beyond our control. So our responsibility is to pursue the goal with all the dedication we can muster, do the best we can but not become fixated on a preconceived notion of a result. Sometimes, actually quite often, our efforts lead to an unexpected outcome that might even be better than what we originally had in mind.

I thought of the Archbishop's comment that it takes time to build our spiritual capacity. "It's like muscles that have to be exercised in order for them to be strengthened. Sometimes we get too angry with ourselves, thinking that we ought to be perfect from the word **go**. But this being on Earth is a time for us to learn to be good, to learn to be more loving, to learn to be more compassionate. And you learn, not theoretically. You learn when something happens that tests you."

Life is constantly unpredictable, uncontrollable, and often quite challenging. Edith Eva Eger explained that life in a concentration camp was an endless selection line where one never knew whether one would live or die. The only thing that kept a person alive was the acceptance of the reality of one's existence and the attempt to respond as best one could. Curiosity about what would happen next, even when she was left for dead in a pile of bodies, was often all she had to pull herself forward to the next breath. When we accept what is happening now, we can be curious about what might happen next.

Acceptance was the final pillar of the mind, and it led us to the first pillar of the heart: forgiveness. When we accept the present, we can forgive and release the desire for a different past.

5.
Forgiveness: Freeing
Ourselves from the Past

have seen remarkable instances of forgiveness carried out by people we would not have thought could possibly do it," the Archbishop began. "In one instance during the Truth and Reconciliation Commission, we had mothers of some young people who had been lured by those working with the apartheid system into a booby trap where they were killed. One of the mothers said she switched on her television set and saw the body of her son being dragged. And apart from her anguish at the death of her son, there was a deep, deep anger at his body being treated as if it were the carcass of an animal.

"You know, when these mothers came to the Commission they were quite amazing, really, because no one demanded that they should forgive these people—they called them **askaris**—who were formerly members of the African National Congress who then turned and supported the government forces. The one who betrayed these young people came and appeared in front of these mothers and asked for their forgiveness.

"When the mother of the young man who had been dragged through the street saw the traitor, she took off her shoe and **threw** it at him," the Archbishop said, laughing and pretending to throw a shoe with his left hand. "We had to adjourn for a little while, but then during the break came a totally fantastic moment as they sat there, and their spokesperson said . . ." The Archbishop closed his eyes, remembering the unbelievable power of her words, "'My child'—she said 'my child' to this one who had been responsible for the death of their children. She said, 'My child, we forgive you.'

"When we asked her about the granting of amnesty, she said, 'What is it going to help us if he were to go to prison? It won't bring back our children.' And there is an incredible kind of nobility and strength. Yes, it's difficult, but it has happened. We talked about Nelson Mandela, but there were these mothers, and many others who were not household names, who had this magnanimity.

"In this group of mothers, the one who was speaking on their behalf got up and went across the room to this guy who had been responsible for the killing of their sons and embraced him and said, 'my child.'

"Just recently I got a message about a white woman named Beth, who was badly maimed in a bomb attack by one of the liberation movements and still had shrapnel in her body. Many of her friends were killed and many were also maimed. She had to be helped by her children to eat, to be bathed. Beth was just . . . I'm overcome . . ." The Archbishop had to pause for a moment. "Beth said . . . Beth said . . . about the perpetrator . . . I forgive him, and I hope he forgives me."

Then the Archbishop told the well-known

story about one of my college classmates, Amy Biehl, who had gone down to South Africa after graduating from university to try to help. She was brutally killed while dropping off one of her friends in a township. "Her parents came all the way from California to South Africa to support the granting of amnesty to the perpetrators who had been sentenced to heavy terms of imprisonment. They said, 'We want to be part of the process of healing in South Africa. We are sure that our daughter would support us in saying we want amnesty to be granted to the murderers.' And more than this, they set up a foundation in their daughter's name and employed these men, who had murdered their daughter, in the project to help the people of that township.

"Now I don't pretend that comes easily, but we do have a nobility of spirit. We've spoken of Nelson Mandela as an amazing icon of forgiveness," the Archbishop said, "but you and you and you and you have the potential to be instruments of incredible compassion and forgiveness. We cannot say of anyone at all that they are totally unable to forgive. I think that all of us have the latent potential, as His Holiness is pointing out, to be sorry for these others who are disfiguring their humanity in this way. Indeed, no one is incapable of forgiving and no one is unforgivable."

"I want to mention," the Dalai Lama said, "one of my friends from northern Ireland, Richard Moore. His story is very, very touching. He was age nine or ten during the troubles in northern Ireland, when a British soldier shot him with a rubber bullet as he was on his way to school." The Dalai Lama was pointing directly between the eyes where the rubber bullet had hit. "He fainted, and when he recovered he was at the hospital, having lost both of his eyes. He realized that he would no longer be able to see his mother's face.

"He continued studying and eventually he got married and had two girls. Then he found the British soldier who shot him in the head so he could communicate his forgiveness. They became very good friends, and on one occasion, at my personal invitation, they both came to Dharamsala. I wanted Richard to share his deeply moving story of forgiveness with Tibetans, especially the students at the Tibetan Children's Village. In introducing Richard

Moore to the students and teachers there, I mentioned that he is my hero.

"Then Richard invited me to visit northern Ireland, and when I saw him with his family there, I teased him. 'Your wife is very beautiful. Your two daughters are also very beautiful. But you can't see. I can, so I can enjoy seeing their beauty.' I describe him as my real hero. That's really a human being."

"Your Holiness, this brings us to a question from a boy named Jack, who writes, 'Your Holiness, I wish you a happy eightieth birthday from the bottom of my heart. I hope that your next year is full of joy, success, and many great things. I have the utmost respect for you and your people and for your undying message of kindness and forgiveness. Yet I wonder, can you forgive China for all of the harm and pain they have caused you and your people? Do they deserve it? Thank you, Your Holiness, and have a wonderful birthday.'"

The Dalai Lama's hands were pressed together as if in prayer as he began, "The other day, I mentioned the 10th of March 2008, when spontaneous protests began in Tibet. I deliberately tried to keep compassion and a sense of concern for the Chinese hard-liners. I tried to take their anger, their fear, into myself and give them my love, my forgiveness. This is our practice of taking and giving, of **tonglen**.

"It was really very helpful to keep my mind calm. In our struggle, we deliberately try to stop ourselves from developing anger or hatred. Of course the Chinese are a wonderful people. But even for the hard-liners, the officials, we deliberately tried to keep a sense of compassion, sense of concern for their well-being."

The Dalai Lama then spoke in Tibetan and Jinpa translated. "Generally, when we speak of cultivating compassion for someone, we are cultivating compassion for someone who is actually undergoing acute suffering and pain. But you can also develop compassion for someone who may not be experiencing acute pain or suffering right now, but who is creating the conditions for their own future suffering."

"So you see," the Dalai Lama continued, "these people are committing such negative actions, committing harmful acts that create lot of pain for others. In the Christian tradition, don't you say they will go to hell?"

The Archbishop nodded, listening.

"In our view also those people who are committing atrocities, including murder, are creating karma that brings very serious negative consequences. So there are many reasons to feel a sense of real concern for their well-being. When you have a sense of concern for their well-being, then there is no place for anger and hatred to grow.

"Forgiveness," the Dalai Lama continued, "does not mean we forget. You should remember the negative thing, but because there is a possibility to develop hatred, we mustn't allow ourselves to be led in that direction—we choose forgiveness." The Archbishop was also clear about this: Forgiveness does not mean you forget what someone has done, contrary to the saying "Forgive and forget." Not reacting with negativity, or giving in to the negative emotions, does not mean you do not respond to the acts or that you allow yourself to be harmed again. Forgiveness does not mean that you do not seek justice or that the perpetrator is not punished.

The Dalai Lama has chosen not to react out of anger and hatred, but that isn't to say he won't speak out against the Chinese occupation and what they are doing inside Tibet until the Tibetan people can live with dignity and freedom.

"I would like to add," the Dalai Lama said, "that there is an important distinction between forgiveness and simply allowing others' wrongdoing. Sometimes people misunderstand and think forgiveness means you accept or approve of wrongdoing. No, this is not the case. We must make an important distinction." The Dalai Lama was speaking emphatically, striking one hand against the other. "The actor and action, or the person and what he has done. Where the wrong action is concerned, it may be necessary to take appropriate counteraction to stop it. Toward the actor, or the person, however, you can choose not to develop anger and hatred. This is where the power of forgiveness lies—not losing sight of the humanity of the person while responding to the wrong with clarity and firmness.

"We stand firm against the wrong not only to protect those who are being harmed but also to protect the person who is harming others, because eventually they, too, will suffer. So it's out of a sense of concern for their own long-term well-being that we stop their wrongdoing. This is exactly what we are doing. We do not let anger and negative feelings develop toward the Chinese hard-liners, but in the meantime we strongly oppose their actions."

"Forgiveness," the Archbishop added, "is the only way to heal ourselves and to be free from the past." As he and Mpho explained in **The Book of Forgiving,** "Without forgiveness, we remain tethered to the person who harmed us. We are bound to the chains of bitterness, tied together, trapped. Until we can forgive the person who harmed us, that person will hold the keys to our happiness, that person will be our jailor. When we forgive, we take back control of our own fate and our feelings. We become our own liberator."

"So what do you say to people," I asked the Dalai Lama, "who say that forgiveness seems like weakness, and revenge seems like strength?"

"There are certain people who act out of the animal mind. When someone hits them, they want to hit back, retaliate." The Dalai Lama made a fist and pretended to hit himself. "With our human brain, we can think, If I hit back, what use will it be in the short-term or in the long-term?

"We can also realize that obviously nobody was born to be cruel, to harm us, but because of certain circumstances, now he or she dislikes me, so hits me. Perhaps my behavior, or attitude, or even my facial expression contributed to this person becoming my enemy. So I was also involved. Who is to blame? So sitting and thinking of the different causes and conditions, then you see that if we are really angry we must be angry toward the causes and conditions— ultimately their anger, their ignorance, their short-sightedness, their narrow-mindedness. So that brings a sense of concern, and we can feel sorry for these people.

"So it is totally wrong," he said emphatically, cutting his hand sharply through the air, "to say that practice of tolerance and practice of forgiveness are signs of weakness. Totally wrong. Hundred percent wrong. Thousand percent wrong. Forgiveness is a sign of strength. Isn't it?" the Dalai Lama said, turning to the Archbishop.

"Absolutely, yes," the Archbishop said with a laugh. "I was just going to say that those who say forgiving is a sign of weakness haven't tried it.

"The natural response when someone hits you," the Archbishop said, "is wanting to hit back. But why do we admire people who don't choose revenge? It is our recognition of the fact that, yes, there are those who think an eye for an eye is going to satisfy you. But in the end you discover that an eye for an eye will leave the whole world blind. We have an instinct for revenge but also for forgiveness."

Indeed, it seems like humans evolved with both impulses and both capacities, for revenge and for forgiveness. When psychologists Martin Daly and Margo Wilson studied sixty different cultures around the world, they found that 95 percent had some form of blood revenge. When psychologist Michael McCullough looked at the same cultures, he found that 93 percent of them also displayed some examples of forgiveness or reconciliation. Forgiveness may actually be so common that it is taken for granted in the other 7 percent.

Primatologist Frans de Waal believes that such peace-making activities are extremely common in the animal kingdom. Chimps kiss and make up, and it seems that many other species do as well. Not only apes like us but also sheep, goats, hyenas, and dolphins. Of the species that have been studied, only domestic cats have failed to show behavior that reconciles relationships after conflict. (This finding will not surprise anyone who has cats.)

In **The Book of Forgiving,** the Archbishop and Mpho outline two cycles: the cycle of revenge and the cycle of forgiveness. When a hurt or harm happens, we can choose to hurt back or to heal. If we choose to retaliate, or pay back, the cycle of revenge and harm continues endlessly, but if we choose to forgive, we break the cycle and we can heal, renewing or releasing the relationship.

Unforgiveness leads to ongoing feelings of resentment, anger, hostility, and hatred that can be extremely destructive. Even short bursts of it can have significant physical effects. In one study, psychologist Charlotte vanOyen Witvliet asked people to think about someone who had hurt, mistreated, or offended them. She monitored their heart rate, facial muscles, and sweat glands.

When people remembered their grudges, they had a stress response—their blood pressure and heart rate increased and they began to sweat. They felt sad, angry, intense, and less in control. When they were asked to empathize with their offenders and to imagine forgiving them, their stress responses returned to normal. As social animals, it is very stressful for us, and for the whole group, when there is rupture in the relationships that bind us together.

In a review of the research on forgiveness and health, Everett L. Worthington Jr. and Michael Scherer found that unforgiveness seems to compromise the immune system in a number of ways, including disrupting the production of important hormones and the way that our cells fight off infections.

want to just come back to you, Archbishop, for our final question before tea," I said. "Often the people that we have the hardest time forgiving are the people who are closest to us."

"Yes, yes."

"You have told me that forgiving your father for some of the things that he did to your mother was very difficult for you and very painful for you. And I wonder, if he were here with us, how you would tell him how that affected you, and how you would tell him that you forgave him. What would you say?"

"Well, I would certainly tell him that I was deeply hurt by how he treated my mother when he was drunk." The Archbishop then closed his eyes and spoke very quietly and slowly as he traveled back in time. "I was very angry with myself for being too small to beat him up. I mean, when he was sober, he was a wonderful person. But my mother was—I just adored my mother—she was just such an incredible human being, a very gentle person. And that just made it worse. And there was a son too small to intervene when she was being roughed up.

"I should tell you one great regret I have. We used to take the children to boarding school in Swaziland, about three hundred miles each way, and we would overnight on the way at our parents' because there were no motels where blacks could stay.

"On this particular time when we were returning from Swaziland, we were going to put up at Leah's home with her mother, which was not in the same township where my parents lived. We had come to say good night and goodbye to my parents, because we were going to leave early to go down to the Cape, where I was working. And on this particular occasion, I was dead exhausted when my father said he wanted to talk to me. There was something he wanted to tell me.

"I was too tired and I was headachy and I said, 'No. Can we talk tomorrow?' And we left to go to Leah's home. And, as sometimes happens only in novels, we were awoken early in the morning by my niece telling us that my father had died the previous evening. And so, I've never known what it was he wanted to tell me. I have a very deep regret. I sometimes shed a tear or two. I hope it was that maybe he had a premonition of his death and wanted to say how sorry he was for the treatment that he had meted out to my mother.

"And so, I regret that . . . I can only say, I hope he rests in peace. I have to accept that I missed an opportunity . . . which was not to come back.

"None of us actually ever knows when it is going to be that moment when something quite crucial might in fact be going to happen and we turn our back on it. And yes, I try to assuage my guilt, but it can't go away completely.

"The fact is he had taken the initiative, and whatever justification I had, it's an initiative that I spurned. And it is a burden on my heart and my spirit. And I can only hope that, he will have forgiven me . . . yah . . ."

We sat in silence for several long minutes, just being with the Archbishop in his grief and regret. He stared off, his eyes wet, remembering his father. He closed his eyes, perhaps saying a prayer. It felt like we were in prayer together, receiving and holding up his grief and loss.

The Dalai Lama was the first one to speak, as he turned finally to Jinpa and spoke in Tibetan.

"He's saying, Archbishop, that you spoke about how wonderful your father was when he was sober," Jinpa said, translating for the Dalai Lama. "It was only when he was drunk that these things happened. So it's the alcohol that is to blame, really."

"So," the Dalai Lama now added, "I think even he is a very, very kind person and when he was drunk, he is not the real person."

"Thank you," said the Archbishop.

6.

Gratitude: I Am
Fortunate to Be Alive

Every day, think as you wake up, 'I am fortunate to be alive. I have a precious human life. I am not going to waste it,'" the Dalai Lama has often said. The topic was gratitude, and it was fascinating to see how often the Archbishop and the Dalai Lama stopped to express their gratitude for each other, for all who were making their time together possible, and for each and every thing that they were witnessing. I had noticed how the Archbishop greets almost every new experience with the word **wonderful**, and it is indeed that ability to see wonder, surprise, possibility in each experience and each encounter that is a core aspect of joy.

"You can be helped to look at the world and see a different perspective," the Archbishop said. "Where some people see a half-empty cup, you can see it as half-full. Perhaps people will be moved to see that there are very, very, very many people in the world today who will not have had the kind of breakfast that you had. Many, many millions in the world today are hungry. It's not your fault, but you woke up from a warm bed, you were able to have a shower, you put on clean clothes, and you were in a home that is warm in the winter. Now just think of the many who are refugees who wake up in the morning, and there's not very much protection for them against the rain that is pelting down. Perhaps there is no warmth or food or even just water. It is to say in a way, yes, it is to say really, you do want to count your blessings."

Neither the Archbishop nor the Dalai Lama spent a great deal of time talking about enjoyment, perhaps because both of their traditions are skeptical of finding lasting happiness through sensual indulgence, but I had been happy to find that neither of them was opposed to the pleasures permitted in their spiritual lives, whether Tibetan rice pudding or rum raisin ice cream. Gratitude is the elevation of enjoyment, the ennobling of enjoyment. Gratitude is one of the key dimensions that Ekman lists in his definition of joy.

Gratitude is the recognition of all that holds us in the web of life and all that has made it possible to have the life that we have and the moment that we are experiencing. Thanksgiving is a natural response to life and may be the only way to savor it. Both Christian and Buddhist traditions, perhaps all spiritual traditions, recognize the importance of gratefulness. It allows us to shift our perspective, as the Dalai Lama and the Archbishop counseled, toward all we have been given and all that we have. It moves us away from the narrow-minded focus on fault and lack and to the wider perspective of benefit and abundance.

Brother David Steindl-Rast, a Catholic Benedictine monk and scholar who spent a great deal of time in Christian–Buddhist interfaith dialogue, has explained, "It is not happiness that makes us grateful. It is gratefulness that makes us happy. Every moment is a gift. There is no certainty that you will have another moment, with all the opportunity that it contains. The gift within every gift is the opportunity it offers us. Most often it is the opportunity to enjoy it, but sometimes a difficult gift is given to us and that can be an opportunity to rise to the challenge."

The Dalai Lama's ability to be grateful for the opportunities that exist even in exile was a profound shift in perspective, allowing him not only to accept the reality of his circumstances but also to see the opportunity in every experience. Acceptance means not fighting reality. Gratitude means embracing reality. It means moving from counting your burdens to counting your blessings, as the Archbishop had recommended, both as an antidote to envy and a recipe for appreciating our own lives.

"I have been able to meet many spiritual leaders like you," the Dalai Lama said, when the Archbishop had been awed by his ability to find gratitude even in fifty years of loss for himself and his people. "It is much more enriching, much more useful. Even suffering helps you to develop empathy and compassion for others.

"Exile really has brought me closer to reality. When you are in difficult situations, there is no room for pretense. In adversity or tragedy, you must confront reality as it is. When you are refugee, when you have lost your land, you cannot pretend or hide behind your role. When you are confronted with the reality of suffering, all of life is laid bare. Even a king when he is suffering cannot pretend to be something special. He is just one human being, suffering, like all other people."

In Buddhism, one can be grateful even for one's enemies, "our most precious spiritual teachers," as they are often called, because they help us develop our spiritual practice and to cultivate equanimity even in the face of adversity. The Dalai Lama's story about his friend who feared losing his compassion for his torturers in the Chinese gulag was a poignant example.

The Archbishop had described earlier in the week how Nelson Mandela had been transformed while he was in prison. Mandela and his fellow political prisoners had used their time to develop their mind and their character so that they would someday be ready to rule the country. They had seen it as an informal university.

These prison stories reminded me of a former inmate I've had the privilege of knowing.

Anthony Ray Hinton spent thirty years on death row for a crime he did not commit. He was working in a locked factory at the time of the crime that he was being accused of. When he was arrested in the state of Alabama in the United States, he was told by the police officers that he would be going to jail because he was black. He spent thirty years in a five-by-seven-foot cell in solitary confinement, allowed out only one hour a day. During his time on death row, Hinton became a counselor and friend not only to the other inmates, fifty-four of whom were put to death, but to the death row guards, many of whom begged Hinton's attorney to get him out.

When a unanimous Supreme Court ruling ordered his release, he was finally able to walk free. "One does not know the value of freedom until one has it taken away," he told me. "People run out of the rain. I run into the rain. How can anything that falls from heaven not be precious? Having missed the rain for so many years, I am so grateful for every drop. Just to feel it on my face."

When Hinton was interviewed on the American television show **60 Minutes,** the interviewer asked whether he was angry at those who had put him in jail. He responded that he had forgiven all the people who had sent him to jail. The interviewer incredulously asked, "But they took thirty years of your life—how can you not be angry?"
Hinton responded, "If I'm angry and unforgiving, they will have taken the rest of my life."
Unforgiveness robs us of our ability to enjoy and appreciate our life, because we are trapped in a past filled with anger and bitterness. Forgiveness allows us to move beyond the past and appreciate the present, including the drops of rain falling on our face.
"Whatever life gives to you," Brother Steindl-Rast explains, "you can respond with joy. Joy is the happiness that does not depend on what happens. It is the grateful response to the opportunity that life offers you at this moment."
Hinton is a powerful example of the ability to respond with joy despite the most horrendous circumstances. As we were driving in a taxi in New York, he told me, "The world didn't give you your joy, and the world can't take

it away. You can let people come into your life and destroy it, but I refused to let anyone take my joy. I get up in the morning, and I don't need anyone to make me laugh. I am going to laugh on my own, because I have been blessed to see another day, and when you are blessed to see another day that should automatically give you joy.

"I don't walk around saying, 'Man, I ain't got a dollar in my pocket.' I don't care about having a dollar in my pocket, what I care about is that I have been blessed to see the sun rise. Do you know how many people had money but didn't get up this morning? So, which is better—to have a billion dollars and not wake up, or to be broke and wake up? I'll take being broke and waking up any day of the week. I told the CNN interviewer in June that I had three dollars and fifty cents in my pocket and for some reason that day I was just the happiest I have ever been. She said, 'With three dollars and fifty cents?' I said, 'You know, my mom never raised us to get out there and make as much money as we can. My mom told us about true happiness. She told us that when you are happy, then when folks hang around you they become happy.'

"I just look at all the people who have so much but they are not happy. Yes, I did thirty long years, day for day, in a five by seven, and you have got some people that have never been to prison, never spent one day or one hour or one minute, but they are not happy. I ask myself, 'Why is that?' I can't tell you why they are not happy, but I can tell you that I'm happy because I choose to be happy."

When you are grateful," Brother Steindl-Rast explained, "you are not fearful, and when you are not fearful, you are not violent. When you are grateful, you act out of a sense of enough and not out of a sense of scarcity, and you are willing to share. If you are grateful, you are enjoying the differences between people and respectful to all people. A grateful world is a world of joyful people. Grateful people are joyful people. A grateful world is a happy world."

Gratitude connects us all. When we are

grateful for a meal, we can be grateful for the food that we are eating and for all of those who have made the meal possible—the farmers, the grocers, and the cooks. When the Archbishop gives thanks, we are often taken on a journey of Ubuntu, acknowledging all of the connections that bind us together and on which we are all dependent. The Eucharist that the Archbishop gave to the Dalai Lama literally comes from the Greek word **thanksgiving**, and saying grace or giving thanks for what we have been given is an important practice in the Judeo-Christian tradition.

Rejoicing is one of the "seven limbs" that are part of the daily spiritual practice in the Indian and Tibetan Buddhist traditions. When we rejoice, we celebrate our good fortune and the good fortune of others. We celebrate our good deeds and the good deeds of others. By rejoicing, you are much less likely to take life for granted and can affirm and appreciate all that you have and have done. Jinpa told me there is a famous passage from Tsongkhapa, the fourteenth-century Tibetan master whose thoughts and writings were an important part of the Dalai Lama's formal education. "It's taught that the best way to create good karma with the least amount of effort is to rejoice in your good deeds and those of others." Rejoicing predisposes us to repeat those good deeds in the future.

Scientists have long known that our brains have evolved with a negative bias. It was no doubt advantageous for our survival to focus on what was wrong or dangerous. Gratitude cuts across this default mode of the mind. It allows us to see what is good and right and not just what is bad and wrong.

Perhaps because of this bias, people are often skeptical of gratitude and wonder if it is a naive point of view or will lead to complacency or even injustice. If we are grateful for what is, will we be less likely to work for what still needs to be? If the Dalai Lama is able to find things in his exile that he is grateful for, will he be less willing to stand up to the Chinese occupation of Tibet?

UC Davis Professor Robert Emmons has been studying gratitude for over a decade. In one study with his colleagues Michael McCullough and Jo-Ann Tsang, they found that grateful people do not seem to ignore or deny the negative aspects of life; they simply choose to appreciate what is positive as well: "People with a strong disposition toward gratitude have the capacity to be empathic and to take the perspective of others. They are rated as more generous and more helpful by people in their social networks." They are also more likely to have helped someone with a personal problem or to have offered emotional support to others.

Emmons and McCullough have also found that people who focus on gratitude, by keeping a list of what they were grateful for, exercised more often, had fewer physical symptoms, felt better about their lives, and were more positive about the week ahead compared to those who recorded hassles or neutral life events. Similarly, those who focused on gratitude were more likely to have made progress toward their important personal goals. So it seems gratitude is motivating, not demotivating. Grateful people report more positive emotions, more vitality and optimism, and greater life satisfaction as well as lower levels of stress and depression.

Gratitude may stimulate the hypothalamus,

which is involved in regulating stress in the brain, as well as the ventral tegmental region, which is part of the reward circuits that produce pleasure in the brain. Research has shown that the simple act of smiling for as little as twenty seconds can trigger positive emotions, jump-starting joy and happiness. Smiling stimulates the release of neuropeptides that work toward fighting off stress and unleashes a feel-good cocktail of the neurotransmitters serotonin, dopamine, and endorphins. Serotonin acts as a natural antidepressant, dopamine stimulates the reward centers of the brain, and endorphins are natural painkillers. Smiling also seems to reward the brains of those who see us smiling making them feel better, too. Smiling is contagious, stimulating unconscious smiling in others, which in turn spreads the positive effects. Did the Dalai Lama and the Archbishop smile because they were happy, or were they happy because they smiled? It sounded a little like a Zen koan. Likely, both were true. Whether we frown in displeasure or smile in appreciation, we have enormous power over our emotions and our experience of life.

Impermanence, the Dalai Lama reminds

us, is the nature of life. All things are slipping away, and there is a real danger of wasting our precious human life. Gratitude helps us catalog, celebrate, and rejoice in each day and each moment before they slip through the vanishing hourglass of experience.

Perhaps it was no surprise to Sonja Lyubomirsky that gratitude is a factor that seems to influence happiness along with our ability to reframe negative events into positive ones. The final factor she found was our ability to be kind and generous toward others, which the Dalai Lama and the Archbishop saw as two separate but related pillars: compassion and generosity. When we recognize all that we have been given, it is our natural response to want to care for and give to others.

7.
Compassion: Something We Want to Become

Too much self-centered thinking is the source of suffering. A compassionate concern for others' well-being is the source of happiness," the Dalai Lama had said earlier in the week. He was now rubbing his hands together in thought as we returned to the topic of compassion. "On this planet, over the last three thousand years, different religious traditions developed. All these traditions carry the same message: the message of love. So the purpose of these different traditions is to promote and strengthen the value of love, compassion. So different medicine, but same aim: to cure our pain, our illness. As we mentioned, even scientists now say basic human nature is compassionate." Both he and the Archbishop had emphasized that this compassionate concern for others is instinctual and that we are hardwired to connect and to care. However, as the Archbishop explained earlier in the week, "It takes time. We are growing and learning how to be compassionate, how to be caring, how to be human." The Buddha supposedly said, "What is that one thing, which when you possess, you have all other virtues? It is compassion."

It is worth taking a moment to think about what compassion really means, since it is a term that is often misunderstood. Jinpa, with the help of colleagues, created the Compassion Cultivation Training at the Center for Compassion and Altruism Research and Education at Stanford University School of Medicine. In his marvelous book **A Fearless Heart: How the Courage to Be Compassionate Can Transform Our Lives,** he explains: "Compassion is a sense of concern that arises when we are confronted with another's suffering and feel motivated to see that suffering relieved." He adds,

"Compassion is what connects the feeling of empathy to acts of kindness, generosity, and other expressions of altruistic tendencies." The Biblical Hebrew word for compassion, **rachamim,** comes from the root word for womb, **rechem,** and the Dalai Lama often says that it is from our mother's nurturing that we learn compassion. He also says that his mother was his first teacher of compassion. It is from being nurtured, and in turn nurturing our own children, that we discover the nature of compassion. Compassion is in many ways expanding this maternal instinct that was so pivotal to the survival of our species.

The Dalai Lama tells a story of flying one night from Japan to San Francisco. Sitting close to him was a couple with two children, a very active boy of around three years old and a baby. At the beginning, it seemed the father was helping to look after the children, often walking about with the young boy, who kept running through the aisles. In the middle of the night the Dalai Lama looked over and saw that the father was fast asleep and the mother was left trying to take care of the two tired and cranky children by herself. The Dalai

Lama handed the boy a piece of candy, as he noticed the mother's swollen eyes and exhaustion. "Seriously," he said later. "I thought about it, and I don't think I would have had that kind of patience." The Dalai Lama's comment echoed a topic I have discussed with quite a few religious seekers and parents: It probably takes many years of monastic practice to equal the spiritual growth generated by one sleepless night with a sick child.

While we all carry what the Dalai Lama calls the "seed of compassion" from our own experience of being nurtured by others, compassion is actually a skill that can be cultivated. It is something that we can learn to develop and then use to extend our circle of concern beyond our immediate family to others. It helps when one recognizes our shared humanity.

"Archbishop, Your Holiness, over the course of the week, you have talked so much about compassion that I thought we might need to rename your collaboration **The Book of Compassion.** In this session, I hope we can explore compassion even more deeply. While everyone agrees that being compassionate is a worthy goal, it is hard for many people to understand or to put into practice. The word **compassion,** as we have said, literally means 'suffering with.' So what would you say to the person who says, 'I have enough problems of my own. Why should I worry about being more compassionate and think about others who are suffering?'"

"As we have discussed," the Dalai Lama began, "we are social animals. Even for kings or queens or spiritual leaders, their survival depends on the rest of the community. So therefore, if you want a happy life and fewer problems, you have to develop a serious concern for the well-being of others. So then when someone is passing through a difficult period or difficult circumstances, then automatically will come a sense of concern for their well-being. And if there is the possibility to help, then you can help. If there is no possibility to help, you can just pray or wish them well.

"Even other social animals have this same concern for each other. I think the other day I also mentioned how scientists have found that when two mice are together, if one is injured, the other will lick it. The injured mouse that is being licked by another mouse will heal much faster than a mouse that is alone.

"This concern for others is something very precious. We humans have a special brain, but this brain causes a lot of suffering because it is always thinking me, me, me, me. The more time you spend thinking about yourself, the more suffering you will experience. The incredible thing is that when we think of alleviating other people's suffering, our own suffering is reduced. This is the true secret to happiness. So this is a very practical thing. In fact, it is common sense."

"So will the mouse that does the licking benefit as well?" I asked.

The Dalai Lama spoke in Tibetan, and Jinpa translated: "One could argue that the mouse doing the licking is better off, and is also in a calmer state of mind."

The Archbishop laughed at all of this discussion of mice and the need for scientific justifications for what, to him, was so obviously at the very core of our humanity. "I would say that one of the ways to show that compassion is something we want to become is the very fact that we admire compassionate people. You know, you don't—very, very few of us—admire a vengeful person. Why do they come to listen to the Dalai Lama?

"It is very largely because of who he has become. They are attracted to him because of his spiritual stature. A stature that has been created by the fact of his caring for others, even in the midst of his own suffering, the suffering of being in exile."

"Still, Archbishop, the question for many people is that they have so many of their own problems. They may admire both of you and say, 'Well that's wonderful, they're incredibly holy men. But I've got to feed my children.' And 'I have to do my job.' And 'I don't have enough money.' Or they say, 'If I am compassionate others will take advantage of me, because it's a dog-eat-dog world.' So why is compassion in their self-interest, how does it help the rest of their goals in life?"

"Yes, I would hope they would try it out, because it's very difficult just speaking about it theoretically. It's something that you have to work out in actual life. Try out being kind when you are walking in the street and say good morning to the people you are passing, or smile, when you are not feeling like it. I bet you my bottom dollar, in a very short period of time this pall of self-regard, which is a bad self-regard, lifts. It's universal. When you try it out, why does it work? We really are wired to be caring of the other. And when we go against that fundamental law of our being, whether we like it or not, it is going to have deleterious consequences for us.

"When you say, 'I, I, I, I, I,' as His Holiness pointed out, you are going to come a cropper. But when you say, 'How can I help?' even in the midst of your deep anguish, it's got an alchemy that transforms your pain. It may not take it away. But it becomes in a way bearable, more than it was at the time when you were just saying 'poor me,' thinking only about yourself.

"When your doorbell rings, and you're going to open it, as a Christian, I would make the sign of a cross over whoever it is who is there, which is just to say let them be blessed. They may not be in desperate need of anything. But they might also be. And you are in that process being helped not to be so self-regarding, so constantly conscious of your anguish. As you remember, yes, compassion is absolutely essential. It is like oxygen."

"Very right, very right," the Dalai Lama said. "Thinking me, me, me automatically brings fear, a sense of insecurity, and distrust. That kind of person will never be happy person. And at the end of that person's life, their neighbor will be happy that that person is gone. Yes?"

"You are quite right, yes," the Archbishop said.

"If you look after others, particularly those who are in need, then when you are passing through some difficulties, there are plenty of people you can ask for help. Then at the end, many people will feel that they have really lost a wonderful person. So it's just common sense," the Dalai Lama concluded, pointing to his forehead.

"And then I want to say," the Dalai Lama now added, passionate and wanting to convince the skeptics, "look at Stalin's picture or Hitler's picture and compare it to the face of Mahatma Gandhi, and also the face of this person." He was pointing to the Archbishop. "You can see that the person who has all the power, but who lacks compassion, who only thinks about control," the Dalai Lama said as he ground one hand into the other, "can never be happy. I think during the night they do not have sound sleep. They always have fear. Many dictators sleep in a different place every night.

"So what creates that kind of fear is their own way of thinking, their own mind. Mahatma Gandhi's face was always smiling. And to some extent I think Nelson Mandela, also; because he followed the path of nonviolence, and because he was not obsessed with power, millions of people remember him. If he had become a dictator, then nobody would have mourned his death. So that's my view. Quite simple."

I was pushing the Dalai Lama and the Archbishop hard because I did not want to leave compassion in the lofty realm of saints and lamas. I knew they were suggesting that it was a pillar of joy for the rest of us, and I wanted to understand why it has been so hard for our modern culture to embrace. "So that same cynic might say, 'If compassion is so natural and it's in many ways the ethical root of all religions and for thousands of years people have been preaching and teaching compassion, then why is there such a lack of compassion in the world?'"

"Our human nature has been distorted," the Archbishop began. "I mean, we are actually quite remarkable creatures. In our religions I am created in the image of God. I am a God carrier. It's fantastic. I have to be growing in godlikeness, in caring for the other. I know that each time I have acted compassionately, I have experienced a joy in me that I find in nothing else.

"And even the cynic will have to admit that it is how we are wired. We're wired to be other-regarding. We shrivel if there is no other. It's really a glorious thing. When you say, 'I will care for only me,' in an extraordinary way that **me** shrivels and gets smaller and smaller. And you find satisfaction and joy increasingly elusive. Then you want to grab and try this and try that, but in the end you don't find satisfaction."

The modern world is suspicious of compassion because we have accepted the belief that nature is "red in tooth and claw" and that we are fundamentally competing against everyone and everything. According to this perspective, in our lives of getting and spending, compassion is at best a luxury, or at worst a self-defeating folly of the weak. Yet evolutionary science has come to see cooperation, and its core emotions of empathy, compassion, and generosity, as fundamental to our species' survival. What the Dalai Lama was describing—explaining that compassion is in our self-interest—evolutionary biologists have called "reciprocal altruism." I scratch your back today, and you scratch my back tomorrow.

This arrangement was so fundamental to our survival that children as young as six months have been shown to have a clear preference for toys that reflect helping rather than hindering. When we help others, we often experience what has been called the "helper's high," as endorphins are released in our brain, leading to a euphoric state. The same reward centers of the brain seem to light up when we are doing something compassionate as when we think of chocolate. The warm feeling we get from helping others comes from the release of oxytocin, the same hormone that is released by lactating mothers. This hormone seems to have health benefits, including the reduction of inflammation in the cardiovascular system. Compassion literally makes our heart healthy and happy.

Compassion also seems to be contagious. When we see others being compassionate, we are more likely to be compassionate. This results in a feeling called "moral elevation," and that is one of the aspects of joy that Paul Ekman had identified. Recent research by social scientists Nicholas Christakis and James Fowler suggests that this ripple effect can extend out to two and three degrees of separation. In other words, experiments with large numbers of people show that if you are kind and compassionate, your friends, your friends' friends, and even your friends' friends' friends are more likely to become kind and compassionate.

We fear compassion because we're afraid of experiencing the suffering, the vulnerability, and the helplessness that can come with having an open heart. Psychologist Paul Gilbert found that many people are afraid that if they are compassionate they will be taken advantage of, that others will become dependent on them, and that they won't be able to handle others' distress.

One of the differences between empathy and compassion is that while empathy is simply experiencing another's emotion, compassion is a more empowered state where we want what is best for the other person. As the Dalai Lama has described it, if we see a person who is being crushed by a rock, the goal is not to get under the rock and feel what they are feeling; it is to help to remove the rock.

Many people are also afraid of receiving compassion from others because they are afraid that others will want something in return or that they will at least feel indebted. Finally, many people are even afraid of being self-compassionate because they are afraid they will become weak, that they will not work as hard, or that they will be overcome with sadness and grief. Gilbert says, "Compassion can flow naturally when we understand and work to remove our fears, our blocks, and our resistances to it. Compassion is one of the most difficult and courageous of all our motivations, but is also the most healing and elevating."

. . .

Self-compassion is closely connected to self-acceptance, which we discussed in an earlier chapter, but it is even more than the acceptance of ourselves. It is actually having compassion for our human frailties and recognizing that we are vulnerable and limited like all people. As a result, it is a fundamental basis for developing compassion for others. It's hard to love others as you love yourself, as both men pointed out, if you don't love yourself.

The Dalai Lama had mentioned during the week how he was shocked to hear from Western psychologists about how many of their patients wrestled with issues of self-hatred. Self-preservation, self-love, and self-care, he had assumed, are fundamental to our nature. This assumption is fundamental to Buddhist practice, so it was shocking to hear that people had to learn to express compassion not only to others but also to themselves.

Modern culture makes it hard for us to have compassion for ourselves. We spend so much of our lives climbing a pyramid of achievement where we are constantly being evaluated

and judged, and often found to be not making the grade. We internalize these other voices
of parents, teachers, and society at large. As a
result, sometimes people are not very compassionate with themselves. People don't rest when
they are tired, and neglect their basic needs for
sleep, food, and exercise as they drive themselves harder and harder. As the Dalai Lama
said, they treat themselves as if they are part of
the machine. People tend to feel anxious and
depressed because they expect themselves to
have more, be more, achieve more. Even when
people are successful and grab all the brass
rings, they often feel like failures or frauds, just
waiting to fall off the merry-go-round. Jinpa
explains, "Lack of self-compassion manifests in
a harsh and judgmental relationship with ourselves. Many people believe that unless they are
critical and demanding, they will be failures,
unworthy of recognition and undeserving of
love."

Psychologist Kristin Neff has identified ways
to express self-compassion: When we treat ourselves with compassion, we accept that there
are parts of our personality that we may not
be satisfied with, but we do not berate our-

selves as we try to address them. When we go through a difficult time, we are caring and kind to ourselves, as we would be to a friend or relative. When we feel inadequate in some way, we remind ourselves that all people have these feelings or limitations. When things are hard, we recognize that all people go through similar challenges. And finally when we are feeling down, we try to understand this feeling with curiosity and acceptance rather than rejection or self-judgment.

The Archbishop and the Dalai Lama had revealed throughout the week one of the core paradoxes of happiness: We are most joyful when we focus on others, not on ourselves. In short, bringing joy to others is the fastest way to experience joy oneself. As the Dalai Lama had said, even ten minutes of meditation on the well-being of others can help one to feel joyful for the whole day—even before coffee. When we close our heart, we cannot be joyful. When we have the courage to live with an open heart, we are able to feel our pain and the pain of others, but we are also able to experience more joy. The bigger and warmer our heart, the stronger our sense of aliveness and resilience.

When Anthony Ray Hinton went to death row after a trial that can only be called a travesty of justice, he was understandably angry and heartbroken at how the American justice system had failed him. "When no one believes a word you say, eventually you stop saying anything. I did not say good morning. I did not say good evening. I did not say a how-do-you-do to anyone. If the guards needed some information from me, I wrote it down on a piece of paper. I was angry. But going into the fourth year, I heard a man in the cell next to mine crying. The love and compassion I had received from my mother spoke through me and asked him what was wrong. He said he had just found out that his mother had passed away. I told him, 'Look at it this way. Now you have someone in heaven who's going to argue your case before God.' And then I told him a joke, and he laughed. Suddenly my voice and my sense of humor were back. For twenty-six long years after that night, I tried to focus on other people's problems, and every day I did, I would get to the end of the day and realize that I had not focused on my own." Hinton was able to bring love and compassion to a loveless place, and in doing so he was able to hold on to his joy in one of the most joyless places on the planet.

While he was in prison, he watched fifty-four people, fifty-three men and one woman, walk by his cell on their way to the execution chamber. He got his fellow inmates to start banging their bars at five minutes before the execution. "I discovered on death row that the other inmates had not had the unconditional love that I had had from my mother. We became a family, and we did not know if they had any other family and friends there, so we were banging the bars to say to those who were being put to death, 'We're with you, we still love you right up to the end.'"

8.
Generosity: We Are
Filled with Joy

think that almost all of us are surprised how our joy is enhanced when we make someone else happy. You know, you go to town, you've gone to do some shopping, and when you get back home you have a bunch of flowers for Rachel. She wasn't expecting them, and the glow of her face and the joy that comes from having made another person joyful is something that you can't actually compute.

"So," the Archbishop said with a laugh, "our book says that it is in giving that we receive. So I would hope that people would recognize in themselves that it is when we are closed in on ourselves that we tend to be miserable. It is when we grow in a self-forgetfulness—in a remarkable way I mean we discover that we are filled with joy.

"I've sometimes joked and said God doesn't know very much math, because when you give to others, it should be that you are subtracting from yourself. But in this incredible kind of way—I've certainly found that to be the case so many times—you gave and it then seems like in fact you are making space for more to be given to you.

"And there is a very physical example. The Dead Sea in the Middle East receives fresh water, but it has no outlet, so it doesn't pass the water out. It receives beautiful water from the rivers, and the water goes dank. I mean, it just goes bad. And that's why it is the Dead Sea. It receives and does not give. And we are made much that way, too. I mean, we receive and we must give. In the end generosity is the best way of becoming more, more, and more joyful."

We had come to the eighth and final pillar of joy.

. . .

Generosity is often a natural outgrowth of compassion, though the line between the two can be hard to distinguish. As Jinpa pointed out, we don't need to wait until the feelings of compassion arise before we choose to be generous. Generosity is often something that we learn to enjoy by doing. It is probably for this reason that charity is prescribed by almost every religious tradition. It is one of the five pillars of Islam, called **zakat.** In Judaism, it is called **tzedakah,** which literally means "justice." In Hinduism and Buddhism, it is called **dana.** And in Christianity, it is charity.

Generosity is so important in all of the world's religions because it no doubt expresses a fundamental aspect of our interdependence and our need for one another. Generosity was so important for our survival that the reward centers of our brain light up as strongly when we give as when we receive, sometimes even more so. As mentioned earlier, Richard Davidson and his colleagues have identified that generosity is one of the four fundamental brain circuits that map with long-term well-being. In the 2015 World Happiness Report, Davidson and Brianna Schuyler explained that one of the strongest predictors of well-being world-wide is the quality of our relationships. Generous, pro-social behavior seems to strengthen these relationships across cultures. Generosity is even associated with better health and longer life expectancy. Generosity seems to be so powerful that, according to researchers David McClelland and Carol Kirshnit, just thinking about it "significantly increases the protective antibody salivary immunoglobulin A, a protein used by the immune system."

So it seems that money can buy happiness, if we spend it on other people. Researcher Elizabeth Dunn and her colleagues found that people experience greater happiness when they spend money on others than when they spend it on themselves. Dunn also found that older adults with hypertension have decreased blood pressure when they are assigned to spend money on others rather than themselves. As the Archbishop had explained, we receive when we give.

I had heard an amazing story that supported what the Archbishop was saying. When I met James Doty, he was the founder and director of the Center of Compassion and Altruism Research and Education at Stanford and the chairman of the Dalai Lama Foundation. Jim also worked as a full-time neurosurgeon. Years earlier, he had made a fortune as a medical technology entrepreneur and had pledged stock worth $30 million to charity. At the time his net worth was over $75 million. However, when the stock market crashed, he lost everything and discovered that he was bankrupt. All he had left was the stock that he had pledged to charity. His lawyers told him that he could get out of his charitable contributions and that everyone would understand that his circumstances had changed. "One of the persistent myths in our society," Jim explained, "is that money will make you happy. Growing up poor, I thought that money would give me everything I did not have: control, power, love. When I finally had all the money I had ever dreamed of, I discovered that it had not made me happy. And when I lost it all, all of my false friends disappeared." Jim decided to go through with his contribution. "At that moment I realized that the only way that money can bring happiness is to give it away."

· · ·

Generosity is not just about the money we give. It is also about how we give our time. In the happiness literature there is a great deal of research on the importance of having a sense of purpose. Purpose, fundamentally, is about how we are able to contribute and be generous to others, how we feel needed by and of value to others. A large meta-analysis by cardiologist Randy Cohen conducted at the Mount Sinai St. Luke's Medical Center found that a high sense of purpose correlates with a 23 percent reduction in death from all causes. In another study conducted by neuropsychologist Patricia Boyle and her colleagues and reported in **JAMA Psychiatry**, people with a sense of purpose were half as likely to develop Alzheimer's disease after seven years. It's no surprise, then, that being generous with our time seems to be equally profound for our health. A large meta-analysis by Morris Okun and his colleagues have found that volunteering reduces the risk of death by 24 percent.

Compassion and generosity are not just lofty virtues—they are at the center of our humanity, what makes our lives joyful and meaningful. "Yes, there are many, many, many ugly things," the Archbishop explained. "But there are also some incredibly beautiful things in our world. The black townships in South Africa are squalor ridden and because of despair and disease, including HIV, children are orphaned. In one of the townships, I met a mother who had collected these abandoned children off the streets. She's got nothing much in the way of resources. But the minute she began doing that, help began coming for her to carry out her work of compassion.

"We are fundamentally good. The aberration is not the good person; the aberration is the bad person. We are made for goodness. And when we get opportunities, we mostly respond with generosity. She has got nothing, but that didn't stop her. And she had about a hundred street children she picked up in a three-room house. And before long people got to know about it who were able to say, 'Okay, we will help. We will build a little dormitory for them.' Others said, 'We will give you food.' And hey, presto, she had a home. And she's becoming a legendary figure. But she wasn't driven by wanting fame or anything of the kind. It was just that she saw these children and her maternal instinct said, 'No, this won't do.' And so yes, I mean, one shouldn't pretend that people don't get overwhelmed by the sense of impotence, but do what you can where you can."

At the Archbishop's eightieth birthday, Rachel and I had gone with the Archbishop and his family to visit the orphanage and to celebrate with a giant cake. As some of the children sat on our laps on the floor in a room that was filled with dozens of other children, it was very hard not to want to adopt them all. The older children held the younger ones in their arms: They had all lashed their lives together in the shelter of the compassion and generosity of the mother who had taken them in. I remembered the Archbishop saying that when he would visit townships, people who had nothing, absolutely nothing, would still open their homes and their hearts to others. Generosity is so deeply rooted in us.

"And you are surprised," the Archbishop continued, "when you go to a monastery or a convent, where people live a very, very simple life, and you just have to accept that they have a peace that we who are always grabbing find elusive. Unless, of course, we sit loosely in relation to all of our wealth and all of our status, then we can be generous because we have really been made a steward of these possessions and these positions. And we don't hold on to them for dear life.

"So it's not the wealth and the status. These are neutral. It's our attitude. It's what we do with them that is so important. We said it on the very first day: When you become so inward looking, so self-regarding, you are going to end up a shriveled human being."

There are ways to give even beyond our time and our money. Jinpa explained that in Buddhist teachings there are three kinds of generosity: material giving, giving freedom from fear (which can involve protection, counseling, or solace), and spiritual giving, which can involve giving your wisdom, moral and ethical teachings, and helping people to be more self-sufficient and happier. This was of course what the Dalai Lama and the Archbishop were giving all week long.

"It's there in front of our eyes," the Archbishop said. "We have seen it. The people we admire are those who have been other-regarding. Who even in the midst of a lot of hard work and so on, when you want to speak with them, they have a way of making you feel that, at that precise moment, you are the most important thing they have to deal with.

"We don't have to bring in religion. I mean it's a secular thing. Companies that are caring of their workers are more successful. Now they could say, 'Well, we pay them so much and that's the end of our concern for them.' Yes, well, okay. Do that. And your workers will be workers who say, 'I work my shift from a certain time to a certain time, and I finish.' But when they have experienced that you care about them as people—you know, you ask after them, you ask after their families or at least have someone in your company whose business is looking after their welfare, as people—it does increase productivity. I don't know what other evidence we want that would tell us that the caring corporation, the caring person, almost always are the ones who do well. In fact do very, very well. And the opposite is true as well."

"Very true, very true," the Dalai Lama added. "It's quite obvious. Many Japanese companies are very successful because of the relationship between the employee and employer. The employees have the feeling that 'this is my company.' So they work wholeheartedly. So with the employer that just cares about the profits, the employees will always be thinking about the lunch break or the teatime, never thinking about the company. If you build the real concept of working together, and the profit is shared together, then real harmony develops. This is what we really need now. Harmony among the seven billion human beings." The Dalai Lama was weaving his hands together, as if he could will the harmony of the world's population with his delicate fingers.

"I want to come back to what you were saying, Archbishop, about how you feel like our human nature's been distorted. What is it about our modern life that distorts our innate sense of compassion and generosity?"

"We have been brought up to think that we have to obey the laws of the jungle. Eat or be eaten. We are ruthless in our competitiveness. So much so that now stomach ulcers are status symbols. They show just how very hard we work. We work hard not only to supply our needs and the needs of our families, but we are trying to outdo the other. We have downplayed the fact that actually our created nature is that we are made for a complementarity. We have become dehumanized and debased. As Martin Luther King Jr., said, 'We must learn to live together as sisters and brothers, or we will perish together as fools.'

"I hope that books such as this one will awaken in us that sense of being human. And then we will realize just how obscene it is for us to spend the billions or trillions that we spend on what we call a budget of defense. When a very small fraction of those budgets would ensure that . . . I mean, children die daily, die because they do not have clean water. That should not be the case if we were aware of our interconnectedness. And there's no way in which one nation is going to be able to prosper on its own. It can't. That's not how we were made. We were wired for this complementarity, this togetherness, this being family. And even if you think it is sentimental, it isn't sentimental. It's for real.

"When you produce a lot, and you don't say, 'by the way there are people over there who are

hungry,' and instead you destroy the surplus—
and you think it's going to be okay—it can't
be okay, because you have broken fundamental
laws of the universe. And things will go hor-
rendously wrong.

"You don't have to have scriptural or religious
teaching. It's just the truth: You can't survive
on your own. If you say you are going to be
totally selfish, in next to no time the person
who is totally selfish goes under. You need
other people in order to be human. That's why
when they want to punish you they put you in
solitary confinement. Because you can't flourish without other human beings. They give
you things that you cannot give yourself, no
matter how much money you have. And so we
speak of Ubuntu. A person is a person through
other persons. And there must have been some
people who said, 'Ah, what a primitive way of
thinking.' It's the most fundamental law of our
being. We flout that—we flout it at our peril."

The Archbishop's eyes were transfixed, and
he was speaking with the passion and power of
an Old Testament prophet who was trying to
save the people from ruin. I knew that speaking
truth to power, as he always did, was exhaust-

ing. However, he did not seem depleted. Perhaps he was feeling energized by his role as a global village elder, who was still desperately needed to bring a moral voice. Nonetheless, I wanted to be careful to protect his limited strength. "Archbishop, I want to be mindful of your energy. We have one last question related to this topic. How are you doing?"

"No, no, I'm fine."

"For one more question?

"You can give us as many as you like."

"This question comes from Micah in South Africa. She asks, 'How can you be of service to people, nature, and causes in need without losing yourself completely to a crisis mentality? How can we help the world heal and still find joy in our own life?'"

"My younger brother, here, go first," the Archbishop said.

"I think you know better."

The Archbishop laughed. "This is the first time, please note, that he said I know better."

"Is the question about Africa?" the Dalai Lama inquired.

"No, this is about the world."

"Okay," the Dalai Lama said, preparing to

answer. "Now, I am always sharing with people that the problems we are facing today are very difficult to solve. An entire generation has been brought up with a certain mentality, with a certain way of life. So when we think about the future, how to build healthy humanity, we really have to think about how we create a new generation of citizens with a different kind of mindset. Here education really is the key. Christianity has wonderful teachings, so does Buddhism, but these teachings and approaches are not sufficient.

"Now secular education is universal. So now we must include in formal education of our youth some teaching of compassion and basic ethics, not on the basis of religious belief but on the basis of scientific findings and our common sense and our universal experience. Just complaining about the present situation is not much help. It is very difficult to deal with our current world crises because of our basic mentality. As you mentioned, your father was usually a very good man, but when he was drunk he behaved badly. Today I think many human beings are drunk. They have too many negative emotions like greed, fear, and anger dominating their minds. So they act like drunk people.

"The only way out of this drunken stupor is to educate children about the value of compassion and the value of applying our mind. We need a long-term approach rooted in a vision to address our collective global challenges. This would require a fundamental shift in human consciousness, something only education is best suited to achieve. Time never waits. So I think it is very important that we start now. Then maybe the new generation will be in a position to solve these global problems in their lifetime. We, the elder generation, have created a lot of problems in the twentieth century. The generations of the twenty-first century will have to find the solutions for them."

"I mean, people are fundamentally compassionate," the Archbishop said, coming back to one of his core points.

The Dalai Lama jumped in. "Yes. That is the basis of our hope."

"I am speaking," the Archbishop shot back, playfully.

The Dalai Lama laughed.

"Even the most selfish person," the Archbishop continued, "must have a modicum of compassion for his family. So we're not speaking about something alien. We are saying that we have discovered that we are interdependent."

"Actually, Archbishop," I said, trying to bring our focus back to the topic, "this question is for people who feel that interdependence profoundly and are so compassionate that it makes them world-sick and heartsick. This person wants to know how she can find joy in her life while there are so many who are suffering."

"Yes. Very good," he said, looking down and reflecting on the question. "As an old man, I can say: Start where you are, and realize that you are not meant on your own to resolve all of these massive problems. Do what you can. It seems so obvious. And you will be surprised, actually, at how it can get to be catching.

"There are very many, many people—I mean, my heart leaps with joy at discovering the number of people—who care. How many people walked in New York City for the environment? I mean, it was incredible. Nobody was going to pay them anything. But there they were in droves. There are many, many people who care. And you will be surprised when you begin to say, Well, I would like to do something relating to the aged. You will be surprised at the number people who come forward and want to help. Why are there so many NGOs? I mean, it is people who say, We want to make a better world. We don't have to be so negative.

"Hey, remember you are not alone, and you do not need to finish the work. It takes time, but we are learning, we are growing, we are becoming the people we want to be. It helps no one if you sacrifice your joy because others are suffering. We people who care must be attractive, must be filled with joy, so that others recognize that caring, that helping and being generous are not a burden, they are a joy. Give the world your love, your service, your healing, but you can also give it your joy. This, too, is a great gift."

The Archbishop and the Dalai Lama were describing a special kind of generosity: the generosity of the spirit. The quality they both have, perhaps more than any other, is this generosity of the spirit. They are big-hearted, magnanimous, tolerant, broad-minded, patient, forgiving, and kind. Maybe this generosity of the spirit is the truest expression of spiritual development, of what the Archbishop had said it takes time to become.

The Archbishop had used a beautiful phrase to describe this way of being in the world: "becoming an oasis of peace, a pool of serenity that ripples out to all of those around us." When we have a generous spirit, we are easy to be with and fun to be with. We radiate happiness, and our very company can bring joy to others. This no doubt goes hand in hand with the ability, as the Archbishop had pointed out repeatedly, to be less self-centered, less self-regarding, and more self-forgetful. Then we are less burdened by our self-agenda: We do not have anything to prove. We do not need to be seen in a particular way. We can have less pretension and more openness, more honesty. This naturally brings ease to those around us, too; as we have accepted ourselves, our vulnerabilities, and our humanity, we can accept the humanity of others. We can have compassion for our faults and have compassion for those of others. We can be generous and give our joy to others. In many ways, it is like the Buddhist practice of **tonglen**, which the Dalai Lama had used on the day he found out about the uprising and brutal crackdown in Tibet. We can take in the suffering of others and give them back our joy.

When we practice a generosity of spirit, we are in many ways practicing all the other pillars of joy. In generosity, there is a wider perspective, in which we see our connection to all others. There is a humility that recognizes our place in the world and acknowledges that at another time we could be the one in need, whether that need is material, emotional, or spiritual. There is a sense of humor and an ability to laugh at ourselves so that we do not take ourselves too seriously. There is an acceptance of life, in which we do not force life to be other than what it is. There is a forgiveness of others and a release of what might otherwise have been. There is a gratitude for all that we have been given. Finally, we see others with a deep compassion and a desire to help those who are in need. And from this comes a generosity that is "wise selfish," a generosity that recognizes helping others as helping ourselves. As the Dalai Lama put it, "In fact, taking care of others, helping others, ultimately is the way to discover your own joy and to have a happy life."

The time had come for a "small" surprise party at the Tibetan Children's Village, where 1,750 children, 300 teachers and staff, and another 700 adult guests from the Tibetan community were eagerly waiting to celebrate the Dalai Lama's eightieth birthday. Like everything we had just read about generosity, we who were there—and all who were watching the live stream around the world—would receive much more from witnessing this extraordinary event than we could ever have hoped to give to the Dalai Lama.

Celebration:
Dancing in the Streets
of Tibet

As we approached the Tibetan Children's Village, we could feel the excitement of the children even before we could see it in their faces. It was a rare occasion for the Dalai Lama to have time to visit the school, and the fact that he was bringing his honored guest made the event a landmark in the school's history.

When we had come in January to plan the trip, we had asked if we could throw a small birthday party for the Dalai Lama. We had met with two of the leaders of the Tibetan Children's Villages, Tsewang Yeshi and Ngodup Wangdu Lingpa, who served as both administrators and surrogate parents for the children, as did all the teachers. They did not want any of the children to miss out on this opportunity, so soon the small gathering had grown to a party of over two thousand. They had kindly offered to bake the birthday cake (we weren't sure how we'd get cake for two thousand in our luggage). We agreed to bring trick birthday candles from America.

The children had been studying how to find joy and happiness in the face of adversity for many months, exploring it in their own lives. They had written about their own wrenching journeys from their families in Tibet, often as young as five. Many had traveled for weeks with family members or strangers over the snow-covered mountain passes out of Tibet, the same dangerous journey that the Dalai Lama had taken a half century before. Because an education based in the Tibetan language and culture is suppressed or severely restricted in many parts of the country, their parents, often poor and illiterate farmers themselves, had sent their children to be educated by the Dalai Lama. After delivering them safely, the family members or guides needed to return to Tibet. Often these children would not get to see their families again until they were adults, if ever.

As our motorcade approached, we heard the children's soaring voices, their welcome song high-pitched and plaintive, yet indomitable and joyful. It was a song they had composed for the Dalai Lama's eightieth birthday. The choir and school staff lined the road. All around them sat waves of students in their school uniforms, the girls in white blouses with green V-neck sweaters and green skirts. The boys wore blue pants and the traditional gray robes over their Tibetan shirts, like the one that had been made for the Archbishop.

The Dalai Lama and the Archbishop's beige SUV drove through the gathered crowd, under the massive circular white tent that had been raised to protect the Dalai Lama and the Archbishop and the children from the midday sun. The car finally arrived at the library, as the children were still singing at the top of their lungs. Once the Archbishop and the Dalai Lama were helped out of the car, long **khatas**, the ceremonial white scarves, were put around the Archbishop's neck. They were then ushered over to a ceremonial red box filled on one side with barley flour mixed with sugar and butter and on the other side with barley grain. Barley, which is able to grow at high altitudes, is the most important crop in Tibet. The flour, or **tsampa**, that is milled from roasted barley is a staple of the Tibetan diet. Colorful barley stalks stuck out of the box. A young woman and young man, elaborately dressed in traditional Tibetan clothing stood next to the box, each of them with their long black hair braided into crowns on their head and large yellow necklaces hanging down to their chest. The young woman held a metal bowl filled with milk, more likely cow or goat than the traditional yak.

The Dalai Lama showed the Archbishop how to toss the barley flour into the air and then dip his ring finger into the milk as part of the ceremonial offering. Long yellow, green, and red sticks of incense burned nearby. The crowd of reporters, photographers, security, monks, and officials, including the bearer of the yellow umbrella, thronged around. We were then led into the library, where the librarians placed more scarves on the Archbishop, and the Archbishop began to shrink under the layers of white fabric. I had been told that one of the librarians had spent three hours scouring the floor to prepare for their visit.

The Archbishop and the Dalai Lama walked past the children who had been selected to share their stories. The children were bowing forward respectfully, holding scarves draped across their hands. The Dalai Lama stopped in front of one of the younger boys, who had a scar running from his nose across his cheek. The Dalai Lama touched it tenderly and asked him how he had gotten the scar, and then showed the boy a scar on his own scalp.

As the Archbishop and the Dalai Lama took their seats, a young woman stepped forward. She looked very studious and stylish in her pink metallic glasses. "A very warm good afternoon to you, Your Holiness and Archbishop Desmond Tutu. My name is Tenzin Dolma, and I am from class twelve. Today, I'm going to share my experience of my journey from Tibet to India. I was born in a small village called Karze in Kham province in Tibet. I am the youngest in my family. My two sisters and I were brought up by our mother, who is a farmer. My oldest memory was of my uncle, who was hiding in our house because the Chinese were looking for him. In 2002, when I was five years old, my mother told me to go to India with my grandma.

"I was very happy because I loved being with my grandma. The journey to India was very long with many difficulties. We had to hide from the Chinese pol—so my grandmo—" She broke down, and started crying, and could not go on. Mpho Tutu stepped forward and put her arm around the girl to comfort her.

As she wept, the Dalai Lama said, "Almost every Tibetan family has had a member of their family either killed, or arrested, or tortured."

After a few minutes, the girl had recovered and was able to continue. "So my grandmother and I hid under the luggage or under the seat of the bus. At the Nepal border, the Chinese police pushed my grandmother away. We were stuck at the Nepal border for a week. One night, my grandmother told me to go with a Nepalese man to Nepal. I was very afraid, but I went with the stranger. The next day, I reunited with my grandma. When we reached India, we first went to Bodh Gaya for Kalachakra."

"Kalachakra," the Dalai Lama explained, "is a big Buddhist ceremony."

"After that, we came to Dharamsala," she continued. "My grandmother started to cry when she saw His Holiness, and he blessed both of us, and my grandmother then told me who he was. I joined TCV, and my grandmother went back to Tibet. I have not been back to Tibet and it . . . it has been thirteen years since I last saw my family." Tenzin was crying again, but still trying to speak. As she cried, I noticed that Jinpa was crying, no doubt moved by her tears, but also perhaps remembering his own early days at a Tibetan boarding school away from his family. The Dalai Lama had the palms of his hands pressed together at his heart.

"I was sad to leave my family, but I have found many things that have brought me joy. I have many friends and I have wonderful teachers and I have Master Lobsang—who is just like my dad." Tenzin was still speaking between tears, her pain spilling over, and I noticed that Ngodup Wangdu, the director of the school, was wiping his eyes with the edge of his gray robe.

"And during my last year of school, I remember and thank all those who have worked together and made me what I am today. With-

416 THE BOOK OF JOY

out the support of His Holiness the Dalai Lama, there would be no TCV. So I thank you, Your Holiness, from the depth of my heart. Thank you." Tenzin was speaking valiantly through her tears. She stepped back as the next student stepped forward, a younger girl.

"**Tashi delek**, Your Holiness. **Tashi delek**, Desmond Tutu," she began, offering the traditional Tibetan greeting. "First of all, I'd like to say my name is Yongzin Lhamo, and I am in class eight. I came to India in 2007. Today, I'm here to share my journey. My journey to India started from Tawo in the Kham province of Tibet. I was only five, and I had to leave my family behind. The pain I went through leaving my family . . ." Yongzin Lhamo stopped and broke down in tears, unable to even start her story; the fact that she had to leave her family was all that really mattered. Mpho came back out and put her arm around the young girl to comfort her.

After a few minutes of witnessing the girl's tears, with concern in his face the Dalai Lama began to speak to her. It was clear she was too overcome to continue, and he now stepped into his role as honorary principal and guardian of the school. "Now, you should think, here you've got complete freedom and have the opportunity to study—not only modern education but also our ancient, thousand-year-old culture. So when you look at your situation that way, you will feel okay.

"We Tibetans, our population is quite small, around six million, but we have a long history, and our own language, and our vast written tradition, so you should feel proud. So then you can feel happy. Now, yes, you can look beyond these sad and difficult experiences. Now you should study hard, because this generation has the responsibility to rebuild Tibet. Then you will feel happy." The Dalai Lama was trying to help her to connect her pain to the larger destiny of the Tibetan people so she could find meaning and comfort beyond her trauma.

"Thank you," the girl said, and returned to the embrace of her teachers.

A young boy stepped forward in his small gray robe and blue pants. "My name is Tenzin Tsering, and I'm from class seven. Now I'm going to share how I escaped from Tibet with my father. As the morning arrived, the moon was still there in the sky. My mother came and told me to study hard and be a brave boy. As soon as my mother was turning away from me, she shed a flood of tears. My father came beside me, patting my back, signaling that it was time for me to say goodbye. I cried my eyes out, not wanting to leave, but my mother insisted that I go, with tears in her eyes.

"Soon the bus came as we were waiting outside my home. I left my home with a heavy heart, and I stood staring through the window of the bus capturing all of the beautiful land and people in my heart so that I could recall them whenever I missed my home. As the snow began to cover the road, my friends and I did not give up. We rode on the yak's back, and the elder ones walked in the deep snow of our land. We wore sunglasses to protect our eyes. I saw a bridge, awaiting us to come and travel through it. My heart was pounding so hard.

"We slept throughout the daytime and walked past the Chinese soldiers at night. My sister had serious pain as we were walking. The day passed with walking and hiding. The pain that I went through while coming to India was nothing compared to the pain of leaving my family far behind. Since I left my family,

I found no joy in everything I did. I no longer enjoyed bus singing, the sight of flowers blooming, the rainbow—the freedom inside me was taken away. I felt myself buried in a deep sorrow with no hope of survival. I was dying slowly inside. The journey to India was the scariest and toughest journey I had ever gone through.

"My father and I came to Dharamsala, and he took me for shopping and left me in the school, saying that he will come the next day, but he lied to me. I waited for him anxiously, crying every single hour that was passing by. Soon, I got many friends, a loving school, and caring teachers, and the blessing of His Holiness. I felt a spot of joy inside me, and I started enjoying my life here in exile. Now I find joy in everything, my loving fellow students, attending classes, and I feel somehow myself again, but I strongly wish to see my mother and to be with her in my own land—that would be the greatest joy of my life. Thank you."

The boy bowed forward and walked back to join the other students. There was a long silence as we absorbed the power and pain of the children's stories. Finally the Dalai Lama turned to

the Archbishop and said, "So, you must congratulate them. Their English is better than me?"

"I must be careful," the Archbishop said, "but
yes. They speak very, very, very, very well. Beautiful. Beautiful. All of them, even the young
ladies, through their pain." The Archbishop said
thank you in English and in Tibetan. Then the
Dalai Lama led the Archbishop over to some
posters where the children had displayed their
pictures and stories about joy. The first one was
titled "Joy in Family," and there were others on
"Joy in Music" and "Joy in Nature."

"'I want to hug my parents,'" the Dalai Lama
read from one of the posters. "'There's deep joy
and love in a hug.' Very good. Wonderful. 'I will
look after my parents when they grow old. I shall
never abandon them.' Very nice." In drawing
pictures of what gave them joy, most of the children mentioned their family or their friends and
teachers at the school, who had become a second
family. More than anything it was the people
they loved who were their greatest source of joy.

At the bottom of one of the posters was a
quote: "True happiness comes from the joy of
deeds well done, the zest of creating things new."
It was a quote from Antoine de Saint-Exupéry,

the author of **The Little Prince,** a story about another boy who was far away from his home.

As we left the library, the girls' choir began singing the birthday song again, this time accompanied by a Tibetan lute.

The Archbishop and the Dalai Lama were led to two chairs at the center of the enormous tent, which displayed the endless knot and other Tibetan symbols overhead. Around the tent hung red, green, and yellow fringes, and strung all along the edges of it were red, green, yellow, white, and blue prayer flags.

The almost two thousand children, who had been waiting patiently, were then invited to stand and sing the Tibetan version of "If You're Happy and You Know It," which involved shaking their heads, clapping their hands, wiggling their hips, and stamping their feet.

Around the Dalai Lama and the Archbishop spread a carpet of cross-legged children. They ranged from five to eighteen years old, from kindergarten to grade twelve. Behind them was a group of adults that had somehow found out about the event—one was patriotically waving a South African flag.

Then the Dalai Lama took the headset and

began to address the students but then turned to his friend and said, "Since you often describe my English as very poor, now I'm going to speak Tibetan." The Dalai Lama slapped the Archbishop's arm playfully, and the Archbishop pretended to rub it as if wounded. The kids were giggling as the two grown-ups, now reconciled, took each other's hands.

"So Archbishop Desmond Tutu is one of my closest friends on this earth," he began. "The Archbishop also has been supporting the Tibetan cause unflinchingly. You are a generation whose parents have suffered, and you also have suffered to be able to come here. And as Tibetans, the Indian government has helped us since the beginning of our exile. Other organizations from all parts of the world have helped us, and because of their kindness and compassion, you have the opportunity to study here. And so you should really work hard in your studies. We are going through a very difficult period in our history, but we have such a rich culture and language. So whether you are monastics or laypeople, you should take great interest in preserving and promoting this culture through education. Our culture should not just be in a museum. All around the world people are facing lots of difficulties and our culture can help the world.

"Today, the main guest is Archbishop Tutu and not me."

The Archbishop put on his headset microphone, which had a little wire along his cheek and fit snugly around his ears. "I look like Bono now, don't I?" he said with a laugh as his microphone was being adjusted.

"Your Holiness, and all of you very, very beautiful children. Some of you are not really children. It is such a great, great honor and privilege to be here. All of us are very, very, very, very proud and privileged to be here in Dharamsala." The Archbishop turned to the Dalai Lama and said, "You are beloved throughout the world." He then turned back to the attentive faces of the children.

"And we want to say to you, young people especially, it might not seem possible that you will one day return to a free Tibet. We in South Africa for many, many years lived under a system of injustice and oppression. And many, many of our leaders and people, young people, went into exile. And it seemed like the chains of oppression would never be broken, that our leaders who were on Robben Island, the prison, would never come home alive. But yow—ha-ha!"

The audience laughed as the Archbishop let out a yelp followed by a triumphant cheer. "But it happened. It happened. In 1990, our beloved Nelson Mandela and others were released from prison. And the exiles came back home." The Archbishop stretched out his arms as if in an embrace to welcome them home. Then he spoke with the force of righteousness and was transformed into the prophet that he had been in South Africa, seer of the future, willing it with his words. "One day you, too, all of you, will see your beloved Tibet. You will be free from the oppression that has driven you to here. The Chinese government will discover that freedom is actually cheaper than oppression." The children burst into applause.

"I am very deeply honored to be the friend of the Dalai Lama. I show off when I'm in other places. I pretend that I am modest, and don't tell too many people that actually he is a very, very dear friend. I just say, well, you know, he's mischievous. He's troublesome. When I'm wearing my cap, he takes it off my head and puts it on his own.

"You know what? The world supports you. The world loves the Dalai Lama. I want to also add my thank-you to the Indian government, the Indian people who opened their arms to welcome you, because they have preserved for us a great treasure. They preserved for us a great treasure that would otherwise have been lost. And so I want to say to you, all of you . . . ooh, look at how beautiful you are. Oh, yo, yo, yo, yo. Ooh, ooh! One day, you will be dancing and singing in the streets of Tibet, your home country. God bless you."

The children now cheered even louder. They were trying to be polite and respectful, but you could see how their hope had been awakened. I scanned the faces of the children, from the older boys and girls who were really almost young men and women, the next generation of Tibetan leaders, down to the very young children, whose memories of leaving their families must still be fresh, the wounds of separation still healing. I felt like my heart was in my throat. Tears streamed down my cheeks as I recalled the anguish we had just witnessed in the library, imagining the children's equally brokenhearted parents. It was not hard to imagine what dancing in the streets of Tibet—reunited with their families—would mean to them. Everything.

After a few questions from the older students, a huge multilayered cake with our trick candles burning was brought on to the stage. At the same time teachers began to pass out little square pieces of cake to all the students. It was an ingenious way to distribute the cake, since we would have been there all day if we had to cut each child a slice.

A group of older children took the stage—this time a band of boys played guitars and drums as the chorus of girls began to sing "We Are the World." Soon the whole school was singing with them: **"We are the world, we are the children. We are the ones who make a brighter day. So let's start giving."**

They waved their arms above their heads together as the Archbishop got up to dance his irrepressible, elbow-waving boogie. He encouraged the Dalai Lama to get up and dance. As a Tibetan Buddhist monk, the Dalai Lama's vows prohibit dancing, but today he got up to dance for the first time in his life. He started to sway and rock his hands back and forth. At first as uncomfortable as a middle school boy on the dance floor, the Dalai Lama started to smile and laugh as the Archbishop encouraged him. They took each other's hands and moved to the music, celebrating the true joy of friendship, the true joy of our unbreakable connection to one another, the true joy of the world coming together as one.

Behind them sewn into the tent were two Tibetan endless knots, symbols for the impermanence and interdependence of all life and the union of wisdom and compassion. Between the knots was an image of two golden fish with large eyes, which represents sentient beings crossing the ocean of existence with the clear sight of wisdom as well as the fearlessness of not drowning in the ocean of suffering.

The song finished, and then the Archbishop began to sing, forcing his usual tenor into a deep and resonant bass: "Happy birthday to you . . . happy birthday to you . . . happy birthday, dear Your Holiness . . . happy birthday to you . . ."

This was followed by "Happy Birthday" sung in Tibetan as the Dalai Lama tried to wave out the candles, which had by now burned down so low that the cake was starting to catch fire.

"Wait, wait," the Archbishop said, encouraging him not to put out the small fire that was starting to burn on top of the cake but to blow it out properly. "Can we have one or two of the children help us blow out the candles? There we go." Two little girls, one in her school uniform and an even younger and tinier one, in pigtails and a green dress, were raised onto the stage between them.

"One, two, three." They blew out the candles, but then the trick candles relit. The Archbishop let out a cackle as they blew again and then the flames came back. But on the third time, as the Archbishop laughed, the Dalai Lama and the girls kept blowing until they finally blew the candles out.

The children were led in a prayer of offering as they held their pieces of cake up high in both hands, giving thanks for their teachers, their teachings, and their community—and perhaps for the opportunity to someday see their families again.

Departure:
A Final Goodbye

The next morning was a brief final session. We had to head to the airport early to fly the Archbishop to yet another funeral of one of his dear friends. So many of the greats were leaving us.

We sat back in the warm pool of light that had enveloped us all week, and got our mikes connected. I thought about how the Archbishop was in his eighties and how the Dalai Lama was joining him in this ninth decade of life. We were all reflecting on the birthday celebration the day before at the school and how these two elders had shared their hard-won wisdom with the students and found hope in the next generation. We all receive a transmission from our role models and mentors, and we all pass it along to those who come after. This was the goal of our project together.

I was sitting across from the Archbishop and was staring at his beautiful, loving face, which had become so familiar over the last decade of collaboration and friendship. He has become a second father and a beloved mentor. I thought of his battle with prostate cancer and how slow the cancer had been to respond to the last round of experimental drugs. We were worried about how long we would have him, not just all those who knew and loved him but the world that still needed him and his moral voice.

The Archbishop's ability to travel had been severely restricted by his doctors, and he had at one time said he was not going to travel outside of South Africa again. This made his decision to come to Dharamsala all the more extraordinary and unlikely to be repeated. Because the South African government would not grant the Dalai Lama a visa, we all knew—most especially the two of them—that this trip might be their last time together.

Death, as the Archbishop had reminded us, is

inevitable. It is the way life should be. A beginning. A middle. And an end. It is this cycle that makes life precious and beautiful. However, it does not make the sorrow any less for those who lose one they love.

"Why are you looking so solemn?" the Archbishop asked me.

"I'm reflecting," I said, "on our time coming to a close."

"Everything has an end."

After the Archbishop's customary prayer, we began our discussion for the last time.

"Archbishop, Your Holiness, what an incredible joy and privilege it has been to join you in this conversation to prepare **The Book of Joy.** Today is just for a few final questions. One we received was, 'Why do you think it is important to write **The Book of Joy** now, and what do you hope it will do for readers around the world?'"

"You obviously hope," the Archbishop said, speaking of himself in the second person, as he often did, "that you could be an agent for helping God's children enter into their heritage so they can have greater fulfillment and can become all that they are meant to be. And you hope that they will realize that it will happen most of all if they are generous, if they are compassionate, if they are caring.

"It is when without thinking about it you help someone who is less well off, when you are kind to someone else and do those things that raise others up, you end up being joyful."

The day before, at the Tibetan Children's Village, the Archbishop had answered one of the children's questions by saying, "If we think we want to get joy for ourselves, we realize that it's very shortsighted, short-lived. Joy is the reward, really, of seeking to give joy to others. When you show compassion, when you show caring, when you show love to others, do things for others, in a wonderful way you have a deep joy that you can get in no other way. You can't buy it with money. You can be the richest person on Earth, but if you care only about yourself, I can bet my bottom dollar you will not be happy and joyful. But when you are caring, compassionate, more concerned about the welfare of others than about your own, wonderfully, wonderfully, you suddenly feel a warm glow in your heart, because you have, in fact, wiped the tears from the eyes of another.

"Why now?" he continued, addressing the second part of the question. "I think that there is so much that is hurting. You almost want not to read the newspapers or watch television when, if you are going to watch television, you will see the beheading of someone's child. When you see the number of refugees, mothers running away from one source of violence and pulling children behind them. Even when you live comfortably it clutches at your heartstrings. It's very . . . it's very distressing. Particularly when we think that during the time of our struggle against apartheid, our people were refugees and exiled and were welcomed in African countries that were a great deal less well off than South Africa is. You have to be quite careless not to be sad. We look like we are hell-bent on competing to show who will be the most exquisitely cruel. I think God wants us to be joyful at every time, but right now, I think God is crying quite a lot." The Archbishop was gesturing to the Dalai Lama. "It's your turn now."

"This is our last session, so perhaps I will

state it this way. I am one human being born in Amdo province in northeast Tibet in a very, very small village in 1935. So, at that time, the Sino-Japanese conflict was about to start. Soon after the Second World War began. Then the Korean War. Then the Vietnam War. Because of these wars, there was immense violence. At those times the human mind, or at least those who were responsible for going to war, believed that using force was the best method for solving disagreement.

"During the Second World War, for example, when a nation declared war on another, the citizens of the country proudly joined the war effort without the slightest question. But since the Vietnam War our way of thinking has changed. More and more people now publicly oppose war; we saw this opposition to war in Kosovo, in Iraq. Many people were against these wars and, from Australia to America, people openly protested against these wars. This is truly a hopeful sign.

"I think as long as we human beings remain here, there will always be some limited violence, as there is with all animals. But serious violence, mass killing, war, this we can eliminate if we have the proper vision and method. I think, certainly, it is possible to achieve a world without such sorrow."

At the Tibetan Children's Village, in response to the question of whether joy can be the ultimate source of world peace, the Dalai Lama had responded, "I think so. I think firstly people should have a clear understanding of joyfulness. You see, you might get a temporary joy in killing your enemy or bullying someone. You may get some kind of temporary satisfaction. But the true joyfulness comes from helping others. This way you get much more satisfaction. So that kind of thinking about joyfulness is really an important factor in building a happy society, peaceful society. In order to create peaceful family, first the individual person himself or herself should create inner peace, joyfulness. Then share with other family members. In that way, one family, ten families, a hundred families. That way, we can change and bring happier community, happier society, then happier humanity. Seven billion human beings, we all have same desire, same right to achieve happy life."

The Dalai Lama then returned to the topic

of why he wanted to write **The Book of Joy** and why now: "We are learning. In 1996, I had an audience with the late Queen Mother. At that time she was ninety-six years old. Since my childhood, I had seen pictures of her round face, so she was quite familiar, and I was really looking forward to the meeting. I asked her, 'Since you have observed almost the whole twentieth century, do you feel the world is becoming better, worse, or staying the same?'

"Without hesitation, she answered, better. When she was young, she said, there was no concept of human rights or the right to self-determination. Now these things have become universal. She shared these two examples of how the world is getting better.

"I think the majority of people everywhere believe that bloodshed is not good and have a desire for peace. Around the time of my meeting with the Queen Mother, I also had a conversation with the renowned quantum physicist Carl Friedrich von Weizsäcker, who was the brother of the then West German president. Von Weizsäcker, too, argued that the world was improving. For example, he said that in the past every German felt that the French were his enemy and every French felt the Germans were his enemy. Now these archenemies have joined together and have formed the Franco-German unified force. They have also been key players in the formation of the European Union. It is not perfect, but it is progress.

"So then eventually, the Berlin Wall disappeared, not by force, but by popular movement, so you see change. Now, China is also changing. Cuba is also changing. North Korea alone perhaps has not changed—yet. So these things are positive signs. Human beings, through wider contact and more education, are becoming more mature. It takes time, and we must take the long view. When we look at our world with a longer time frame, say, of a hundred years, we can then envision a world that is very different. A better, kinder, a more equitable, more joyful world. But we must start the process of that change now, not wait for some ideal time. The ideal time is now."

The Dalai Lama was arguing for this longer perspective, and I could not help but think of Sir Martin Rees's comment that we were only halfway through our evolution as a species on this planet. When one thinks of the long parade of the human journey, it is really quite extraordinary to think what we can become in a century, in a millennium or more.

"After meeting with so many people, thinkers, scientists, educators, health-care professionals, social workers, and activists," the Dalai Lama continued, "it is clear that the only way to truly change our world is through teaching compassion. Our society is lacking an adequate sense of compassion, sense of kindness, and genuine regard for others' well-being. So now many, many people who seriously think about humanity all have the same view." He was pointing both his index fingers at his temple to emphasize the logic of their conclusion. "We must promote basic human values, the inner values that lie at the heart of who we are as humans.

"Religion is not sufficient. Religion has been very important in human history, and perhaps for another thousand years it will continue to bring benefit to humanity." The Dalai Lama knew he was being controversial, calling the long-term value of religion into question, and he had taken the Archbishop's hand to comfort him and reaffirm that he was not planning to put either of them out of a job anytime soon.

"So now we have to think seriously. Just to pray or rely on religious faith is not sufficient. It will remain a source of inspiration, but in terms of seven billion human beings, it's not sufficient. No matter how excellent, no religion can be universal. So we have to find another way to promote these values.

"I think the only way really is, as we have said, through education. Education is universal. We must teach people, especially our youth, the source of happiness and satisfaction. We must teach them that the ultimate source of happiness is within themselves. Not machine. Not technology. Not money. Not power.

"We are not talking about heaven or hell or Buddhahood or salvation; these are too far away." He laughed. "So our book is part of this important process to help spread the message that love, kindness, and affection are the source of joy and happiness.

"As you already made clear, our basic human nature is good, is positive, so that can give us a basis for courage and self-confidence. So that's why we spend a lot of time discussing all of this. There must be some real concrete purpose and result, or if not, it's better to sleep." The Dalai Lama pretended to lean over on his elbow toward the Archbishop, as if falling asleep, and then laughed.

I turned to Archbishop Tutu and said, "I'd like to invite you, Archbishop, to address your readers directly and offer them a blessing." He turned to the camera and began to speak.

"Dear Child of God, you are loved with a love that nothing can shake, a love that loved you long before you were created, a love that will be there long after everything has disappeared. You are precious, with a preciousness that is totally quite immeasurable. And God wants you to be like God. Filled with life and goodness and laughter—**and joy.**

"God, who is forever pouring out God's whole being from all eternity, wants you to flourish. God wants you to be filled with joy and excitement and ever longing to be able to find what is so beautiful in God's creation: the compassion of so many, the caring, the sharing. And God says, Please, my child, help me. Help me to spread love and laughter and joy and compassion. And you know what, my child? As you do this—hey, presto—you discover joy. Joy, which you had not sought, comes as the gift, as almost the reward for this non-self-regarding caring for others."

"Thank you. Your Holiness, what final words would you like to leave the reader with so that they can experience more joy and create more joy in our world?"

"I hope this book will leave you with more hope and a sense of greater responsibility rooted in genuine concern for others' well-being. You see, in order to become a happy person, we need to live more from the compassionate part of our nature and to have a sense of responsibility toward others and the world we live in. In this century if we make an attempt with realistic effort and clear vision, perhaps in the later part of the century, we can really have a happier world. A more peaceful world. A kinder and more compassionate world. So, my hope is that this book can be a contribution toward bringing about this happier humanity.

"Nobody expects this book alone will change the world. No, that's impossible, but from various quarters, with a common effort, and a vision that thinks about humanity, we can achieve unity and harmony with a sense of brotherhood and sisterhood, with the oneness of humanity. And all these small problems here and there, I think, ultimately, we will solve, but we must also address the bigger problems. When the larger systemic problems are addressed, then the smaller problems will also be solved quite easily. So all of us, spiritual brothers and sisters, have a special responsibility, have a special role to make clear that the ultimate source of a meaningful life is within ourselves. If you live in this way, until your last breath comes you will be a happy, happy person. That's the goal of human life—to live with joy and purpose."

We were done with the interviews, but before we ended the session, the Archbishop thanked all who had been involved, most especially his friend. "I want to say a very big thank-you to the Dalai Lama for his generosity and his hospitality here. Thank you very, very much for opening your home so we could come and be cared for and have this very important project undertaken. Would you please tell your household and staff that we are very deeply indebted to them?" He then turned to me: "Now you can say your piece."

"Actually, I think you said it so wonderfully, which is to thank each and every one for the incredible work of making these dialogues possible, but as a representative of all those who will benefit from this work, I want to thank you both so profoundly for your life-sustaining and life-changing words. May the merit of this book benefit all of God's children and all sentient beings."

As we got ready to leave, the Dalai Lama said, "I was very sad to miss your birthday. When I found out that you might come here, I was really surprised. I knew your health was not good and that you were also very old, and to reach here is not easy."

"Yes," the Archbishop said, "that's quite right."

"But," the Dalai Lama continued, "when I heard that everything was finalized, and the date and hour was approaching, I really felt happy and excited. I really appreciate your friendship and your sense of responsibility to do what you can for a better humanity."

Earlier in the week, the Archbishop and the Dalai Lama had reflected on what was so special about their friendship with characteristic humor.

"He's always teasing me," the Archbishop said with a laugh. "Almost the first time we met— do you remember? Maybe the first time you were a little reserved, but by the second time you were taking my cap off my head. I don't know that you wake up in the morning and say, I'm going to become a friend to the Dalai Lama. It just happens. Scientists will come afterward and analyze it. But I don't think that he woke up either—at three—and said, I think I'm going to be friends with that large-nosed black man from Africa. I think it was a communication of the heart. When we kept quiet, our hearts discovered that they were kindred spirits.

"I admire him enormously. Oh, he's going to get proud. But I always say to people, 'After being in exile over fifty years, how many would show the same serenity, the same joy, and the eagerness to spread goodness and compassion in the world?'

"I think I would be very sulky, and I think there'd be a part of me that was always sad and it would show in my face. It doesn't in his. I mean, I'm just saying he is there for us as a beacon to tell us that you can, in fact, overcome some of the most horrendous circumstances and emerge on the other side, not broken. So he is a very great gift to the world. And maybe the Chinese, without intending it, have given the world a wonderful gift."

"Thank you," the Dalai Lama said quietly, perhaps humbled by the praise.

"Pay me, pay me," the Archbishop said, reaching out his hand and rubbing his fingertips together.

"I will pay. I will pay with a few nice words."

"At our first meeting I notice this person. I always look at people, firstly, human level, so I do not consider importance of their rank or position. So, on the human level, this person very nice, humble, I think very, very, very joyful."

He was holding the Archbishop's arm. "And

then, you see, once you connect on the human level, you become close friends and that friendship never changes. But on another level, this person is a very funny person," he said, slapping the Archbishop's arm playfully. "I love that. He is always teasing me, and also I am teasing him. So we really become something quite special.

"And finally, right from the beginning, you always speak out about the truth and the justice of the Tibetan cause. As a Tibetan, I very much appreciate it.

"Whenever he is at Nobel Peace Prize Laureate meetings, they are full of joy. The atmosphere is something different. Then in recent years, because of his age and also his physical condition, you see, he could not attend. Of course, there are many other Nobel Peace Prize Laureates and many other Nobel Peace Prize Laureates are wonderful **ladies**—"

"You are a monk, remember?" the Archbishop scolded.

"But when you are not there, something missing, really. Really, really. The other Nobel Peace Prize Laureates also feel it, I think. So the relationship is something unique and something very special."

"Thank you. I paid him," the Archbishop said, pretending to stage whisper.

The Dalai Lama erupted into a belly laugh and then began pointing at the Archbishop. "His face, his face," he said, gesturing to the Archbishop's bald head. "He looks like a monk now, doesn't he?" Then the Dalai Lama drew his hand into the shape of an eye. "When I see your eyes"—then he squeezed his nose playfully— "and, of course, your nose—"

The Archbishop could not help but giggle at the mention of his much joked about nose.

Then the Dalai Lama's playful tone changed as he pointed at the Archbishop's face warmly. "This picture, special picture." Then he paused for a long moment. "I think, at time of my death . . ." The word **death** hung in the air like a prophecy. ". . . I will remember you."

I could hear everyone in the room, even the camera operators, take a deep breath, we were all so moved. The Archbishop looked down and hummed deeply, obviously humbled and touched by the Dalai Lama's words. Could there be a truer sign of love, to see another's face at the time of death?

"Thank you. Thank you," was all the Archbishop could say, all that could be said.

"So perhaps," the Dalai Lama said, "according to your religious tradition, we may meet in heaven in the presence of God. You as a good Christian practitioner will go first." The Archbishop now chuckled heartily and the room seemed to breathe again. "You may help me and bring us together." We laughed imagining the Archbishop bargaining with St. Peter at the pearly gates, trying to get special admission for the Dalai Lama.

"But from the Buddhist viewpoint," the Dalai Lama continued, "once in a life, you develop some sort of special close connection, then that sort of impact will carry life after life. That's Buddhist viewpoint. So maybe even then. But now, I'm looking forward to another occasion to see you again—somewhere that only God knows."

After some final photographs were taken, we had to rush to the airport. As the Archbishop leaned on his cane now, walking perhaps a bit slower than before, his age showing just a little more than it had earlier in the week, I could see the Dalai Lama's forehead wrinkling with concern and worry. He had said God only knew where they would meet again, and perhaps he was thinking about whether God would give them another opportunity in this life.

The two leaders had told us over the course of the week that there is no joy without sorrow, that in fact it is the pain, the suffering that allows us to experience and appreciate the joy. Indeed, the more we turn toward the suffering, our own and others, the more we can turn toward the joy. We accept them both, turning the volume of life up, or we turn our backs on life itself, becoming deaf to its music. They had also told us and demonstrated that true joy is a way of being, not a fleeting emotion. What they had cultivated in their long lives was that enduring trait of joyfulness. They had warned us that we cannot pursue joy as an end in itself, or we will miss the bus. Joy comes, rather, from daily thoughts, feelings, and actions. And they had told us repeatedly the action that gets us on the bus: bringing joy to others.

At the car, the two old, mischievous friends were joking and laughing again. The Dalai

Lama was rubbing the Archbishop's hand tenderly through the open window of the car. I could still see the signs of worry, or perhaps it was just sadness at saying goodbye. As the engine started to hum, the Dalai Lama looked at the Archbishop in the car, staying with him to the last minutes of his visit. He put the palms of his hands together in front of his face and bowed his head forward in a sign of deep respect and affection.

The motorcade to the airport began to move, and the Dalai Lama still stood, bowed slightly forward, eyes twinkling, and fingers waving goodbye brightly, as children do. As we drove away, the Archbishop looked back through the window of the SUV and gave one last smile and laugh to his improbable and invaluable friend.

The next day the rest of the film crew flew out of the airport in Dharamsala on a clear day. Forty-five seconds after their plane took off, an enormous 7.8 magnitude earthquake struck in Nepal.

The devastation was enormous and the tremors were felt all the way in Dharamsala. We thought of all the people we knew and cared for in the region and we mourned the thousands who had died. We witnessed as people from all around the world poured in to help the displaced, repair the broken, and heal the thousands who were wounded. It was hard not to think of the Dalai Lama's comment on the first day of the dialogues that the suffering of natural disasters we cannot stop, but so much of the rest of our suffering we can. Adversity, illness, and death are real and inevitable. We choose whether to add to these unavoidable facts of life with the suffering we create in our own minds and hearts, the chosen suffering. The more we make a different choice, to heal our own suffering, the more we can turn to others and help to address their suffering with the laughter-filled, tear-stained eyes of the heart. And the more we turn away from our self-regard to wipe the tears from the eyes of another, the more—incredibly—we are able to bear, to heal, and to transcend our own suffering. This was their true secret to joy.

Joy Practices

DEVELOPING MENTAL IMMUNITY

During the week, as the Dalai Lama and the Archbishop joked about who got up too early and who was praying and meditating too much, it was clear that both believed strongly that spiritual practices were the essential ground of their being, sustaining and supporting them through their lives.

These daily times of prayer and meditation kept these two masters in spiritual alignment. I thought about what the Archbishop had said about the even greater importance of these practices for those who are not spiritual teachers but who must live and die in the blur and buzz of the marketplace. During the week, we had had a chance to discuss some of the spiritual practices that help to cultivate and sustain their joy.

Here we present some simple practices that can help overcome the obstacles to joy and support the eight pillars of joy. We have book-ended this section with practices that Tibetan Buddhist monks typically do at the beginning and end of each day. The other practices can be tried on a regular basis or when needed. Like physical exercises, spiritual practices are not ends in themselves. They exist to support our mental health and mental immunity. The more we practice, the more we benefit. There is no spiritual competition. Do whatever you need to adapt them to your life for maximum benefit. (Remember the Dalai Lama adapting his morning practice to accommodate his aging knees.)

As the Dalai Lama said, he finds the science very motivating when he is trying to decide whether to wake up or hit the snooze button. Earlier we mentioned Daniel Siegel's explanation of the brain on meditation. It seems that we are literally using our attention and awareness to establish neural firing patterns that help the brain avoid the destructive reactivity that the Dalai Lama said was so toxic to our mental and physical health. Many of these practices appear to integrate and harmonize the brain so that we can respond to the inevitable challenges of life with less fragmentation and more integration, less fear and anger and more ease and joy.

In our age of instant gratification, any information can be googled in a matter of seconds, but real knowledge and wisdom take time. These practices reward and deepen through continued effort. Usually when we start meditating or praying, we can experience what the Archbishop has called "spiritual sweets," or the tingling and calming that comes from beginning to pay attention to our inner life. Like sweets, these are tasty, but the real benefits occur as we create a temporal container into which we can pour our heart and soul as we experience the joys and sorrows of life.

The nature of contemplative life is that it is very personal, and not all practices will work for all people. Find what works best for you. What is presented here are simply sample practices, including many that the Dalai Lama and

the Archbishop use. We hope these will inspire
your own practice.

MORNING INTENTION SETTING

Every conscious action begins with intention,
which is simply setting goals. Many Tibetan
monks do this each morning as a way of preparing their mind and heart for how they wish
to face the day. They also check in with their
intentions regularly, when preparing to sit in
meditation or when undertaking any important task. Another way to focus your intentions
is to read short inspirational passages that support your highest ideals. The Archbishop celebrates the Eucharist each morning, which
involves reading (and pondering) Biblical passages. He observes the liturgies of the hours
(morning, noonday, and evening prayer), for
which there are a cycle of designated readings.
He also likes to read passages from the great
mystics to guide his heart and mind.

   **1. Sit comfortably, either on a chair
      with the soles of your feet on the**

ground or cross-legged. You can also do this exercise while still lying in bed before getting up in the morning—after the alarm goes off and before the rush of the day has begun. You can rest your hands on your legs or on your belly.

2. **Close your eyes and take several long breaths through your nose.** Feel your stomach rise and fall as you breathe from your diaphragm.

3. **Now ask yourself: "What is my heart's desire? What do I wish for myself, for my loved ones, and for the world?"** Our deepest desires usually lie beyond our temporary wishes and wants. They are likely to involve living with profound human values that lead to our greatest happiness, calling us back to our place within the fabric of life. The Dalai Lama has a simple way of testing our intentions: "Is it just for me, or for others? For the benefit of the few, or for the many? For now, or for the future?" This litmus test can help guide us toward what we truly wish for.

4. Then state your intention for the day. For example: "Today may I greet everyone with the love that is in my heart." Or "Today may I be less judgmental." Or "Today may I be patient and loving with my children." It can be specific or it can be general. If you do not know your intention, you can repeat the following four lines adapted from the traditional Tibetan prayer of the Four Immeasurables, which has guided many on their journey to more compassion and greater happiness:

May all beings attain happiness.
May all beings be free from suffering.
May all beings never be separated from joy.
May all beings abide in equanimity.

OVERCOMING THE OBSTACLES TO JOY

Focus and Stress Relief—A Breathing Practice

Our breath is so important as a focus of spiritual practice in many religious traditions because it is the hinge between our self and the world. Our breath is internal, but it is also external. Breath is also both voluntary and involuntary. It is therefore an ideal doorway through which we can develop our self-cultivation. Focus, as you may remember, is so important that neuroscientist Richard Davidson found that one of the four neural circuits of well-being was dedicated to our ability to focus the mind. Simply observing **quiet time,** which the Archbishop maintains in the pre-dawn hours, afternoon, and evening, is another way to focus our mind, relieve stress, and concentrate on what matters most.

1. **Find a quiet place where you can practice consistently.** This way the

physical space—a room, a corner, a cushion—will help signal to your body that this is a time for your practice.

2. **Sit comfortably.** If you are sitting on a cushion or chair, try to lean slightly forward, away from the back of the chair so that your back will be straight. If you have chronic back pain, adjust as necessary.

3. **Close your eyes or keep them slightly open in a restful position.**

4. **Place your hands gently on your knees or in your lap.**

5. **Focus your attention on your breath.**

6. **Breathe in deeply through your nose as your belly expands. As a jug of water fills from the bottom, your lungs should also fill from the bottom.**

7. **Breathe out slowly.**

8. **On each inhalation you can think in, and on each exhalation you can think out. Alternatively, you can count each breath after each exhalation.**

9. **You can count out five to ten breaths and then repeat.** If you lose your focus

and your mind begins to wander, as minds do, just gently bring your attention back to your breath. You can start by doing this for five to ten minutes and extend the time as your practice develops.

10. **If you are feeling particularly stressed,** you can imagine each breath bringing in calming cool air and it spreading throughout your body. Then, as you release your breath, you can imagine the stress leaving your body from the neck, shoulders, back, tummy, or wherever you tend to hold on to stress.

Morning Meditation Walk or Exercise

The Archbishop takes a morning meditation walk or constitutional each morning, and he continued to do so throughout the anti-apartheid struggle, even when he experienced death threats. I had the opportunity to accompany him on one of his meditation walks when we were working together in Florida. We walked silently for half an hour when the walkway abruptly ended at a wall. I will never forget seeing him walk right up to the very end of the path, right to the wall, so that his nose was practically touching it. It was at that moment I saw the man who was willing to walk around the world to end apartheid, no shortcuts, no turning back, going to the very, very end. Walking, hiking, running, or any other exercise can be made into a meditative experience. The key is to avoid all external distractions like talking, music, or television. The goal is simply to listen to the wisdom of the spirit that often comes through the wisdom of the body.

Fear, Anger, and Sadness—An Analytic Meditation

As the Dalai Lama said, fear, anger, and sadness are natural human responses. Fear and anger are natural stress responses, and these emotions carry important information for us. Sadness, too, can tell us that we are unhappy with something in our life. These three emotions no doubt evolved to motivate us to change our situation. As the Archbishop said, to be human is to feel, and these emotions will arise at times, regardless of our spiritual mastery. Yet responding to a situation constantly with fear, anger, or sadness tends to perpetuate negative energy. It is the irrational and obsessive components of these emotions that are destructive. Meditation is a profound way to develop our ability to escape our fight-or-flight reflex and extend the pause between stimulus and response to act with intention rather than just react out of emotion.

"The word 'meditation' is quite vast," explained the Dalai Lama. "One form of meditation, for example, involves thoughtlessness. When I pull back the curtains in the morning and I see pigeons on the windowsill, I really think those pigeons are also doing something similar to this kind of meditation. They are not asleep but in a state of thoughtlessness. There is also meditation that involves maintaining focused attention. For example, for religious believers, single-pointed focus on God is a very powerful way to meditate and to quiet the mind.

"Now, in my own practice I engage mostly in analytical meditation. This is a form of mental investigation where you can see your thoughts as thoughts and learn not to be chained to them, not to identify with them. You come to recognize that your thoughts do not necessarily reflect the truth. In analytical meditation, you are constantly asking, What is reality? What is that self, or 'I,' that we hold so dear and that is the focus of so much of our concern? In analytic meditation, we contemplate on impermanence and on the transient nature of our existence.

"Some forms of meditation are just trying to create a state of thoughtlessness. This works like a painkiller, where fear and anger go away for a short moment but then come back when the meditation ends. With analytical meditation, we can get to the root cause of the fear or the anger. We can discover, for example, that ninety percent of our anger is mental projection. We can discover that the angry words were in the past and no longer exist, except in our memory. When you think about these things, the intensity of the anger reduces and you develop your mental immunity so that anger arises less.

"Many people think that meditation simply means sitting and closing your eyes," the Dalai Lama continued, closing his eyes and taking a stiff posture. "That kind of meditation even my cat can do. He sits there very calmly purring. If a rat comes by, it has nothing to worry about. We Tibetans often recite mantras so much, like **Om Mani Padme Hum**, a mantra invoking the name of the Buddha of Compassion, that we forget to really investigate the root causes of our suffering. Maybe my purring cat is actually reciting **Om Mani Padme Hum**." The Dalai Lama laughed hard at the thought of his devout Tibetan Buddhist cat. Nothing, not even one of the most sacred phrases of the Buddhist tradition, was above his analytic investigations and his sense of humor. The Dalai Lama was interested in truth wherever it might lie, and analytical meditation was one of his most effective tools for discerning it.

1. **Sit comfortably.**
2. **You can close your eyes or keep them open.** If you keep them open, keep your gaze soft and your focus inward. When the Dalai Lama meditates, his eyes remain open but with his gaze pointed slightly downward, not looking at anything specifically.

3. **Now pick a topic or experience that is troubling you, or simply watch your thoughts and feelings arise and recognize that they are temporary, without judging or identifying with them.** Some will be bright and pleasant and some will be dark and stormy, but they all pass in time. Let them float through your mind like clouds in the sky.

4. **Now ask yourself, "Is my thought true? How do I know for sure? Does it help the situation?** Is there a better way of thinking about it or approaching the situation?" Let's look at how we might analyze the three fundamental, and often challenging, negative human emotions.

- **For fear, it can help to face the fear directly.** You can think of the worst thing that could happen if your fear comes true. Now, could you or your loved one survive what might happen? Could it actually be beneficial for you or your loved ones? What

could you or they learn if this were
to happen? How might this allow
you or them to grow and deepen as
a person? For example, perhaps you
are worried about your child who
is struggling in school and you are
afraid that some bad outcome will
come to pass. Ask yourself, "Is it true
that this outcome will definitely happen? How do I know for sure? Does
my worry help the situation? Is there
a better way of thinking about it or
approaching the situation? What
might my child learn from this experience? How might they grow and
develop as a person?" When we turn
and embrace what we fear, it loses its
power to frighten us. We no longer
need to fight it, but can instead work
with it.

- **For anger, you can ask yourself
  what is its use?** It may help to think
  of the Dalai Lama's story of his driver,
  who was so angry about banging his
  head into the fender of the car that
  he banged his head into the fender

of the car. Anger often involves some disappointment or frustrated expectation. Ask yourself, "What was my expectation? Can I release it and accept what is or how others are rather than how I think they should be? Can I also acknowledge my part in the conflict? Can I see my part in contributing to the situation I am angry about? If I am angry about what has been said, can I see that these are just words that no longer exist, that, like all things, they are impermanent? Will my anger benefit anyone, including me?" You could also reflect on how, if not contained, anger can lead to destructive action—from saying hurtful things to outright violence—that we later regret. Contemplate how anger can destroy relationships, alienate others, and rob you of your peace of mind.

- **For sadness, we can reach out for comfort or count our blessings.** As we saw, sadness is an emotion that expresses our need for one another, and our sorrows are halved when shared. We can also recognize that while sadness may last longer than other emotions, it, too, will pass. All life, the sadness and sorrow included, is impermanent and will end. There are always going to be highs and lows in any life, in any year, in any day. So much of our mood comes from what we focus on. We can choose to focus on what is going well for us and for the people in our life. As the Archbishop said, we can count our blessings. By putting our attention on the things we are grateful for, we can shift how much time we spend in sadness and how quickly we return to joy. The Dalai Lama's ability to focus on what has been enriching about life in exile rather than all that has been lost has allowed him to go beyond sadness, grief, and even despair.

Frustration and Anger—A Prayer

During the days of apartheid, the Archbishop would pray daily for the government officials who were maintaining the oppressive system. He prayed for them to transform their hearts and to transform the racist system that they created, but he also prayed sincerely for their well-being. It helped him to love them rather than hate them, and ultimately made it possible to work with them to help transition the country to democracy.

1. **Close your eyes and turn your attention inward.**
2. **Think of the person who is upsetting you and say a prayer for them.** Pray for their joy and happiness. Sincerely wish them well. See them as a child of God deserving of God's love, or as another human being who shares your desire to be happy and avoid suffering.
3. **Try to do this each day for two weeks.** See how your relationship is transformed.

Loneliness—A Common Humanity Practice

The Dalai Lama speaks constantly of our common humanity at the "first level." The things that divide us (our ethnicity, our race, our nationality, even our gender) are much less significant than the things that unite us: our common humanity, our human emotions, and our fundamental desire to be happy and avoid suffering. Because we each have a human body, a human brain, and a human heart, we each have the same human longings, and, as the Archbishop often points out, the same human frailties and vulnerabilities. The common humanity practice reminds us that despite appearances and our fears of rejection, we are really deeply connected even when we do not see it.

The Archbishop was born just a short distance from the Cradle of Humankind, the place where our species is supposed to have originated. In a mere thousand generations, we have spread all across the world. As the Archbishop has said, "We are all cousins, really, perhaps just a few thousand times removed."

1. **Think of someone you love—a child, parent, close friend, or even a cherished pet.** Bring their image into your mind and allow yourself to feel the love that you have for them. Notice the sense of warmth and openheartedness that comes from feeling your love for them.

2. **Imagine their desire to be happy and to avoid suffering.** Reflect on how they live their life to achieve these aspirations.

3. **Think of someone you know but do not know well.** You could think of a colleague at your job, someone in your class at school, or someone who works at one of the stores where you shop. Allow yourself to recognize how your feelings for this person are different from the feelings you have for the person you just had in mind. We often do not feel empathy or connection for those who we consider strangers. Perhaps you feel indifference, perhaps a sense of separation, or perhaps even judgment. Now try to imagine being this person. Imagine their life, their hopes, their dreams,

their fears, their disappointments, and
their suffering. Recognize that, just
like you, they wish to achieve happiness and to avoid even the slightest
suffering. Let your mind dwell in this
realization and understand that you do
not need an introduction because you
already share the greatest bond—your
humanity. They may be just as lonely
as you, and your reaching out to them
might be a gift to them.

4. **Take this awareness into the world.**
Start living from this newfound connection by opening your heart to those
around you. You can start by smiling or
acknowledging the other person by looking at them warmly and nodding your
head. Different cultures have different
ways of acknowledging others, but find
what is appropriate in your situation
and begin greeting your human family. Do not get discouraged if some are
suffering from their own loneliness and
isolation and do not acknowledge you.
You can have empathy from your own
feelings of loneliness. Greet the world

with greater trust, kindness, and compassion, and the world will greet you
with greater trust, kindness, and compassion. When you smile at the world,
the world does tend to smile back.

Envy—A <u>Mudita</u> Practice

When we are envious, we have a nagging sense
of dissatisfaction that effaces joy, as we are able to
see only what we do not have and not what we do
have. Envy is a poison tinged with guilt and self-
criticism. It kills our happiness and empties the
world of its riches and wonders. As with the common humanity practice above, Buddhism has a
practice that breaks down the bonds of isolation
and jealousy that keep us separated: It is called
mudita, the practice of rejoicing in others'
good fortune. Just as a parent can rejoice in
the good fortune of their child, we can rejoice
in the good fortune of others when we expand
our identity to include them and when we open our
heart to experience their joy as our own.

**1. Imagine the person who has some-
thing that you envy.**

2. **Recognize your shared humanity.** You can refer to the previous practice or simply focus on the hopes, dreams, fears, disappointments, and suffering of the person you envy. Recognize that, just like you, the person you envy wishes to achieve happiness and to avoid even the slightest suffering.

3. **Imagine how happy what they have must make them.** Think about what it must mean to them and to their family that they have what you envy. The car, the house, or the position may be a source of great satisfaction. Try to expand your heart to include them and their good fortune. Rejoice in their good fortune. Rejoice in the fact that they do not need your help because they have helped themselves.

Suffering, Adversity, and Illness— A Lojong Practice

A fundamental premise of Tibetan mind training, or **lojong,** is to take whatever suffering and adversity you experience into your spiritual practice and use it to help you grow and develop. Let's say you have a difficult boss. You can see this as a challenge to become more responsible, tougher, and more resilient. If you are in a car accident and your car was totaled, rather than focusing on the loss of your car, you can be grateful that you were not harmed. If you experience a financial crisis, or even bankruptcy, you can see the experience as an opportunity to empathize with others who are going through similar hardship and to expand your capacity for empathy and compassion. As the Archbishop said, there are some aspects of empathy and compassion that can only be discovered through suffering.

1. **Think of where you are experiencing suffering or adversity.**
2. **Think of others who are experiencing the same situation.** Can you think of others who might be in a similar situation or are perhaps even worse off? Can you feel empathy and compassion for them?
3. **How might this situation be useful to you?** What might be gained from

this experience? What lessons can be learned? How might this circumstance help you grow and mature as a person?

4. **Try to feel grateful for the opportunity that this suffering and adversity has given you.**

5. **Try saying the sentence: "May my suffering spare others from a similar suffering."** How can you use your suffering to alleviate the suffering of others? Can your actions help to prevent others from experiencing similar suffering, or contribute to reducing the suffering of others?

Suffering, Adversity, and Illness of Others—A <u>Tonglen</u> Practice

The famous **tonglen** practice allows us to be present and helpful to others when they are suffering, facing adversity, or confronting illness. This practice is the culmination of the Compassion Cultivation Training and is based on a widespread and powerful Buddhist practice. In this practice, we take suffering from others and offer our love, our courage, our strength, and our joy. In **A Fearless Heart,** Jinpa tells a powerful story of **tonglen**: One person who took the Compassion Cultivation Training was a hospital chaplain who recounted how the practice had helped her when she was called to the emergency room because of a drowning accident involving a child.

"I felt myself cringe inwardly because I knew the magnitude of this kind of situation—the hardest call for all concerned is when it involves a child. I prayed for strength as I hurried toward the ER. The RN told me there were actually two children, siblings, and doctors were performing CPR but it didn't look good at all. I felt my whole body tighten as I entered the room to see the young mother bent over and sobbing from the depths of her being. . . . I felt overwhelmed, as if I was going to collapse under the weight of the suffering and my task. What could I offer? Then I remembered the "giving and receiving" technique of **tonglen**. . . . So I breathed in the suffering as if it were a dark cloud and breathed out golden light from my heart into the room and to everyone I encountered. A whole new level of integration happened. I could open to the experience of suffering and found something necessary and precious to sustain me. The suffering became fluid with each breath and washed over me so that I began to become unstuck. I began to feel the liberation of not being trapped in the experience of suffering but the freedom that happened as a result of actively engaging in it."

Tonglen can also be used to reduce our own suffering by freeing us from our own excessive self-concern and focusing our attention on others. Jinpa tells another story, about Tibetan musician Nawang Khechog, who suffered a horrible car accident and had to have multiple lifesaving surgeries. It was **tonglen** practice that had sustained him during the weeks of pain and of not knowing whether he would live. He would spend hours in bed thinking of others who were experiencing physical and emotional pain. He would breathe in their suffering and breathe out his compassion and concern for their recovery. Khechog recovered completely and was able to return to playing music.

Tonglen can allow us to become oases of peace and healing. The Dalai Lama used this practice to transform not only the suffering of the Tibetan protesters who were being injured during the 2008 demonstrations in Tibet but also the anger and hatred of the Chinese soldiers who were cracking down on the protesters. As the Dalai Lama explained, whether or not it actually helped those on the ground, it transformed his relationship to the suffering and allowed him to respond more effectively.

1. **Begin by settling your mind with several long breaths through your nose.**
2. **Think of someone who is suffering.** You can choose a loved one, a friend, or even a whole group of people, such as refugees.
3. **Reflect on the fact that, just like you, they wish to overcome suffering and to be joyful.** Try to feel a sense of concern for the well-being of the person or group you are focusing on. Feel deep within your heart the desire for them to be free of suffering.
4. **Taking their suffering.** As you inhale, imagine the pain being drawn from their body and dissolving when it encounters the warmth and bright light

of your compassionate heart. You can see their pain as dark clouds that are dissolving as they encounter the bright light of your heart. If the idea of taking in others' suffering is concerning or unsettling, you can imagine their suffering dissolving into a bright orb of light in front of you that is radiating out from your compassionate heart.

5. **Give out your joy.** As you exhale, imagine that you are sending the person rays of light filled with your love and compassion, your courage and your confidence, your strength and your joy.

6. **Repeat this practice of taking the suffering and transforming it by giving your joy.** If you have done this practice for an individual or loved one, you can extend the practice to others who are suffering all around the world. If you are taking the suffering of someone who is being harmed by others, you can take the cruelty and hatred that is causing the harm and give your love and kindness. If you feel able, you can practice taking on the suffer-

ing of all beings and giving them your compassion and your joy. Stay quiet as your love and joy radiate out from your heart.

Silent Retreat

The Archbishop once or twice a year goes on a seven- to ten-day silent retreat. He will work with a spiritual director who will design a retreat to meet his needs. For the Archbishop, the silent retreat is an undisturbed time for intensive prayer, reflection, self-examination, and deep rest. Retreat is also an important feature of the Dalai Lama's life. In addition to several shorter retreats at his residence, he also spends a month in retreat during the monsoon summer, mostly in Ladakh. In the whirling blur of our lives, these times of retreat are even more important than ever. You don't need to be a world leader to need one.

Death Meditation

All spiritual traditions remind us that death is an unavoidable part of our life, and contemplating our own mortality can help bring a sense of urgency, a sense of perspective, and a sense of gratitude. St. Benedict famously said, "Keep death before your eyes." Like all fears, the fear of death grows in the shadows. Death is the ultimate reminder of impermanence and the ephemerality of all life. It can help us remember that there are no days to waste and that every moment matters. This death meditation is much less involved than the one that the Dalai Lama described, but it shares the same goal: using the reminder of death to help us be truly alive.

1. **Reflect on the words: "Anything that has a birth has a death, and I am no exception."**
2. **Consider the following: "There are many conditions that can lead to death.** Death can never be stopped. Nothing can prevent the inevitable."
3. **Now imagine that you are on your deathbed.** Ask yourself the following questions: "Have I loved others? Have I brought joy and compassion to others? Has my life mattered to others?"

4. **Imagine your funeral.** Imagine your loved ones making preparations for your funeral and referring to you as "the late so-and-so."
5. **Reflect on what people would say about you.** Are you happy with what they might say? What might you need to change now to change what will be said then?
6. **Conclude with the resolve "I shall always live my life with purpose.** Time never remains still, and it's up to me to use my time in the most meaningful way. I shall live in harmony with my deeper aspirations so that when my final day arrives I will be able to leave with ease and without remorse."

CULTIVATING THE EIGHT PILLARS OF JOY

Perspective—A Self-Distancing Practice

Many of the practices already offered are useful for cultivating perspective. Meditative practices work to shift our perspective from our reactive emotional brain to our more reflective, more evolved higher-brain centers. Getting a "wider perspective," as the Dalai Lama calls it, is possible by stepping back from our situation to see the bigger picture. Scientists have called this practice "self-distancing," and it allows us to think more clearly about our problems, as well as to reduce our stress response and our negative emotions. This broader perspective also allows us to get beyond our own limited and immediate self-interest and into a perspective that takes into account the interests of others. As the Archbishop says, it allows us to see what serves all of God's children when we are taking this "God's-eye" perspective. This ability to go beyond our own self-interest is essential for any good leader, whether of a nation, an organization, or a family.

1. **Think about a problem or situation that you are facing.**
2. **Describe your problem as if it were happening to someone else**—using your name rather than the words **I**, **me**, or **mine**.

3. **Imagine this problem from the perspective of a week, a year, or even a decade from now.** Will this issue or event still have an impact on you? Will you even remember it? What will you have learned from the experience?

4. **Witness your life from a God's-eye, or universal, perspective.** See your fears and your frustrations from this point of view. Now see all of the other people who are involved as having equal value and being worthy of love and respect. Then ask what will serve the whole.

Humility—A <u>Lojong</u> Practice

Humility helps us to remember our common bond with others. It helps us to avoid isolation, judgment, and indifference. It helps us remember that we are all equally beloved children of God, as the Archbishop would say, and to remember that we are just one of the seven billion people on the planet. It helps us remember that we are all in it together.

1. **Reflect on all the people who are responsible for your life.** Think of your parents, who gave you life, your teachers who taught you, the people who grew your food and who made your clothes, the countless others who are responsible for your having the life that you have each and every day. Now think of all those who discovered and created all of the things we take for granted, the housing, the crops, and the medicines that keep you alive. Think of all the ancestors who had to live, and survive, so that you could be born, who braved enormous hardship so that you could have the life that you do. Now think of the family and friends who give your life meaning and purpose.

2. **Allow your heart to open and experience love and appreciation for all of these people.** Experience the enormous joy and appreciation that comes from being in touch with all that has been given to you, in realizing how

dependent we are on others, how weak
in our separateness and yet how strong
in our togetherness.

Laughing at Ourselves to Develop Humor

Humor seems like something that is spontaneous and natural and cannot be cultivated,
but the ability to laugh at ourselves and to see
the rich ironies and funny realities in our lives
is actually, like perspective, something that we
can learn with practice over time.

1. **Think of one of your limitations,
   human faults, or foibles.** Think of
   something about yourself that is actually quite funny when you can have
   some perspective. The Dalai Lama can
   laugh at his limited English. The Archbishop can laugh at his big nose. What
   can you laugh at about yourself? When
   you can laugh at yourself, you will let
   others feel closer to you and inspire
   them to accept their own limitations,
   faults, and foibles.

2. **Laugh at yourself.** The next time you are in a situation where you act in a funny way, or say something in a funny way, or are just less than perfect, chuckle at yourself and make a joke of it. Humor is one of the best ways to end conflict, especially when you are able to make fun of yourself or admit that you are overreacting or being silly.

3. **Laugh at life.** The next time you are delayed or something does not go your way, try being amused by the situation rather than getting angry or outraged. You will notice how your amusement puts others at ease and can often smooth the situation. Similarly, when you encounter certain ironies in your day-to-day life, try to see the humor.

Acceptance—A Meditation

Any possibility of joy requires an acceptance of reality. As the Archbishop and the Dalai Lama both explained, this is the only place from which one can start to work for change, personal or global. Meditation is a practice that allows us to accept our life moment by moment without judgment or the expectation for life to be other than what it is.

1. **Sit comfortably, either on a chair with your feet on the ground, or cross-legged.** You can rest your hands on your legs or in your lap.
2. **Close your eyes and take several long breaths through your nose.** Feel your stomach rise and fall as you breathe into your belly.
3. **Pay attention to what you hear around you.** Notice how the world is alive with sound. As thoughts about these noises arise—judgments, assessments, irritations—let these observations and evaluations drift away.
4. **Release your focus on your breath and, while staying in the present moment, notice as any thoughts or feelings arise.** Perhaps you will notice some discomfort in your body or have a feeling arise, or you may have a thought about what you need to accomplish or remember to do today.

5. **As the thoughts come up, let them float away without judging them or getting caught up in them.** Begin to start seeing thoughts as thoughts without identifying with them. Just observe each moment without judgment.

6. **Think of a situation that you are having a hard time accepting.** Perhaps it is your difficulty finding a job or a life partner, or it may be a friend's illness or a collective reality such as war.

7. **Remind yourself that this is the nature of reality.** These painful realities do happen to us, to those we love, and in our world.

8. **Acknowledge the fact that you cannot know all the factors that have led to this event.**

9. **Accept that what has happened has already happened.** There is nothing you can do to change the past.

10. **Remind yourself: "In order to make the most positive contribution to this situation, I must accept the reality of its existence."**

11. **You can also choose to recite or**

reflect on one of the following two passages, one from the Buddhist tradition, the other from the Christian tradition:

If something can be done about it,
what need is there for dejection?
And if nothing can be done about it,
what use is there for being dejected?
—Shantideva,
The Way of the Bodhisattva

God, give us the grace to accept with
   serenity
the things that cannot be changed,
courage to change the things
which should be changed,
and the wisdom to distinguish
the one from the other.
—Reinhold Niebuhr,
The Serenity Prayer

The Fourfold Path of Forgiveness

The Archbishop became the world's leading spokesperson on forgiveness when he was asked to chair the Truth and Reconciliation Commission in South Africa by then president Nelson Mandela. Over the many decades since that pioneering effort to use truth, forgiveness, and reconciliation to move beyond violent conflict, the Archbishop has been asked, how exactly do we forgive? While most spiritual leaders, including the Archbishop and the Dalai Lama, are adamant about the importance of forgiveness, very few people talk about the actual process of forgiveness. In **The Book of Forgiving,** the Archbishop and his daughter Mpho Tutu presented a universal fourfold path to forgiveness. This step-by-step process has been made available to the world in the Global Forgiveness Challenge (forgivenesschallenge. com), and has now been used by people from over 170 countries. Forgiveness can be a rather involved process, and those two resources may be helpful to those who are working to forgive major sources of pain and trauma. The resources also address how we can ask for forgiveness and learn to forgive ourselves. The following are the basic steps of the fourfold path, combined with some of the latest neuroscience research.

1. **Telling your story.** All forgiveness must begin by facing the truth. You can write down in a journal or tell a trusted friend what happened. Telling your story also allows you to integrate the memories in your consciousness and defuse some of your emotional reactivity. To help heal the memories and avoid retraumatizing yourself, it is helpful to imagine that you are watching the event happen in a movie. This way you may reduce the chances of triggering the brain's neural stress response. One scientific protocol by Ethan Kross and his colleagues suggests recalling your experience this way: **Close your eyes. Go back to the time and place of the emotional experience and see the scene in your mind's eye. Now take a few steps back. Move away from the situation to a point where you can watch the event unfold from a distance and see yourself in the event, the distant you. Watch the experience unfold as if it were happening to the distant**

you all over again. Observe your distant self.

2. **Naming the hurt.** The facts are the facts, but these experiences caused strong emotions and pain, which are important to name. **As you watch the situation unfold around your distant self, try to understand his or her feelings. Why did he or she have those feelings? What were the causes and reasons for the feelings? If the hurt is fresh, ask yourself, "Will this situation affect me in ten years?" If the hurt is old, ask yourself whether you want to continue to carry this pain or whether you want to free yourself from this pain and suffering.**

3. **Granting forgiveness.** The ability to forgive comes from the recognition of our shared humanity and the acknowledgment that, inevitably, because we are human we hurt and are hurt by one another. Can you accept the humanity of the person who hurt you and the fact that they likely hurt you out of their

own suffering? If you can accept your shared humanity, then you can release your presumed right to revenge and can move toward healing rather than retaliation. We also recognize that, especially between intimates, there can be multiple hurts, and we often need to forgive and ask for forgiveness at the same time, accepting our part in the human drama.

4. **Renewing or releasing the relationship.** Once you have forgiven someone, you must make the important decision of whether you want to renew the relationship or release it. If the trauma is significant, there is no going back to the relationship that you had before, but there is the opportunity for a new relationship. When we renew relationships, we can benefit from healing our family or community. When we release the relationship, we can move on, especially if we can truly wish the best for the person who has harmed us, and recognize that they, like us, simply want to avoid suffering and be happy in their life.

Journaling for Gratitude

Gratitude, as we have seen, is an extremely important part of joy because it allows us to savor life and to recognize that most of our good fortune in life comes from others. The gratitude practice is very simple. To expand it you can go back to the humility practice, which also involves gratitude and appreciation for all those who have made it possible for you to be you. The gratitude practice below is meant to be one you can do daily, to help you appreciate large and small blessings. This practice can also be done at the end of the day, when reflecting on whether you fulfilled the intention you set in the morning. You can also do this practice together with a spouse or friend.

1. **Close your eyes and recall three things from your day for which you are grateful.** They can be anything from the kindness and generosity of a friend to the bounty of a meal to the warmth of the sun to the beauty of a night sky. Try to be as specific as you can be in recalling what you are grateful for.

2. Write these three things down in a journal. While you can do this exercise in your head, keeping a list of what you are grateful for has been shown to have many physical and emotional benefits over time. Each time you journal, try to write down three different things. Variation is the key to effective gratitude journaling.

Compassion Meditation

There is probably no word that the Dalai Lama and the Archbishop use more when describing the qualities worth cultivating than **compassion**. In short, the Dalai Lama feels that educating our children to have more compassion is the single most important thing we can do to transform our world, but we do not need to wait for the next generation to grow up before we can start to experience the benefits of compassion. Indeed, cultivating compassion for even ten minutes a day, the Dalai Lama said, can lead to twenty-four hours of joy. Expanding our circle of concern is essential for both our well-being as well as that of our world. The

following practice is adapted from the Compassion Cultivation Training program. A more
extensive series of compassion practices can be
found in Jinpa's **A Fearless Heart**.

1. **Find a comfortable sitting position.**
2. **Take several long breaths through
   your nose and follow this with a
   minute or two of breath-awareness
   meditation.**
3. **Think of someone you love very much,
   a relative or friend or even a pet.** Try
   to either see their face in your mind's eye
   or feel their presence, and notice how
   your heart feels when you think of them.
4. **Feel whatever arises.** If you feel
   warmth, tenderness, or affection, stay
   with these feelings. If not, just stay with
   the thought of your loved one.
5. **Silently say the following lines:**
   • **May you be free from suffering.**
   • **May you be healthy.**
   • **May you be happy.**
   • **May you find peace and joy.**
6. **Breathe in, and as you breathe out
   imagine a warm light coming from**

the center of your heart, carrying your love to your loved one, and bringing them peace and joy.

7. **Rejoice in the thought of your loved one's happiness for a minute or more.**

8. **Remember when this person was having a difficult time.**

9. **Notice what it feels like to experience their pain.** Does your heart ache? Do you have a feeling of unease in your stomach? Or a desire to help? Simply notice the feelings and stay with them.

10. **Silently offer the following phrases:**
    • **May you be free from suffering.**
    • **May you be healthy.**
    • **May you be happy.**
    • **May you find peace and joy.**

11. **Imagine that a warm light emerges from the center of your heart and touches the person you have in mind, easing their suffering.** Finish with the heartfelt wish that they be free of suffering.

12. **Think of a time when you experienced great difficulty and suffering—when**

you were a child, or perhaps even now.

13. Place your hand on your heart and notice feelings of warmth, tenderness, and caring toward yourself.

14. Reflect on the fact that just like all people, you want to be happy and free of suffering.

15. Silently offer the following phrases:
   • May I be free from suffering.
   • May I be healthy.
   • May I be happy.
   • May I find peace and joy.

16. Imagine someone you neither like nor dislike, someone you might see frequently at work or the store or the gym but do not have strong positive or negative feelings toward.

17. Reflect on the fact that just like all people, this person wants to be happy and free of suffering.

18. Imagine this person being faced with suffering—in conflict with a loved one or experiencing despair or grief. Allow your heart to feel warmth,

tenderness, and caring for this person and an urge to help them.

19. **Now silently offer the following phrases:**
    - **May you be free from suffering.**
    - **May you be healthy.**
    - **May you be happy.**
    - **May you find peace and joy.**

20. **Reflect on the fact that everyone on the planet has the fundamental desire to be happy and to be free of suffering.**

21. **Fill your heart with the desire that all be free of suffering, perhaps even someone with whom you have a difficult relationship, and silently repeat these phrases:**
    - **May all beings be free from suffering.**
    - **May all beings be healthy.**
    - **May all beings be happy.**
    - **May all beings find peace and joy.**

22. **Allow your feelings of compassion and concern to fill your heart, and feel the warmth, tenderness, and caring.** Radiate this feeling of compassion out to the world.

Compassion—A Prayer

The Archbishop often has a long prayer list for those who are in need. This happens during designated liturgies and in times of personal prayer. This ability to open our mind and our heart to others who are suffering, whether we know them by name or from only the news, helps us to reorient our heart to compassion from the inevitable self-preoccupations of our day. You can ask God to help them, or simply ask that they be given what they need. You can ask God to bless them, or send them your own blessings that they will be made whole and may be happy.

Compassion—A Fast

The Archbishop fasts on a weekly basis. Fasting not only helps us develop discipline and self-control but also to foster compassion, as when we fast, we experience some of the hunger that others do not choose but are forced to endure. Letting go of our focus on food, which is a preoccupation for so many, can free more time to spend on thought and prayer. As the

Archbishop got older, his doctors encouraged him to drink during his fasts, so he began a practice of having "hot chocolate fasts." You can choose to fast in a way that makes sense for your body, mind, and heart.

Generosity Practices

Compassion, as we have discussed, is necessary but not sufficient. It is the impulse to help others, but the action that follows from that desire is generosity. Generosity practices are so important that they are formalized and even mandated in many of the world's religions. Here we have presented three forms of giving that are prescribed in Buddhism, which involve material giving, giving freedom from fear, and spiritual giving. Many Christians tithe their income, giving one-tenth of what they earn, and others expand this to giving one-tenth of time, talent, and treasure. It is in this regular concern for others that we experience the most joy.

1. **Material giving.** There is no substitute for helping to lessen the inequality

and injustice that are such enduring features of our world. Whether you tithe or give **dana**, this is really the beginning of weekly and even daily practice of thinking about how you can give to others.

2. **Giving freedom from fear.** This can involve giving protection, counsel, or solace. This is how we can give our time and attention to others. Who needs your presence today? Do your children, your spouse, your parents, your colleagues, your friends, or even the stranger on the street need your compassion and your caring? To whom can you reach out to support?

3. **Spiritual giving.** You don't have to be a holy man or a spiritual teacher to give in this way. Spiritual giving can involve giving wisdom and teachings to those who may need them, but it can also involve helping others to be more joyful through the generosity of your own spirit. Seek to be an oasis of caring and concern as you live your life. Simply smiling at others as you walk down the

street can make an enormous difference in the quality of human interaction in your community. And it is this interaction that is most responsible for the quality of human life on our increasingly crowded and lonely planet, our affluent and still impoverished world.

Joy Meditation—The Eight Pillars

This is a meditation that allows you to review the eight pillars and to use them when you encounter a problem, confront pain, or face suffering, whether these are major life challenges or daily dissatisfaction (or **dukkha**). This meditation is meant to smooth the ride on the bumpy road of life. It builds on the earlier meditations but can be used independently. The eight pillars are the practices that lead to greater inner peace and greater joy.

1. **Sit comfortably.** You can sit in a chair with your feet on the floor or cross-legged. Place your hands comfortably on your legs or in your lap.
2. **Take several long breaths through**

your nose. Let your body begin to relax. Reflect on each of the pillars, and notice as your body relaxes even more and your heart feels lighter.

3. **Let your problem come to mind.** Reflect on the situation, person, or challenge that is causing you pain or suffering.

4. **Perspective.** See yourself and your problem from a wider perspective. Try to step back from yourself and your problem. See yourself and your struggle as if you were watching a movie about your life. Now think about this problem from the future, from a year or a decade from now. Recognize that your problem will pass. See how your problem shrinks as you see it in the wider context of your life.

5. **Humility.** Now see yourself as one of the seven billion people and your problem as part of the pain and suffering that so many human beings experience. You can see your problem as part of the unfolding and interdependent drama of life on our planet and

even see yourself from space, or from a God's-eye perspective. See how deeply connected we are with one another. You are part of the flowering of the universe in your particular place and time. Your connection to others makes you much stronger and more capable of solving your problem. Let yourself feel love and appreciation for all of those who have contributed to who you are and who support you in your life.

6. **Humor.** Smile and see if you can chuckle at your problem, at your shortcomings, at your frailties. Try to find the humor in the situation and in your struggle. Even if it is a very grave or serious situation, there is often some humor that can be found. The human drama is often a comedy, and laughter is the saving grace. This ability to laugh allows us to accept life as it is, broken and imperfect, even as we aspire for a better life and a better world.

7. **Acceptance.** Accept that you are struggling and accept that you have human

limitations. Remind yourself that these painful realities do happen to us, to those we love, and in our world. Acknowledge that you cannot know all the factors that have led to this event. Accept that what has happened has already happened and that there is nothing you can do to change the past. Now remind yourself: "In order to make the most positive contribution to this situation, I must accept the reality of its existence."

8. **Forgiveness.** Place your hand on your heart and forgive yourself for any part you have played in creating this problem or this situation. Recognize that you are only human and that you will inevitably fall short of your aspirations. You will hurt and be hurt by others. See the shared humanity of any others who are involved and forgive them for their part and for their human limitations.

9. **Gratitude.** Think of three or more people or things that you are grateful for in this problem or your life right now. Can you find ways in which your

problem is actually contributing to
your life and growth? Are there people
or things that are supporting you to
face this challenge?

10. **Compassion.** Put your hand on your
heart or place the palms of your hands
together at your heart. Have compassion for yourself and for how you are
struggling. Remember it takes time to
grow and learn. You are not meant to
be perfect. Suffering is inevitable. It
is part of the fabric of life. There are
going to be frustrations in any life. The
goal is to use them as something positive. Feel the light of loving-kindness
shining from your heart throughout
your body. Now send that compassion
to your loved ones, to anyone you are
struggling with, and out to all who are
in need of love and compassion.

11. **Generosity.** Feel the deep generosity
that is in your heart. Imagine yourself
radiating this generosity of the spirit to
all around you. How can you give your
gifts? How can you transform your

problem into an opportunity to give to others? When we give joy to others, we experience true joy ourselves.

REJOICING IN YOUR DAY

How we close the day and go to sleep is an important part of our practice. Both Buddhist and Christian monks, like people in many traditions, have a practice of reflecting on the day. St. Ignatius Loyola called it the Daily Examen. Buddhist monks call it Making a Dedication. The practice has different aspects, but all involve reflecting on the events of the day as a way of noticing whether one has fulfilled one's intention, experiencing gratitude for one's blessings, and turning toward the next day on the journey of life. The following is a shared practice reflecting the major features of the two traditions. If you have a religious faith, you can adapt this into a prayer practice in which you are in conversation with the divine. If you do not, you can focus on the highest and best part of yourself.

1. **Reflect on the day.** Before going to bed or while lying in bed, take a few minutes to reflect on your day. Consider important experiences, conversations, emotions, and thoughts, although it is important not to focus too much on what you did or did not do. The point is simply to note the major features of your day and to consider whether your day was in alignment with the intention you set in the morning.

2. **Pay attention to your emotions and accept your experience.** Reflect on the emotions that came up during the day. If negative thoughts or feelings arise, just be present with them. Do not try to push away the negative or grasp after the positive. Just acknowledge what happened. If you are disappointed with some aspect of how you acted, put your hand on your heart and say, "I accept myself as I am, flawed and human like everyone else." Notice where you have fallen short of your intention, because that is part of what will allow you to

grow and learn. If something painful happened in your day, you can gently acknowledge it by saying, "That was painful. I am not alone. We all suffer at times."

3. **Feel gratitude.** The most important quality to have toward your day is gratitude for what you have experienced, even for what was hard and what allowed you to learn and grow. If you are keeping a journal of what you are grateful for, you may wish to write these down now.

4. **Rejoice in your day.** Pick something you did during the day that you feel good about—helping someone, keeping your cool during a conflict. If you can't think of anything, you can rejoice in the fact that you are doing this practice. Now dedicate the merit of your day and let it be a blessing to all.

5. **Look to tomorrow.** You can finish by turning your attention to the next day and setting your intention for how you wish to face the challenges that may come. Trust that you will be able to

handle whatever the next day may hold and release your concerns for the night as you go to sleep.

RELATIONSHIP AND COMMUNITY— THE GREATEST JOY

Almost all of the above practices assume a degree of solitude, but we would be missing the main message of the Dalai Lama's and the Archbishop's teachings if we did not emphasize that the source of true joy, as evidenced all week long and in their lives, is in our relationships with other people. Both men are embedded in deep and profound spiritual communities that they have nurtured and been nurtured by. Seek out your own communities of love and practice and bring the teachings of joy to them in whatever way is meaningful to you and your community. This may be your existing religious community or it may be a community you help to create, even if that community is simply another friend, a relative, or a group with whom you can read and reflect on this book and others. If you invite others to do these joy practices, you will experience far greater joy than just doing them by yourself. Relationship is the true proving ground for spirituality. Ultimately, joy is not something to learn, it is something to live. And our greatest joy is lived in deep, loving, and generous relationships with others.

For more information about this book and for video footage from the week in Dharamsala, please visit bookofjoy.org.

ACKNOWLEDGMENTS

We would like to begin by thanking former chair of the Dalai Lama Foundation James Doty, MD, who first suggested the idea of a joint book at Leah Tutu's eightieth birthday party. It was immediately apparent what the topic would be: joy. The book itself and our time together in Dharamsala has indeed been a true joy, and we want to thank all who have made it possible.

We give thanks for our extraordinary editors and publishers, who are taking joy out to the world and who work so tirelessly to publish books that will make our world the kind of place that we all know it can be: Mauro Palermo, Vanda Ohnisková, Tiiu Kraut, Pernille Follmann Ballebye, Henrikki Timgren, Patrice Hoffman, Florent Massot, Ulrich Genzler, Jakob Mallmann, Adam Halmos, Artem Stepanov, Paolo Zaninoni, Talia Markus, Julia Kwon, Heleen Buth, Halfdan Freihow, Knut Ola Ulvestad, Damian Warszawski, Anastasia Gameza, Marija Petrovic, Martin Vydra, Laura Alvarez, Carlos Martinez, Claes Eriksson, Yunyi Wu, Yingyi Yeh, Alex Hsu, Jocasta Hamilton, Susan Sandon, Megan Newman, Brianna Flaherty, Andrea Ho, Justin Thrift, and Caroline Sutton. We would especially like to thank Caroline, who worked on many drafts of the manuscript to make sure that this book truly conveyed not only our words but also our hearts.

We also want to thank our devoted and talented foreign rights agents, who have worked so hard to make sure our book found its way to the right publishers: Chandler Crawford, Jo Grossman, Mary Clemmey, Peter Fritz, Erica Berla, Zoe Hsu, Gray Tan, Trine Licht, Kristin Olson, Maribel Luque, Maru de Montserrat, Jennifer Hoge, Ludmilla Sushkova a Sushkova, Vladimir Chernyshov, Sue Yang, Jackie Yang, Efrat Lev, Deborah Harris, Eliane Benisti, Filip Wojciechowski, Marcin Biegaj, and our much missed and still cherished Lynn Franklin. We would especially like to thank our gifted translators.

We'd also like to thank Tenzin Taklha, Chhime Rigzing, Kaydor Aukatsang, and Ken Norwick at the Office of His Holiness the Dalai Lama and the Dalai Lama Trust for their help in creating this project and in arranging everything so skillfully for our time in Dharamsala. Their extraordinary sense of responsibility and their efforts on our behalf were essential to the success of this project.

We would also like to thank Tsewang Yeshi, Ngodup Wangdu Lingpa, and their colleagues at the Tibetan Children's Villages for hosting the eightieth birthday celebration and for all they do on behalf of so many children who are in need of love as well as learning.

We would like to thank the film crew and support team that made our dialogue in Dharamsala possible and recorded it so we could share it with others: Tenzin Choejor, Chemey Tenzin, Tenzin Phuntsok, Lobsang Tsering, Ven. Lobsang Kunga, Don Eisenberg, Jason Eksuzian, Juan Cammarano, Zachary Savitz, Miranda Penn Turin, Andrew Mumm, Michael Matkin, Lara Love Hardin, Siby Veliath, Satbir Singh, Jesse Abrams, Lama Tenzin, Michele Bohana, Pat Christen, Shannon Sedgwick Davis, John and Ann Montgomery, Scott and Joanie Kriens, Joe Lombardo, Matt Grey, Don Kendall, Rudolph Lohmeyer, Niko von Huetz, and Lloyd Sutton. We would especially like to thank Peggy Callahan, who produced the event and is working to turn the footage into a documentary. She made sure that not only did everything run like clockwork, and not only did the international team work together smoothly, but with the magic of studio lighting, she also managed to make two old men look surprisingly handsome. We would also like to thank the Archbishop's American doctor, Rachel Abrams, MD, who made sure that everyone stayed healthy and well during the trip. Thanks to Mary Ellen Klee and Gordon Wheeler too.

We would also like to thank the rest of the international members of Team Joy including Mike Mohr, Lalita Suzuki, Sarah Steven, Lindsay Gordon, Anne Kosmoski, Farin Schlussel, Casey Maloney, Alexandra Bruschi, Najma Finlay, Charlotte Bush, Andrew

Mumm, Mark Yoshitake, Ivan Askwith, Anna Sawyer, Savannah Peterson, Kevin Kelly, Mark Daley, Ryan Brounley, Ty Love, Jess Krager, Erin Roberts, and Kelsey Sheronas for using their great talents to help spread our message of joy.

We would also like to thank our beloved families and friends who were there: Mpho Tutu van Furth, Marceline Tutu van Furth, and Tenzin Choegyal. The Archbishop would also like to thank Leah Tutu, who could not make the journey, but who was there, as always, in his heart. We especially want thank Pam and Pierre Omidyar, without whom our time together and this book would never have been possible. They have been treasured friends and tireless supporters of both of our offices and campaigns to create a more compassionate and peaceful world.

Doug would like to thank his family and friends and especially his parents, who have supported him on his lifelong journey to joy—every step of the way. He would also like to give special thanks to his wife and children, Rachel, Jesse, Kayla, and Eliana, who are his greatest joy.

We would like to give very special thanks to Thupten Jinpa. His help before, during, and after the dialogues could not have been more essential to the realization of this book. He worked closely with Doug at every stage of the process, and this book truly would not have been possible without his profound knowledge, his spirit of generosity, and his commitment to creating a more compassionate world where all can have a fearless heart.

We would like to thank our cowriter and the Archbishop's longtime collaborator and friend, Doug Abrams. We asked him to clean up our spoken words for the written page, especially since one of us is not a native English speaker (guess who?). He has done an extraordinary job conveying our words faithfully and our hearts truthfully. He has also brought in a great deal of valuable science and has captured an incredible amount from our time together, which was filled with so much laughter, good fun, and the true joy of friendship. He has been a wonderful gift and has shared his splendid giftedness with us and with all who will read this book. As our literary agent, our interviewer, and our cowriter, this book really would not have happened without him. Thank you profoundly. You really are so very special.

Finally, we would like to thank you, our readers, who are doing so much to create a world filled with joy and love, where the future we create together will live up to our bravest and boldest dreams.

His Holiness the 14th Dalai Lama, Tenzin Gyatso, describes himself as a simple Buddhist monk. He is the spiritual leader of the Tibetan People and of Tibetan Buddhism. He was awarded the Nobel Peace Prize in 1989 and the US Congressional Gold Medal in 2007. Born in 1935 to a poor farming family in northeastern Tibet, he was recognized at the age of two as the reincarnation of his predecessor, the 13th Dalai Lama. He has been a passionate advocate for a secular universal approach to cultivating fundamental human values. For more than three decades the Dalai Lama has maintained an ongoing conversation and collaboration with scientists from a wide range of disciplines, especially through the Mind and Life Institute, an organization that he cofounded. The Dalai Lama travels extensively, promoting kindness and compassion, interfaith understanding, respect for the environment, and, above all, world peace. He lives in exile in Dharamsala, India. For more information, please visit www.dalailama.com.

Desmond Mpilo Tutu, Archbishop Emeritus of Southern Africa, became a prominent leader in the crusade for justice and racial reconciliation in South

Africa. He was awarded the Nobel Peace Prize in 1984 and the Presidential Medal of Freedom in 2009. In 1994, Tutu was appointed chair of South Africa's Truth and Reconciliation Commission by Nelson Mandela, where he pioneered a new way for countries to move forward after experiencing civil conflict and oppression. He was the founding chair of The Elders, a group of global leaders working together for peace and human rights. Archbishop Tutu is regarded as a leading moral voice and an icon of hope. Throughout his life, he has cared deeply about the needs of people around the world, teaching love and compassion for all. He lives in Cape Town, South Africa. For more information, please visit tutu.org.za.

Douglas Abrams is an author, editor, and literary agent. He is the founder and president of Idea Architects, a creative book and media agency helping visionaries to create a wiser, healthier, and more just world. Doug has worked with Desmond Tutu as his cowriter and editor for more than a decade. Before founding his own literary agency, he was a senior editor at HarperCollins and also served for nine years as the religion editor at the University of California Press. He believes strongly in the power of books and media to catalyze the next stage of global evolutionary culture. He lives in Santa Cruz, California. For more information, please visit idea-architects.com.